P9-EDG-564

The Elegiac Cityscape

The Elegiac Cityscape

PROPERTIES AND THE MEANING OF ROMAN
MONUMENTS

Tara S. Welch

The Ohio State University Press
Columbus

Copyright © 2005 by The Ohio State University.
All rights reserved.

Library of Congress Cataloging-in-Publication Data

Welch, Tara S., 1967–
The elegiac cityscape : Propertius and the meaning of Roman monuments / Tara
S. Welch.
p. cm.
Includes bibliographical references (p.) and index.
ISBN 0–8142–1009–0 (alk. paper)—ISBN 0–8142–9087–6 (CD-ROM)
1. Propertius, Sextus. Elegiae. Liber 4. 2. Augustus, Emperor of Rome, 63 B.C.–14
A.D.—In literature. 3. Augustus, Emperor of Rome, 63 B.C.–14 A.D.—Influence. 4.
Elegiac poetry, Latin—History and criticism. 5. City and town life in literature. 6.
Politics and literature—Rome. 7. Literature and society—Rome. 8. Public architec-
ture—Rome. 9. Architecture in literature. 10. Masculinity in literature. 11.
Imperialism in literature. 12. Monuments in literature. 13. Rome—In literature. I.
Title.
PA6646.W45 2005
874.'01—dc22
2005012368
2005012352

Cover design by Laurence Nozik.
Text design and typesetting by Jennifer Shoffey Forsythe.
Printed by Thompson Shore, Inc.

The paper used in this publication meets the minimum requirements of the
American National Standard for Information Sciences—Permanence of Paper for
Printed Library Materials. ANSI Z39.48–1992.

9 8 7 6 5 4 3 2 1

CONTENTS

PA
6646
W45
2005

ILLUSTRATIONS

ABBREVIATIONS

BMCRE Mattingly, H. 1965–1966 (1923–1936). *Coins of the Roman Empire in the British Museum. Vols. I-VI.* London.

CIL *Corpus inscriptionum Latinarum.* Berlin.

FGrH Jacoby, F. 1957. *Fragmente der griecischen Historiker.* Leiden.

Inscr.It. *Inscriptiones Italiae.* Vols. 1–13. Rome.

OLD P. G. W. Glare, ed. 1982. *Oxford Latin Dictionary.* Oxford.

RIC Mattingly, H., et al. 1923–1981. *The Roman Imperial Coinage.* London.

RRC Crawford, M. H. 1974. *Roman Republican Coinage.* Vols. I-II. Cambridge.

TLL *Thesaurus linguae Latinae.* Leipzig.

All periodicals are abbreviated following the rubric of *L'Année Philologique*. For ancient texts and authors I have followed the abbreviations given in the *Oxford Latin Dictionary* (1997 [1962], ed. P. G. W. Glare), and the *Greek-English Lexicon* (1983 [1940], ed. H. G. Liddell, R. Scott, and H. S. Jones).

ACKNOWLEDGMENTS

IT IS A PLEASURE to thank, in everlasting print, those who have helped bring this book to completion. It began as a dissertation at UCLA under the watchful eye of Carole Newlands, who inspired me with her discernment and her passion for the beauty and complexity of Latin poetry. She has continued to inspire and improve this project in its growth from a dissertation to the book you are now holding. I was lucky to have two advisors at UCLA; Bernard Frischer was always ready to share with me his considerable expertise in both Latin literature and Rome's landscape. In classes and in conversation I learned from Bernie much that appears in this book.

My colleagues and friends at the University of Kansas, generous with their ideas, knowledge, and much-needed criticism, have improved this book immeasurably. I cannot imagine a more supportive or exciting environment in which to work. I owe special thanks to two colleagues in the Department of Classics whose influence is seen on every page that follows. Anthony Corbeill read and reread various portions of the text and offered countless suggestions and valuable criticism with his characteristic good humor and patience; and Stan Lombardo helped me draw nearer the spirit of Propertius' poetry in my translations. Additionally, two graduate research assistants, Brian Walters and Brad Engelbert, helped me check details, clarify arguments, and voice them consistently. Undergraduate assistant Corbett Bennett assisted in preparing the index. KU's good influence extends beyond the classics department; grants from the New Faculty General Research Fund, General Research Fund, and Office of International Programs subsidized research trips to Italy and enabled me to devote three summers to the project.

I am grateful, too, for the help and insight of many esteemed colleagues elsewhere. Micaela Janan, Allen Miller, Ellen Greene, David Konstan, Natalie Boymel Kampen, and Lawrence Richardson Jr. each read all or part of the manuscript, in various stages of polish. Their insights and suggestions enriched the book greatly and rescued it from some embarrassing defects. I am afraid I made myself quite a pest to all these kind and busy people—but they responded with such good will and acumen that I know now to what I aspire. I also thank two anonymous readers whose suggestions sharpened the book in many ways, and Eugene O'Connor at The Ohio State University Press, whose enthusiasm for the project and calm efficiency have made working with Ohio State a true pleasure.

In completing this book I have relied on friends and family for encouragement and support. Celia Schultz has been a steadfast friend and sane interlocutor on both the ideas and the process. My parents, Henry and Diane Silvestri, have seen this project from beginning to end and have borne with me the bumps and disappointments that are inevitable in such an endeavor. My mother also drew all the maps you will see throughout. I can barely express my debt to my husband, Kelly, for his unfailing support, patience, and love; his presence in my life is my *sine qua non*.

I dedicate this book to my brother Tony Silvestri, who took me, a wide-eyed *hospes* but eighteen years old, on my first tour of the eternal city. Thank you, Tony, for giving me such a precious gift as Rome.

INTRODUCTION

AUDIENCES BOTH ancient and modern have been fascinated by the dignity and grandeur of Roman remains. Though the ancient city grew gradually, building by building, throughout its millennium-long heyday, the city experienced periodic growth spurts during which large-scale building programs dramatically transformed the urban landscape. Such sweeping changes in the urban fabric usually coincided with political or social crises or periods of transition in Roman identity. We see such building programs not only at obvious cruxes in Rome's history, e.g., between Republic and Empire, or between pagan and Christian, but also in times of more subtle changes, such as the transition from national to international power, or from the Julio-Claudian principate to a more autocratic state under the Flavian emperors of the late first century CE.

This book explores the interaction of Roman places and Roman ideas in the Augustan age by examining the late poetry of the elegiac poet Propertius, published soon after 16 BCE. For his fourth and final book, Propertius sets out a new artistic program: aetiological poetry celebrating Rome's origins. Departing from the love elegies to his elusive mistress Cynthia that characterized his earlier poetry—a program defiant for its insistence on a life of love rather than public duty—he turns his poetic voice to Roman institutions:

Roma, faue, tibi surgit opus, date candida ciues
    omina, et inceptis dextera cantet auis!
sacra diesque canam et cognomina prisca locorum:
    has meus ad metas sudet oportet equus.

1

Rome, approve: this work rises for you. Grant favorable omens, o citizens, and may the bird of prophecy sing propitiously at what I have begun! I shall sing of the rites and festivals of Rome, and of the hallowed names of its places. My steed rightly pants toward this goal.[1] (4.1.67–70)

In the pages that follow, I focus on these places and situate them in the context of Augustus' extensive building program after his victory at Actium in 31 BCE. This last battle in the civil wars after Julius Caesar's assassination made Augustus sole master of the Roman world. Caesar's adopted son thus became the first Roman emperor, and a new social and political order was born, now called the Principate after its Princeps, or "first man." Augustus as Princeps set about repairing, literally and figuratively, a broken Rome. The fact that Propertius shifts his theme from love to the re-emerging city does not mean that he aligns himself with Rome's ruling power—far from it. Combining the approaches of archaeology and literary criticism, I examine how Propertius' poems on the origins of Roman places explore and comment on the ways Augustus used the city to solidify his position as first emperor of a new Rome. In this way the poet establishes himself as a rival to Augustus in the creation of Rome's urban identity.

BUILDING THE AUGUSTAN CITY

With his broad program of gradual urban renewal, Augustus eased the transition between Republic and Principate by blending old and new visual elements and architectural forms and by endorsing traditional Roman values in the structure and decoration of his monuments. The new emperor thus invited Romans of his day to consider themselves and their new state as the destined and deserving heirs of Rome's glorious legacy. Archaeologists and art historians of the Augustan age, such as Paul Zanker, Diane Favro, and Barbara Kellum have been concerned with understanding the monuments of Augustan Rome as a form of imperial propaganda. Zanker's *The Power of Images in the Age of Augustus* (1988), now almost two decades old, makes a sustained and persuasive case that all forms of material culture—public and private—reflected the evolving ideologies of the Principate. Favro's *The Urban Image of Augustan Rome* (1996), a response to Zanker that employs modern urban theory to understand the topography of Rome, demonstrates how Augustus's building program created a more cohesive cityscape that matched the new central locus of power. Kellum's substantial body of work, in articles such as "Sculptural Programs and Propaganda in Augustan Rome: The Temple of Apollo on the Palatine" (1993 [1986]) and "Concealing/Revealing: Gender and the Play of Meaning in the Monuments of Augustan Rome" (1997), suggests some of the ways Rome's new buildings and public works encoded values and behaviors conducive to the new state. Such approaches as these have vastly expanded our understanding of the Augustan age, moving us beyond Sir Ronald Syme's chapter on "The Organization of Opinion" in his seminal *The Roman Revolution*, published in 1939, and demonstrating, among other things, how the forms and goals of the new system might have reached audiences across the political spectrum, even those unaffected by the constitutional reforms.[2] An understanding of the Augustan cityscape as a form of imperial propaganda raises an important question: to what extent was the message received by its intended audience? Zanker's study suggests one way to find out. Examining how patrons gradually adopted for the private sphere some themes and motifs of imperial works and ignored others, Zanker argues that the Augustan visual program was not a product but a process, not a revolution but an evolution of ideas and images.[3]

There is another way to gauge the reception of imperial urban propaganda: through words about images. The Augustan age is uniquely rich in literature that engages Roman places, as Vergil, Vitruvius, Horace, Tibullus, Propertius, Dionysius, Strabo, Livy, and Ovid all include images of the city to a greater or lesser extent in their work. Propertius' topographical poems offer insight into how one Roman adopted different voices and perspectives regarding the new city around him. His works reveal that he interpreted the new monuments as attempts to coerce morality, identity, and behavior into forms more in tune with the new state. The poems thus offer ways of looking at the monuments that perhaps differ from the ways Augustus intended them to be seen. Indeed, Propertius' reactions to the monuments as coercive do much to shape our reception of them as propagandistic. By reading Propertius' poems as multiple responses to the changing cityscape, we begin, like Zanker, to understand Augustan monuments not simply as one-way propagandistic statements by the emperor, but as part of a dialogue with Roman citizens about the unique development of their state and their collective identity, a dialogue made even more complex by the fact that it is conducted in both images and words, i.e., through both visual and verbal sign systems that encode experience and expectations. As Alessandro Barchiesi puts it, " . . .

most people would agree that ideology plays some part in this process of turning images into meanings. And once ideology is perceived in terms of a discourse, there is no way of keeping the discourse simple or monolithic."[4]

This book rests on the premise that Augustan literature—richly self-conscious, politically aware, and sensitive to the nuances of all forms of art—reads and responds to the emerging city.[5] In one sense, this premise indicates that for Propertius, Vergil, and others, the cityscape is simply another sort of "text" in the densely woven fabric of Augustan poetry, or even that the city acts as a metaphor for something else, such as power, the state, the Golden Age or its decline. Diane Favro's work poses a method of reading the city-as-text that rescues it from such oversimplification: by controlling access to monuments and urban nodes, Augustus effectively created a sequence of viewing, a "narrative" that structured people's experience of the Roman cityscape.[6]

Propertius' responses to the new city demonstrate that he was keenly aware of the dynamics of the city-as-text, and of the differences between the visual and verbal arts. His topographical poems capitalize on that difference in two primary ways. On the one hand the elegiac poet draws attention to the physicality of the city and to its experientiality—i.e., that individuals experience the city by moving through it in space and time. The statue of Vertumnus, for example, is in Propertius' elegy 4.2 venerated and decorated by its visitors as they bustle to and from the Forum along the Vicus Tuscus, and Hercules in elegy 4.9 approaches the sanctuary of the Bona Dea as a suppliant who can hear sounds beyond its closed door. This experiential dynamic goes beyond Propertius' visual sensibility, a quality of Propertius' poetry examined by scholars such as Jean-Paul Boucher, D. Thomas Benediktson, and Theodore Papanghelis.[7] As these scholars have demonstrated, visual imagery pervades Propertian elegy, in part because the poet in Rome was always surrounded with works of public and private art.[8] Propertius' city is imbued with this visual sensibility, to be sure—but his poems on the city appeal not only to his readers' eyes but to their ears, noses, and feet as well, and to their memories of places and their expectations of what will happen there. Propertius' urban landscape is thus more than a text for his readers; it is a context.

On the other hand, the elegist also draws attention to the textuality of his own poetry and to the ability of words to suggest specific interpretations. By lingering on certain details and occluding others, by punning on the names that identify places, and by imposing narratives that explain their existence, Propertius invites his readers to view the monuments he treats from certain perspectives—sometimes even from several perspectives within one poem. This presentation from a certain viewpoint is often called "focalization," a critical term of narratological theory.[9] As a visual metaphor borrowed from photography, "focalization" articulates the relationship between the one who sees (e.g., a character within a literary work) and the one who speaks (e.g., the author): the author who speaks focalizes the narrative through the lens of a character who sees. The combination of visual and verbal perspectives captures the spirit of the poems in Book 4.

However temporarily, Propertius' techniques of focalization not only reframe Roman places in his audience's imagination, but also suggest a hierarchy of semantic influence: words may have power over images, a case that Horace makes in a very general sense in *Carm.* 3.30 (*exegi monumentum perennius aere*).[10] This relationship between words and images is similar to that which arises in instances of ekphrasis. While only one of the poems to be discussed in this book constitutes an ekphrasis *per se* (elegy 2.31 on the temple of Palatine Apollo), the other poems implicate both the poet and the reader in the interpretation of the places or monuments that are their subject. As Stephen Harrison points out in a discussion of ekphrasis in Greek and Latin poetry, the effectiveness of ekphrasis depends in large part on what the reader brings to the experience—namely, her knowledge of aspects both within the text and outside of it that interpret and are interpreted by the artwork being described.[11]

Propertius' topographical poems are instances of ekphrasis with a twist: the places he describes are real works, seen and experienced by his audience in Rome. Propertius' poems and the monuments they interpret engage each other via the reader/viewer, since Propertius' Roman readers also were the primary viewers of Roman monuments. These readers brought to Propertius' poems their prior experiences with the Roman places at issue, and took from the poet's works new ways of viewing Roman monuments. Don Fowler's work on narratology and ekphrasis points the way to the importance of this dynamic for understanding Propertius' poetry.[12] Contrasting descriptions of works that are imagined by the poet or by a character within the poem with works that have existence outside the text, Fowler posits that ekphrasis (and indeed art criticism) is most effective when it describes a real work of art, available to many viewers and discutants: "Art and literature do not exist to be understood or appreciated, but to be discussed and argued over, to function as a focus for social dialogue . . . ekphrasis proves to be not a minor aspect of the relationship between visual art and literature, but the central activity which gives all art meaning."[13] The underlying discourse about art and words that always operates in instances of ekphrasis thus also becomes, in the presence of Propertius' real places, a discourse about lived reality and the cultural identity embedded in it.

ELEGY, MONUMENTS, AND ROMAN IDENTITY

After biographical readings of Propertius' poetry from the mid-twentieth century gave way to readings of the poet-lover as a persona created and not necessarily real, criticism on Propertian elegy has focused on the ways the poet situates himself and his poetry vis-à-vis other discourses. This shift in focus from *love* poetry to love *poetry* has enabled exploration of Propertius and the discursive codes of gender, genre, and Augustan ideology, among others. In recent decades criticism influenced by poststructuralism, drawing renewed attention to discourse and representation as themselves problematic, has stressed elegy's broad resistance to any consistent or stable discourse.[14] The male lover in elegy, for example, does not conform to traditional gender roles, either normative or inverted. He is feminine in his passivity and his subservience to his mistress, but masculine in his control of the poem and of the representation of the mistress.[15] Likewise, he cannot be easily defined by social category. He is nobly born, and his lifestyle depends upon the money and status that nobility provides,[16] but he refuses to engage in the pursuits typical—indeed expected—of his class: military service and political office.

The incongruity of the elegiac lover and the dissolution of stable discourse that operate in Roman elegy are more than "part of the fun"; more importantly, they reflect the crisis of identity that pervaded Roman culture at the end of the first century BCE.[17] With the gradual transition from Republic to Principate, Roman men could no longer define their masculinity through political activity. The accumulation of military honors such as the triumph and the *ouatio* within the imperial household (and their concomitant denial to outsiders) restricted access to another avenue for masculine self-definition.[18] With the displacement of the nobility from traditional positions of authority came the ascent of freedmen and even slaves into positions of wealth, authority, and rank.[19] It is striking that elegy's short life span as a genre in Roman literature, from the issue of Catullus' poems in the 50s BCE to Ovid's last publication in the genre in 17 CE, roughly coincides with the fall of the Republic and the birth of the Principate.

Equally striking is the dramatic renovation of Rome's urban fabric at that time. Rome's most vibrant and venerable civic area, the Forum Romanum, was transformed into a Julian monument through the rebuilding of existing structures and the creation of new ones. New imperial forum complexes likewise became monumental testaments to the transfer of power from the people to the imperial family. In this period Augustus decorated his own Forum Augustum with statues of the heroes of myth and history, including Rome's founders Aeneas and Romulus. Romans and visitors to Rome were invited to consider themselves but a small part of something much grander, participants in a sweeping history of success and rebirth.

In his 1995 book *Art and the Roman Viewer*, Jas Elsner offers a framework for understanding the effect of art on Roman identity. To Elsner, a work of art acts upon a viewer by reinforcing previously held perceptions through familiar elements, and also changes those perceptions by adding something new.[20] Augustus' monuments and their decorative programs, by incorporating new details into traditional forms, bridged the gap between the old and new orders and helped redefine what it meant to be a Roman citizen. At the same time, the Augustan age saw a sharp rise in the number, length, and size of public inscriptions in the city; such inscriptions marked and sometimes interpreted Roman places and monuments, enabling them to "speak" more clearly to the viewing public.[21] These changes in turn affected the processes of cognitive mapping—the ways in which people oriented themselves to and moved through Roman places.[22] In this context, Propertius' elegies on Rome's monuments in Book 4 offer much to the scholar seeking to understand not only elegy's evolution throughout these years but also Rome's evolving civic identity.

While analyses of individual poems have addressed the interrelationship between text and place in Book 4,[23] recent comprehensive studies of Propertius' last book have focused on themes other than Propertius' Roman places. Two notable exceptions are the parallel analyses of the pastoral landscape in Book 4 by Kenneth Rothwell and Elaine Fantham.[24] Rothwell traces the lack of a romanticized Golden Age and the tenacity of the natural world as linked themes in the topographical elegies, concluding that for the poet, nature is a force that can—and will—overpower any of man's achievements in the physical world, which were never laudable in the first place. Fantham offers a more optimistic view, arguing that Propertius' depiction of Rome's untamed early landscape overshadows the city's contemporary manu-factured splendor and indicates the poet's preference for the lost inno-cence of Rome's distant past. I see Propertius' portrait of early Rome as neither naturalist nor nostalgic; on the contrary, I argue that the elegist's ancient landscape is already darkened by the shadow of what it will become—an emblem of a state that demands too many sacrifices from its citizens. Propertius' elegiac discourse on Rome resists this presence of an intrusive state by reading its past pessimistically, thus resisting the invited perspective on Roman identity and behavior.

My approach is heavily influenced by two recent studies on the interaction between Roman texts and monuments. Ann Vasaly's *Repre-sentations*, published in 1993, demonstrates how Cicero's speeches employ space as a rhetorical device to aid persuasion, not only by exploiting the connotations of the monuments in view as Cicero deliv-ered his speeches, but also by evoking preconceptions about places not immediately visible to the audience, places both inside and outside Rome. Cicero uses what Vasaly calls a "'metaphysical topography'— that is, the meaning these places would have held for a Roman audi-ence in Cicero's time."[25] Catharine Edwards, in her 1996 volume *Writing Rome*, examines the conceptual city in Latin literature, and the ways Latin texts have informed the Romans' and our own opinions about the great city, i.e., "these literary resonances of the city and also the city's resonance in literature."[26] These approaches form a complemen-tary pair: while Vasaly searches for the influence of monuments—or, better, of monuments' metaphysical topography—on texts, Edwards focuses on the influence of texts on the metaphysical topography of monuments. Propertius' poetic engagement with local monuments and places responds to and reshapes their "metaphysical topography," making his poetry a unique and fruitful locus for understanding Roman identity in the Augustan age.

I should make it clear that by *identity* I do not mean the private, inte-rior identity felt by individual Romans, much less any essential or nat-ural Roman cultural identity. In this respect I follow Eve D'Ambra in her 1998 volume *Art and Identity in the Roman World* and Duncan Kennedy in his 1993 *The Arts of Love: Five Studies in the Discourse of Roman Elegy*. By *identity* I mean social identity—that is, various pub-licly sanctioned and performed roles that are encoded in, for example, behavior, dress, habit, and manner of speaking.[27] Whatever an individ-ual Roman's private, interior identity might be, Lacanian approaches demonstrate that it must always stand in relationship with social forces external to the self. Identity is the ever-changing product of this interaction. In recent years two scholars have teased out for elegiac poetry some of the implications of the Lacanian model of identity. Paul Allen Miller's *Subjecting Verses* of 2003 explores how elegy as a generic discourse is enabled—even necessitated—by an increasing gap (called the Real) between the self (called the Imaginary) and the external world of shared codes and norms (called the Symbolic). Micaela Janan's 2001 volume *The Politics of Desire* locates that gap at its widest in Propertius' fourth book, which reframes the elegiac view of the external world.[28] It is a primary argument of my project that Roman monuments constitute a crucial part of the external world that forms and informs identity in the Augustan era.

Likewise, by *Roman* I mean precisely "having to do with the city of Rome," rather than ethnically Roman (whatever that is), or even under Rome's broader political or geographic sway. Recent cultural studies have demonstrated the inability to label and contain Roman culture, focusing instead on the variety of ways people respond to and understand Rome and their own relationship to it.[29] As W. R. Johnson argues, "what we need is a history of literature that searches for traces of such conflictedness, such indeterminate feelings, in all the Roman writers who are émigrés (which means, most of them)."[30] To be sure, many of the monuments of Augustan Rome were known to outsiders through their appearance on coins and in descriptions, and even from hearsay. Yet Propertius' poetry is quite sensitive to the distinction between local inhabitant and visitor, and the very first line of Book 4 introduces a guest, *hospes*, to a city not his own. What is more, we must always keep in mind—and Propertius frequently reminds us to do so—the fact that Propertius was himself a son of another land, Umbria's Assisi some one hundred miles north of Rome. With one exception (the temple of Palatine Apollo), the places Propertius treats in Book 4 arose as the result of Rome's conquest of the Italian peninsula. Their history is the history of Rome's imperialist expansion, and in engaging that history Propertius necessarily engages the negotiation between Roman and non-Roman that pervades the urban landscape. With these understandings of the terms *identity* and *Roman* I aim to indicate that Propertius resists Roman identity as something natural, essential, or inevitable: Roman identity—whatever that is—is always under negotiation, and is available to anyone for adoption or rejection.

THE ELEGIAC ACHIEVEMENT OF BOOK 4

A young Muse with young loves clustered around her
        ascends with me into the aether, . . .
And there is no high road to the Muses. (Ezra Pound, *Homage to Propertius* 1)[31]

Propertius' earlier poetry is guided by twin stars: Cynthia, the mistress under whose sway the poet suffers and rejoices, and Callimachus, the great Alexandrian poet, master of delicate verse, and father of the poetic form—self-contained, first-person poems in elegiac meter—that gave voice to the poet's feelings.[32] Cynthia's presence in his poetry allows Propertius to explore personal themes, such as the extent to which the male lover is master of his own feelings, actions, and relationships, or whether instead he is subject to another, lost in his desire. Related to this are questions about Cynthia herself—is she a flesh-and-blood lover? a metaphor for poetry? grist for the poet's mill? Or is she a means for the poet to describe and negotiate his selfhood to the third parties who are his addressees?[33] In all cases, the dominance of the first-person voice indicates that the poetry is focused more on Propertius than on Cynthia, and on his reaction to her, whoever or whatever she is. Cynthia is the presence around which Propertian elegy organizes questions of the self: she is a focal point for elegy's personal themes.

Callimachus' presence in Propertius' poetry contextualizes these personal themes, this selfhood, within broader conversations about discourse. Callimachus' poetry, highly self-conscious of its jewel-like style and confident of its privileged status vis-à-vis other poetic practitioners and genres, had become in the first century BCE a popular model for Roman poets who wished to distance themselves from the political and rhetorical discourses of traditional Republican literature.[34] By introducing Callimachus and Callimachean literary style into his poetry, Propertius invites his readers to contemplate how various types of discourse, such as epic, epigram, or history, facilitate or inhibit the personal voice. Indeed, it is in Callimachus' name that Propertius claims to be unable to write "high" epic poetry, as in elegy 2.1.39–42, glossed by Pound in the epigram above: "there is no high road to the Muses."

Both Cynthia and Callimachus situate the poet as a nonconformist vis-à-vis Roman mores. Whatever the relative social station of the lover and his mistress, his love affair is not sanctioned by the hallowed traditions of Roman marriage.[35] Regardless of this sanction, his conduct in the affair undermines the poet's very masculine identity.

Under the spell of his mistress, the male poet as lover plays a passive role in the relationship, unable or unwilling to assert control over his beloved or even himself. His passivity and lack of self-control style him as effeminate, a self-characterization that is one of the hallmarks of Propertian elegy and that flies in the face of traditional Roman gender roles. Likewise, his choice of Callimachus as a poetic model excuses him from ennobling the Roman way. Looking to the great Greek poet as his model allows Propertius to claim a worthy poetic enterprise while keeping his eye focused on something other than Rome. Callimachean aesthetic values such as refinement and esotericism promote a scale of composition too small to do Rome justice, in any case.

Book 4 breaks sharply from this defiant stance and turns instead to Rome's history and institutions. Scholars of Propertius' last book, confronted with this break, have focused their attention on the renegotiation of the poet's position vis-à-vis the dominant ideology. Do Propertius' aetiological poems celebrate Roman institutions, as argued by such scholars as Luigi Alfonsi, Pierre Grimal, Jean-Paul Boucher, Salvatore d'Elia, and Jeri Blair DeBrohun?[36] Or rather, despite the public themes he treats, does Propertius maintain a posture that is critical of the the dominant ideology? Hermann Tränkle, Hans-Peter Stahl, John Sullivan, Robert Gurval, and Micaela Janan have seen in Book 4 the same seeds of discontent with normative values that characterize Propertius' earlier work.[37]

However we are to interpret Book 4, it is important to recall (as do all the scholars mentioned above) that Propertius' final work does not abandon the themes explored in his earlier books. In Book 4 Propertius has created the perfect end to his life's work, throwing into high relief the attitudes and stances of the first three books by confronting head-on those mores that Cynthia and Callimachus had previously helped him avoid. "Rome, this work rises for you," he asserts at 4.1.67 (*Roma . . . tibi surgit opus*). Yet Cynthia and Callimachus still linger: Book 4 contains one of the best, if the most perplexing, Cynthia poems in the whole collection (4.7) and a bold assertion that his new project is the work of the Roman Callimachus (*Romani . . . Callimachi*, 4.1.64).[38] The book thus continues to engage the themes of selfhood and discourse that dominate his earlier work, while introducing new levels of complexity. Nearly half the poems in Book 4 are voiced by speaking subjects other than the poet himself (Horos in 4.1, Vertumnus in 4.2, Arethusa in 4.3, Cornelia in 4.11, and cf. the extended voices of Tarpeia in 4.4 and Cynthia in 4.7). To a much greater extent than in the earlier books, in which Propertius' voice predominates, these many voices in Book 4 expand the book's horizons of subjectivity, interacting with the lover-poet and offering "external" ways of evaluating the personal voice of Propertius, his relationship with Cynthia, and his Callimachean aesthetic commitment.[39] These different speakers are situated in the cultural, historical, and physical setting of Rome, with poems on Roman legends and places, mention of consuls and wars, and inclusion of marriage and death. By examining Rome as this setting, and more particularly the ways it confines or enables identities and discourses, we may come closer to understanding to what extent Book 4 aligns itself with the dominant ideology. Rome's presence in Book 4 allows the poet a medium through which to discuss more overtly public themes, such as Rome's imperialism and normative gender roles. More powerfully, Propertius' poems also demonstrate that Rome is itself the means by which such themes are constituted as public. Propertius rejects the use of Rome as a tool for such service.

Propertius' achievement of Book 4—its multivalence, its artistry, and its relevance to the self and to society—had never been seen before in Latin elegiac poetry and, arguably, would never be seen again. To be sure, Ovid would recombine and adapt the forms of his predecessor's elegiac swan song, writing love elegies in the *Amores,* letters from abandoned women to their absent lovers in the *Heroides,* and aetiologies in the *Fasti.* The topographical dynamics of the last poem have found new voice in recent critical treatments. Boyle's map of Ovid's festival city examines how political ideology meets literary and cultural aesthetics at the intersection of building/viewing and writing/reading in Augustan Rome.[40] Ovid's contribution to our understanding of this intersection is not to be underestimated, but neither is the achievement of his predecessor in the task. Ovid found his archetype in Propertius' fourth book, a text that persistently voices the tension between the individual thinking subject and the subjectifization enacted upon him by Rome. The elegies in Book 4 make audible the process of self-expression, individuation, and even defection all but drowned out by the overwhelming—and persuasively symphonic—legacy of Augustus' city of marble. In this way, Propertius' final book is more than Propertius' own triumph: it is the acme of personal elegiac poetry.

ORGANIZATION OF *THE ELEGIAC CITYSCAPE*

In the chapters that follow I examine in turn each of Book 4's poems on

Roman places. In each chapter I first orient the reader to the monument at hand, exploring what resonance that place might have held for a Roman audience in the first century BCE. With attention thus focused on the monument on the ground, I turn to the poem itself and explore the ways Propertius engages with that meaning—sometimes challenging it, sometimes endorsing it, always changing it. Though the structure of each chapter is thus consistent, the content is not: the variable and shifting ways Propertius incorporates these monuments into his different poems, and sometimes even the shifting perspectives on Roman places to be found within one poem, necessitate a variety of approaches to the poems themselves.

Likewise, Propertius' treatment of Roman monuments often blends the actual (or the probable) with the fanciful, especially when he provides an ancient "history" for them. While Francis Cairns attributes this to his "lack of pure intellectual curiosity,"[41] this gives Propertius too little credit. His reconstructions of Rome's past are designed to indicate that monuments have no fixed, real, or zero-grade meaning, but rather that their meaning is always open to (re)interpretation. Indeed, this malleability is one of the keenest lessons Propertius wanted to teach his readers with this collection of poems. Thus each of these chapters may stand alone as a thematic reading of the poem at hand, but the reader who engages *The Elegiac Cityscape* as a whole will, I hope, better realize the extent to which Propertius sustains his scrutiny of Rome's urban identity throughout his final oeuvre.

In the first chapter I explore elegy 4.1, Propertius' own introduction to his grand finale. This programmatic poem does not dwell on any one monument, but rather traces the outline of the city as a whole, introducing several ways of viewing it and of reading the poems that follow. Time, culture, genre, gender, and astrology are all interpretive lenses that color the Roman horizon in elegy 4.1, combining with each other in ways that magnify the possibilities and tensions inherent in defining the city. The proliferation of Romes that embellish this introductory elegy sets the tone for the multiple perspectives on specific Roman places that we see throughout the rest of the book.

In elegy 4.2, the focus of chapter 2, Propertius applies the interpretive lenses of elegy 4.1 to a particular monument: the talking statue of Vertumnus that stood close behind the Forum's edge. Vertumnus revels in his flexibility in adapting to the needs and viewing habits of passersby—man, woman, soldier, lover, farmer, statesman—resisting any one interpretation of his representation or even of his name. Likewise, Vertumnus asserts his own cultural plurality: he is at once Etruscan in origin, Roman by current residence, Oscan in craftsmanship, and Sabine by historical coincidence (he arrived in Rome along with the Sabines). With this talking monument asserting that his meaning is not fixed, even to himself, Propertius challenges his reader to approach Roman monuments with an open mind, and to be wary of what pre-dispositions she might bring to viewing and interpreting the cityscape.

Chapter 3 offers a reading of elegy 4.4, on the legendary traitoress Tarpeia and the tomb named after her. This poem lends voice to an individual at odds with the city around her. In Propertius' poem, Tarpeia, confined to a small part of the city and surrounded on all sides by places resonant of Rome's political and imperial power, enacts her disobedience not only toward the Roman state but toward its places as well, betraying the citadel to enemy forces. I argue that this elegy has as a subtext the use of Tarpeia's myth as part of the urban landscape—her rock, her tomb, and the monumental relief sculpture of her punish-ment in the Basilica Aemilia. Tarpeia's demise is not only set within but even caused by the urban structures that surround her; the whole city turns out to be Tarpeia's tomb. Hers is a cautionary tale about how much influence is exerted by Rome's places over the people who move among them.

The grand temple of Apollo on the Palatine hill inhabits elegy 4.6 and chapter 4. In this elegy, Propertius promises to discuss the Prin-ceps' magnificent new temple, dedicated in 28 BCE but, curiously, says nothing about it. Instead, his poem dwells on the battle of Actium as the victory that the temple commemorates, and on Apollo as Octa-vian's helper and patron in that battle. The grim Apollo of elegy 4.6 who fought at the future Princeps' side bears little resemblance to the elegant god of art displayed in the temple itself, as described by Prop-ertius in an earlier elegy written at the temple's dedication (2.31). The two elegies read together sever the cause (battle) from the urban effect (temple), unsettling the relationship between the Princeps' authority earned in that victory and his patronage of the urban landscape, and posing a subtle criticism of the way monuments were used to endorse power in Rome. What is more, in both elegies 2.31 and 4.6, Propertius claims Apollo as his own patron god, who watches over and inspires his poetry. With this move Propertius appropriates the honor of the temple of Palatine Apollo for himself: it commemorates his poetic achievement rather than the Princeps' victory in battle.

In chapter 5 I move with Propertius through the Forum Boarium and the Aventine hill, following the hero Hercules as he establishes the Ara Maxima ("Greatest Altar") in elegy 4.9. This poem stretches Hercules' elastic masculinity as he meets and is rejected by the women who stand in his way: the priestesses who guard the sanctuary of the Bona Dea's sacred spring. Both the Ara Maxima and the sanctuary of the Bona Dea were dear to Augustus and his wife, Livia, whose associations with these monuments served to reinforce their status as models of traditional gender roles for Roman men and women, i.e., warriors and wives. Propertius' feminized Hercules falls short of the Princeps' model of manly virtue, as the cavorting devotees of the Bona Dea fall short of Livia's matronal decorum. In the elegist's city, therefore, the Ara Maxima and the sanctuary of the Bona Dea do not reinforce, but rather undermine, the traditional gender roles encoded into them.

The final chapter examines elegy 4.10, the poet's unpacking of the temple of Jupiter Feretrius, since with this temple Propertius closes his poetic tour of Roman monuments. This small temple, perched atop the Capitoline hill, contained the rare relics of Rome's highest military honor: the *spolia opima*, armor taken by a Roman commander from an enemy commander whom he defeated in hand-to-hand combat. These spoils were rare indeed: only three men in Roman history had achieved this honor. As Propertius tells their tales, he dwells on neither the spoils nor the honor of dedicating them, but rather on the violence of the combat itself. Where he does mention spoils, they are blood-soaked. His poem thus casts a shadow on the way martial valor is programmed into the Roman city. As in elegy 4.6, in elegy 4.10 Propertius simultaneously draws attention to an alternative way of earning glory: by writing poetry about the city. By beginning and ending the poem with a focus on the poet's own achievement rather than on that of the military men who dedicated *spolia opima* or on that of Augustus, who had restored the temple, the poem makes a fitting finale for Propertius' walk through Rome. It leaves in the poet's hands both the power to shape the way we read the Roman cityscape and the glory of having built his own Rome.

I conclude the book by examining briefly some verbal correspondences between this final topographical poem (on the fall of Rome's victims) and the introductory poem (on Rome's rise to greatness). In elegy 4.1 Propertius introduces the contrast between Rome's current splendor and its rustic beginnings. Elegy 4.10 reverses this technique, juxtaposing the former splendor of the great Etruscan city Veii, defeated by Rome, with its current, conquered obscurity. This reversal in elegy 4.10 of the trope of humble origins leaves the reader with the impression of the transience of the built environment and of the identity built into it and fostered by it. Like Veii's, Rome's monuments will

FIGURE 1. Plan of Rome with the sites of Propertius' aetiological elegies noted by poem number. Their cluster shows their focus on the city's public center, in contrast with the minor sites mentioned in the book's non-aetiological poems. After Favro 1996: 278.

inevitably fall. Though unspoken, the complement to this notion inheres: unlike Rome's monuments, Propertius' poetry will remain.

Before beginning, I offer two notes on style and selection. The elegiac couplet lends itself perfectly to Book 4's project. As a self-contained unit, the couplet offers to the poet the ability to shift perspective quickly. These shifts happen thus not just between poems, but within poems as well. In Books 1–3 the couplet both enables the rapid twists and turns in the poet's feelings about Cynthia, and permits him to insert, without warning, statements about his aesthetic values and goals. Luigi Alfonsi has argued that the quicksilver nature of the couplet is one reason Propertius didn't approach Book 4 as a comprehensive, sustained aetiological project like Vergil's *Aeneid;* rather, each poem stands independently of the others.[42] While his poems do not follow a single narrative thread, the couplet's versatility, I believe, unifies Propertius' city in an important way. Applied to Roman buildings and monuments in Book 4, the couplet facilitates movement through and around Roman places—not just physical movement and shifts in direction and visual perspective (such as Hercules' rapid movement from the Forum Boarium to the sanctuary of the Bona Dea in elegy 4.9), but also emotional, or conceptual perspective (as in the way the sanctuary of the Bona Dea is, in one moment, a doublet for the secluded bath of Pallas but, in the next, a haven for giggling girls). In this way, though the poems remain discrete, as Alfonsi argues, the poetic form itself enables the variety of approach to Roman monuments that characterizes the Propertian landscape. I do not pretend that the translations I offer for Propertius' couplets are poetry in any sense and have thus left them in prose format, but I have tried to recapture in their pacing and tone the movement and shape of the elegiac couplet.

Likewise, though I do not attempt to interpret the remaining, non-topographical elegies in Propertius' book, much can be learned by considering the movement of the book as a whole. A map of the places discussed in the topographical elegies (Figure 1) reveals an important feature of the fourth book: Propertius' aetiological poems focus on public places in the city's center.

In contrast, the places mentioned in the non-aetiological poems lie nearer the city's periphery, such as the Esquiline bedroom of elegy 4.8; on its very edge, as in the city gate that bears Arethusa's votive wishes in elegy 4.3; or even beyond its walls, such as Cornelia's and the *lena*'s tombs from elegies 4.11 and 4.5. The contrast between private and public is strongly marked and suggests that Propertius' readers must always keep in mind that the city is made up of both sorts of places.

In this way, the questions I raise about the topographical poems can be fruitfully adapted to those more private poems as well: what is Roman identity, and how is it shaped and enforced? The presence in Book 4 of familiar elegiac themes, such as love outside of marriage (4.7, 4.8) helped or hindered by a *lena* (4.5) or magic (4.5, 4.7), and the introduction of new themes, such as marital fidelity (4.3 and 4.11) and the interrelationship of death and *fides* (4.7, 4.11), are intertwined with and around poems on Roman places, suggesting that all forms of human experience are implicated in the cityscape, and vice versa: the cityscape is implicated in all forms of human experience. Just as the individual feels, acts, and loves in the context of Rome's urban landscape, moving through it and being shaped by it, so too that landscape is formed of individual experiences and perceptions, lived and seen by people, not institutions. The relationship between the individual and the city that unfolds in Book 4 is, indeed, as faithful and fickle, as rewarding and painful, as pure and as complex as the love Propertius once expressed for Cynthia. Cynthia might be first, as the poet says in his first published verse, elegy 1.1.1: *Cynthia prima* (1.1.1); but Rome, as he asserts at the beginning of his final book (4.1.1), is greatest: *maxima Roma est.*

CHAPTER 1

Fallax Opus

READING ROME(S) IN ELEGY 4.1

AS AN INTRODUCTION to the sorts of questions Propertius asks of the Roman cityscape in Book 4, this chapter explores the interplay of places and poetic styles in elegy 4.1, Book 4's controversial programmatic poem that has much to say about topography but little about any one monument. Elegy 4.1 takes the reader on a verbal tour of Propertius' Rome. Acting as tour guide, the poet introduces several ways of reading the city around him, several responses to Roman places. The most obvious instance of this multivalent reading is the fact that the poem is split into halves in which different speakers espouse contrasting views on the material of the fourth book—the first, a celebratory and grand view seemingly voiced by the poet himself; the second, a skeptical and more restricted view offered from the perspective of the astrologer Horos.[1]

Yet even within each "univocal" half, the poet organizes and approaches the urban subject material in various ways that will inform the rest of the topographical poems in the book. In the first half of the poem, for example, Propertius offers (at least) three different ways of interpreting Rome. First, its opening lines, in which the poet introduces a guest to the ways the city he sees differs from the settlement it was long ago, introduce Rome as a city that changes over time. As the poem progresses, Propertius adds another element: cultural perspective. Highlighting his dual allegiance to his native Umbria and to his current homeland, Rome, Propertius suggests that Rome offers different faces to visitors with different cultural backgrounds. Third, homing in on the way his own poetry will shape and glorify the city, Propertius introduces Rome as a place built of words rather than of brick and stone. In the second half of the poem, Horos adds to the list two additional perspectives: genre and gender. Taking aim at the enthusiasm expressed in the first half of the poem, Horos argues that the elegist must stick to a more modest Rome fitting for delicate and personal elegy. Similarly, the astrologer's focus on women and the feminine suggests that men and women inhabit different Romes.

On a broader level, the poem's two parts engage in a dialogue about how Rome fits into other physical models that inform identity. In the first half, Propertius promises to discuss Roman monuments in the context of rituals and festivals, i.e., in the context of other structures, intangible ones that helped Romans organize their lives in meaningful ways. In the second half, Horos broadens this context by posing an alternative architectural framework that influences actions and behaviors: the sky, whose paths and monuments direct our very fates. Horos' claim reminds us all that Rome's landscape—multiple though it is—is but one part of a larger material world. Ironically, Horos' knowledge of a grander celestial city returns the focus to the smallest of units: the individual. Telling fortunes, Horos repopulates Rome (and other cities) with individuals—the poet included—each with his or her personal perspective, resisting or conforming to the ideologies built into the city around them.

ROMES PAST, PRESENT, AND FUTURE

The first half of the poem is spoken, it seems, by Propertius himself, acting as a spectator of Rome's glorious monuments. In the opening lines, Propertius juxtaposes the splendors of the city around him with its rustic roots:

> hoc quodcumque uides, hospes, qua maxima Roma est,
>   ante Phrygem Aenean collis et herba fuit;
> atque ubi Nauali stant sacra Palatia Phoebo,
>   Euandri profugae procubuere boues.
> fictilibus creuere deis haec aurea templa,
>   nec fuit opprobrio facta sine arte casa.
> Tarpeiusque pater nuda de rupe tonabat,
>   et Tiberis nostris aduena bubus erat.

qua gradibus domus ista Remi se sustulit, olim
   unus erat fratrum maxima regna focus.
Curia, praetexto quae nunc nitet alta senatu,
   pellitos habuit, rustica corda, patres.
bucina cogebat priscos ad uerba Quiritis:
   centum illi in prato saepe senatus erat.

All that you see here, visitor, where great Rome stands now, was but hill
and grass in the days before Trojan Aeneas. And where stands the Palatine sanctuary for Phoebus Protector of the Sea, the exiled cattle of Evander used to take their rest. These golden temples arose out of clay spirits,
nor was it any shame to live in a house built without pretense. The
Tarpeian Father thundered from his bare rock, and Tiber was a neighbor
to our cattle. Do you see where the house of Remus rises up yonder on its
high steps? Once a single hearth was the extent of the brothers' kingdom. The Curia, which now gleams aloft with the Senate in its ceremonial toga, once held skin-clad Elders, humble hearts those. A shepherd's
horn used to assemble Romans of yore: then "the Senate" was often any
hundred men in a field. (4.1.1–14)

In this passage, contemporary Rome is the Rome of Augustus; all of the
specific monuments mentioned in these opening lines can be linked to
Augustus' urban activity.[2] The four-line emphasis on the Palatine Hill
and the possibility of a view of the Capitol, the Tiber, the Forum, and
the Quirinal suggest to Stahl that the speaker is located on the Palatine
Hill, perhaps even near the Temple of Palatine Apollo; this would make
the opening lines' viewpoint "Augustan in the most literal way."[3] One
problem inherent in the trope of Rome's humble beginnings is the tension between nostalgia for a better past (a "Golden Age" rhetoric, such
as can be seen in Tibullus 1.10) and pride in a glorious present (an "evolution of justice" rhetoric, such as the one found in Lucretius *De Rerum
Natura* Book 5). Like Vergil in *Aeneid* 8, in which Aeneas takes a tour of
the rustic locale that will become Rome's splendors,[4] Propertius must
straddle the line between progress and degeneration, planting seeds of
the present in the past and finding the virtues of the past in the present.[5]
For Stahl, Propertius solves this problem precisely by means of the
Augustan viewpoint mentioned above: the repeated images of Aeneas
and his followers weave the *gens Iulia* throughout the story of Rome's
growth. Stahl's reading of this poem thus sees continuity between
Rome past and Rome present, continuity guaranteed by the recent
extensive attention given by the Julian family to urban progress.

Yet like its mirror-image in *Aeneid* 8, this trope also requires that readers always be aware of the differences in, or discontinuities among, Romes then, now, and yet to be. Indeed, so broad is the gap between then and now that Propertius must explain Rome's humble past to his visitor, to whom it is not readily apparent in the modern, golden city. Newman refers to this distance as a type of estrangement,[6] a concept confirmed by the poet's own statement that the Roman has but a thin connection to his heritage:

> nil patrium nisi nomen habet Romanus alumnus:
>   sanguinis altricem non putet esse lupam.

> The Roman foster child has nothing from his ancestors except the name:
> he would not wish to believe that a she-wolf nursed his bloodline.
> (4.1.38)

In temporal terms, the Roman foster child is alienated from his own past.[7] DeBrohun, in her recent study of this poem, argues that the gulf between past and present raises questions about *how* Rome grew.[8] The unsettling answer that Propertius provides, she argues, is that Rome grew through the use of *arma,* a method that problematizes not only the growth and development of Rome but also the parallel growth of Propertius' poetry from small to great. To highlight a slightly different element of DeBrohun's complex argument, these *arma* are equally problematic for both temporal frames of the physical city: the sophistication and scale of Roman/epic arms are at odds with Rome's simple forebears, and with the peace that seems manifest in the current city's splendors. Rome's past and present are thus both connected by means of *arma* and differentiated by them.

In its refusal to choose between connecting Rome's past and present and severing them, this opening passage poses the tension between continuity and discontinuity that operates in all aetiology, and so provides a fitting introduction to the themes the poet will discuss later in the poem and throughout Book 4. As Bing points out, the very need to explain something from the past "bespeaks at once an awareness of the enormous gulf separating past and present, and the desire to bridge it."[9] Bing notes that interest in aetiology increased dramatically in the Hellenistic period; whereas Homer's heroic age, unattested in the Greek landscape but for the tomb of Achilles, is to remain remote, Greeks of the Hellenistic period felt a greater need to forge linkages to the past. I believe this rise in interest reflects a growing insecurity about cultural identity in a period following tremendous social and political upheaval—i.e., in a period that marks a strong break from a past now lost.[10] Similarly, the temporal play of Propertius' opening poem and of the aetiological poems that pepper Book 4 has strong implications for Roman identity. As one critic states, the simultaneous bridge/gap drawn between past and present in this passage, as in aetiology in general, constitutes a search for what is "Roman" that has no stable answers.[11] Is it what was, what is, or what will be in the destiny implied by the forward march of time? The presence of Romes divergent over time thus multiplies the ways one may interpret Roman monuments.

WHOSE CITY?

At the end of elegy 4.1's first half, the poet rounds off his tour with a surge of patriotism—but for which *patria* is unclear:

> moenia namque pio coner disponere uersu:
>   ei mihi, quod nostro est paruus in ore sonus!
> sed tamen exiguo quodcumque e pectore riui
>   fluxerit, hoc patriae seruiet omne meae.
> Ennius hirsuta cingat sua dicta corona:
>   mi folia ex hedera porrige, Bacche, tua,
> ut nostris tumefacta superbiat Umbria libris,
>   Umbria Romani patria Callimachi!

> For I should try to lay out these walls in my holy verse: alas, that there is such a tiny voice in my throat! But all the same, whatever trickles from my puny breast, it will all go to serve my fatherland. Let Ennius decorate his words with a bristly crown: decorate me with leaves from your ivy, Bacchus, so that Umbria might grow proud, swollen with my books, Umbria, fatherland of the Roman Callimachus! (4.1.57–64)

Since Propertius has been describing monuments in Rome, the *moenia* of 4.1.57 surely are Rome's walls, and *patria* in 4.1.60 would seem to refer to Rome, glorified in the poet's verse. But Propertius' *patria* in 4.1.64 is explicitly Umbria. The repetition of the word *patria* draws attention to the fact that the poet is at home in two cities, and that he brings with him the perspective of a resident of each. Similarly, at 4.1.63 his goal is to glorify Umbria (*ut . . . tumefacta superbiat Umbria*), but two lines later he complicates the matter with the claim that his written city rises for Rome's benefit (4.1.67):

> Roma, faue, tibi surgit opus, date candida ciues
>   omina, et inceptis dextera cantet auis!

> Rome, approve: this work rises for you. Grant favorable omens, o citizens, and may the bird of prophecy sing propitiously at what I have begun! (4.1.67–68)

The combined purposes of Roman and Umbrian glorification emphasize his ambivalent viewpoint on Rome, and open the possibility for variations across Italy in ways of viewing Rome. The seer Horos, skeptical speaker of the poem's second half, draws renewed attention to Propertius' culturally divided perspective on Rome. Pointing out that Propertius is Umbrian (4.1.121–30), Horos warns that Apollo forbids the poet to thunder in the Forum (*uetat insano uerba tonare Foro*, 4.1.134). Not only is thundering antithetical to the Callimachean elegist,[12] but more importantly for the present argument, the Forum is no place for an Umbrian to speak out. Horos' point is all the more powerful for the reader who recalls the end of Vergil's second Georgic, in which the poet contrasts the happy Italian who cultivates the rustic gods (*ille deos qui nouit agrestis*, G. 2.493) with the unhappy Roman who witnesses the insane Forum (*ferrea iura / insanumque forum aut populi tabularia vidit*, G. 2.501–2).[13]

The poem elsewhere hints at other people with plural cultural identities. At 4.1.33–38 Propertius lists towns that have been absorbed not just into the Roman polity but into the very city itself, now suburbs and satellite towns dwarfed by great Rome:

> quippe suburbanae parua minus urbe Bouillae
>   et, qui nunc nulli, maxima turba Gabi.
> et stetit Alba potens, albae suis omine nata,
>   ac tibi Fidenas longa erat isse uia.
> nil patrium nisi nomen habet Romanus alumnus:
>   sanguinis altricem non putet esse lupam.

Indeed Bovilla was less a suburb when the city was small, and the Gabines, who are now nothing, were a great horde. And Alba stood strong in those days, born from the omen of a white sow, and the road to Fidenae used to be considered a long one. The Roman foster child has nothing from his ancestors except the name: he would not wish to believe that a she-wolf nursed his bloodline. (4.1.33–38)

Given how many foreigners have become Romans—Fidenates, Bovillans, Gabines, Albans, Umbrians, Propertius himself—we might wonder from how far afield the *hospes* comes to whom Propertius gives his tour of the great city (4.1.1). The last couplet of this passage emphasizes Rome's immigrant population: Romans are all *alumni*, foster children.[14] As Johnson points out, such naturalized citizens are at once Roman and not Roman, self and other: "But who," Johnson asks, "is an Umbrian to explain to Romans the truth of their city? It is he, after all, who stands as *alumnus*, the naturalized citizen, in this equation between those who know that their mother's milk was from the famous wolf and those who don't believe in that myth."[15] It is worth noting that everywhere Propertius uses the word *alumnus*—four times overall, three in Book 4—he connects it to a place rather than a person.[16] Identity comes from places as much as from parents. What do Rome's monuments mean to Romans? Which Romans? With these tensions between native and foreign, self and other, elegy 4.1 calls into question the entropic impact of cultural perspective on the meaning of a culturally diverse city.

A CITY OF VERSE

In marking out his new poetic endeavor, the poet establishes a tension between monuments made of stone and brick and those he constructs out of his words. Turning from Rome's glorious past to his own task as its poet, Propertius sets Romulus' walls (and what they have become) side by side with his own poetic walls:

optima nutricum nostris lupa Martia rebus,
    qualia creuerunt moenia lacte tuo!
moenia namque pio coner disponere uersu:

> ei mihi, quod nostro est paruus in ore sonus!
> sed tamen exiguo quodcumque e pectore riui
>   fluxerit, hoc patriae seruiet omne meae!

Wolf of Mars, best of nursemaids for our commonwealth, what walls grew from your milk! For I should try to lay out these walls in my holy verse: alas, that there is such a tiny voice in my throat! But all the same, whatever trickles from my puny breast, it will all go to serve my fatherland. (4.1.55–60)

Scholars often note the Callimachean resonance of these lines;[17] they are topographically important as well: Propertius establishes the theme of himself as builder. *Disponere* has strong spatial force, and the word is normally used of laying out or positioning buildings in space.[18] The metaphor continues with *versu*, emphatic at line's end, all the more startling as the nominal partner for the adjective *pio* earlier in the line. It is worth noting how succinctly line 4.1.56 poses a contrast to the *incipit* of Vergil's *Aeneid*, with its very different combination of walls and piety (*Aen.* 1.7 and 1.10, respectively). What is more, since the walls that grew from the she-wolf's milk surely refer to Romulus' archaic city, and to the contemporary walls the speaker points out to the visitor, the repetition of *moenia* at 4.1.56–57 (*qualia creuerunt moenia . . . moenia . . . coner disponere*) makes clear the parallel between Rome's first founder, its refounder, Augustus, and its latest founder, Propertius, each an architect of the city in his own way and with his own tools.[19]

As this *Callimachus Romanus* builds to a conclusion in the first half of the poem, he urges visitors to judge monuments by his own poetic talent:

> scandentis quisquis cernit de uallibus arces,
>   ingenio muros aestimet ille meo!
> Roma, faue, tibi surgit opus, date candida ciues
>   omina, et inceptis dextera cantet auis!
> sacra diesque canam et cognomina prisca locorum. (4.1.65–69)

Whoever sees these citadels rising above the valleys, let him judge their walls by my genius! Rome, approve: this work rises for you. Grant favorable omens, o citizens, and may the bird of prophecy sing propitiously at what I have begun! I shall sing of the rites and festivals of Rome, and of the hallowed names of its places.

As Newman points out,[20] we might have expected a different line: *ingenium muris aestimet ille meum!* (let him judge my genius by those walls!), a claim such as the poet often makes about Cynthia: she is (paradoxically) the source and product of his *ingenium* (2.1.4 and cf. 2.30b.40) and has power over his words. Instead, the poet chooses to reverse the common trope about his talent—instead of his subject conferring fame on his talent, his talent confers fame on his subject. The astrologer Horos will mimic Propertius' language with the same message at 4.1.125–26: *scandentisque Asis consurgit vertice murus, / murus ab ingenio notior ille tuo* (the wall of Assisi climbing upon its hilltop—a wall made more famous because of your genius). Words have power over people—and cities. Architecture has now replaced the *puella* as the beneficiary of the poet's skill. It is also important to note that this injunction about judging fame is given not to his readers *per se*, but to anyone who sees monuments; the poet's effect is not confined to poetry and its readers. Rather, those who see monuments are to judge them by Propertius' words.

Propertius continues to hold in balance the physical and verbal cities in the next couplet. *Tibi surgit opus*, he says at 4.1.66: this work rises for you. *Opus* has strong poetic connotations, and *surgo* is commonly used of architecture.[21] We might press these nuances of the phrase, by translating it thus: this (poetic) work rises (into the skyline) for you. In the pentameter, Propertius once again sets himself up as a new Romulus, founding a new city: a bird on the right (*dextera auis*) will approve his endeavor, just as birds on the right had shown favor to Romulus's city when it was new.[22] Finally, and most importantly, his famous programmatic statement draws attention to the names of places—*cognomina prisca locorum*—not the places themselves. These names, moreover, are not simply *nomina*, names given at birth, but rather *cognomina*, names bestowed afterward to clarify and redefine existing identities.[23] Throughout this programmatic section, therefore, Propertius' words juxtapose the monuments themselves with what is said about them. There is a Rome of stone, and a Rome of words.

ROME FOR THE ELEGIAC LOVER

In the second part of this introductory poem, the seer Horos interrupts the enthusiastic poet with a warning against this new and ambitious program. Horos—himself embodying another voice, a self-styled

defender of elegiac norms—introduces still more variables in interpreting Roman places, the first and foremost of which is genre. As he
begins his rebuttal to Propertius' new grand designs, Horos picks up
the theme of the city of words only to turn it on its head:

> quo ruis imprudens, vage, dicere fata, Properti?
>   non sunt a dextro condita fila colo.

> Where are you rushing, Propertius you fool, to utter the fates? These
> threads were not set up on a favorable distaff. (4.1.71–72)

With *dextro . . . colo* Horos recalls the *dextera . . . auis* Propertius had sum-
moned four lines earlier to sanction his poetic city, but he re-appropri-
ates divine favor for the poetic mission; though line 4.1.72 surely refers
to the literal activity of the Parcae, who weave and mete out the
threads of fate, the line also plays on spinning as a metaphor, as old as
Homer, for poetry. Horos also plays on the double meaning of *condita*,
an obvious term for city building, especially after the proem to Vergil's
Aeneid (1.33). Horos' interruption itself seems to indicate a fundamen-
tal incompatibility between urban subject matter and finely spun poetry. After the seer demonstrates his own credentials, he makes his point
about this incompatibility even more explicit. Apollo, erstwhile patron
of Propertius' former love poetry, forbids it:

> tum tibi pauca suo de carmine dictat Apollo
>   et uetat insano uerba tonare Foro.
> at tu finge elegos, fallax opus: haec tua castra!—
>   scribat ut exemplo cetera turba tuo.

> Then Apollo tells you a few things about his type of poetry, and he for-
> bids you to thunder in the frenetic Forum. No—you craft elegies instead,
> a tricky task: this is your tour of duty!—so that the rest of the crowd may
> write from your example. (4.1.133–36)

Again, Horos turns the poet's own words to new meaning: where
Propertius had promised that his opus would rise up for Rome (*tibi surgit opus*, 4.1.67), Horos encourages him to stick with elegiac poetry, a
fallax opus. Propertius' poetic city is antithetical to elegiac poetry.
Horos is responding to the poet's own promise of a grander style for
Book 4: words such as *tumefacta* and *superbiat* (4.1.63), *surgit* (4.1.67),
and images such as the poet's chariot racing toward a new goal

(4.1.70), all suggest a higher style.[24] Horos' response to this inflated program is that the poet is forbidden by his patron Apollo to thunder, *tonare*, in the Forum. The phrase is multivalent. On one level it speaks about the sort of poetry Apollo's poet is best suited to write: the word *tonare* at once evokes Callimachus' famous statement that thundering was Zeus's province, not Apollo's:

"βροντᾶν οὐκ ἐμόν, ἆα Διός."
καὶ γὰρ ὅτε πρώτιστον ἐμοῖς ἐπὶ δέλτον ἔθηκα
γούνασιν, Ἀπόλλων εἶπεν ὅ μοι Λύκιος·
" . . . ἀοιδέ, τὸ μὲν θύος ὅττι πάχιστον
θρέψαι, τὴν Μοῦσαν δ᾽ ὠγαθὲ λεπταλέην."

"It is not my job to thunder, but that of Zeus." For as soon as I put the tablet on my knees Lykian Apollo said to me, "Poet, feed the victim to be as fat as possible, but keep your Muse slender." (*Aitia* fr.1.20–24)

Because of the Callimachean intertext, I read Propertius' *suo de carmine* as "about his song" rather than "from his song;"[25] I believe Apollo is feeding the poet guidelines, not words. Thundering, says the god, is not the sort of thing appropriate to Apollo's poet. On another level the phrase *vetat tonare* forbids Propertius from engaging in a public career such as would be boomed in the Forum.[26] Yet thundering also summons the image of Jupiter Tonans from 4.1.7, a temple built by Augustus in 23 BCE to commemorate the special favor shown to him by the sky-god. In forbidding thundering, Apollo thus vetoes not only a grand, un-Callimachean poetic style but an Augustan monument as well. Add to this the explicit interdiction from the Forum, and we are left with the impression that grand poetry may treat some sorts of urban places—some parts of Rome—while elegiac poetry inhabits different places—some other parts of Rome, parts without thunder or the bustle of the Forum. This relationship between—or rather severance of—genre and urban location offers yet another way of reading Rome: it changes according to the matrix of genre.[27]

GENDERED SPACE

Furthermore, the stories Horos tells to validate his own authority are all about women—not the men who had featured in the more patriotic first half of the poem. The reader may recall that in the poem's first half, against a catalogue of Evander and Aeneas, the Patres, Fabius Lupercus, Lucumo, Titus Tatius, Romulus and Remus, Caesar, Iulus, the Decii and the Bruti (both the founder of the Republic and the tyrannocide),[28] the poet includes only Vesta, *armigera* Venus, the Sibyl, the prophet Cassandra, and the she-wolf as representatives of the softer sex—hardly *puellae* in any sense, except for Cassandra, but, as DeBrohun argues, all these women serve and operate in an exclusively male world.[29] Horos, on the other hand, focuses closely on women and women's concerns. Various examples of female sexuality fill his own prophetic *cursus honorum*—Arria, a mother who lost two sons to warfare (4.1.89–97); Cinara, who suffered a difficult childbirth (4.1.99–102); Iphigeneia, virginal sacrificial victim of the Trojan War (4.1.109–14); and Cassandra again, now the rape victim of Ajax (4.1.114–18). These women and their experiences are the antithesis of the masculine experience outlined in such inflated terms by Propertius in the first half of the poem.

When the seer turns to the poet's own stars, he draws attention to the fact that Propertius' life has been guided by a feminine, not masculine, influence. After the loss of his father in the civil wars, a loss inappropriate for one as young as the poet presumably was, Horos reveals that Propertius took up the toga of manhood under his mother's guidance, not his father's:

> ossaque legisti non illa aetate legenda
> > patris et in tenuis cogeris ipse lares:
> nam tua cum multi uersarent rura iuuenci,
> > abstulit excultas pertica tristis opes.
> mox ubi bulla rudi demissa est aurea collo
> > matris et ante deos libera sumpta toga.

> And you collected the bones of your father, which should not have been collected at such a young age, and you are forced into a lowly estate. For although many bulls used to turn over the soil in your fields, a grim surveyor's rod took away the riches you had cultivated. Soon, when the golden amulet was released from your young neck, you took up the free man's toga before the watchful gods of your mother. (4.1.127–32)

A ceremony normally involving fathers and sons has become, in the wake of war, one between mothers and sons. Propertius is thus shepherded into manhood by his mother;[30] in this way he is, the seer suggests, more in tune with feminine concerns than with the traditionally masculine exploits promised in the poem's first half.

Horos' focus on mortal women, and on Propertius' mother, offers yet another outlook on the split city that emerges from this split poem. Just as the seer pits the grand Callimachean city against the softer elegiac town, he suggests a difference between man's Rome and woman's. He follows his famous urban injunction (*uetat . . . tonare Foro . . . at tu finge elegos*, 4.1.134–35) with a plea to attend to the ladies:

> militiam Veneris blandis patiere sub armis,
> > et Veneris pueris utilis hostis eris.
> nam tibi uictrices quascumque labore parasti,
> > eludet palmas una puella tuas.

> You will endure a tour of duty under the soft weapons of Venus, and you will be a useful foil for Venus' boys. For whatever conquests you have earned with your own work, one girl will make sport of your victory palms. (4.1.137–40)

Horos has transformed martial Venus, advancing Caesar's arms at 4.1.46, into Martial Venus, waging her war for and with lovers. One woman will win this war against the poet, cheating him out of the tokens of victory. "Avoid the Forum," Horos tells Propertius: it is the poetically correct thing to do, and a girl will keep you from such male pursuits anyway. Gender difference, too, influences the way one interprets Roman places and the places one interprets.[31]

HOROS' *OMINA* AGAINST THE POET'S *COGNOMINA*

It is widely agreed that the intrusion of a second voice at 4.1.71 retracts and amends the program set out in the first half of the poem.[32] Horos urges a return to personal elegiac poetry and an awareness of the woman that foils all grander plans. He also demonstrates a broad interest in the interconnection of physical environment and identity. Like Propertius, Horos follows a physical structure: that of the sky. Horos' knowledge of the sky, he contests—that is, his expertise in its topography—gives him special authority to interpret the city on the ground. Horos presents a lengthy argument that identity is better revealed and shaped by the celestial city than the terrestrial one; that the terrestrial city obscures its own cost in human suffering, while his heavenly architecture reveals it; and that the city on the ground will always be shaped and seen by persons, rather than institutions or categories.

As mentioned above, Horos opens his rebuttal by discrediting the city Propertius promised to celebrate a few lines earlier:

> quo ruis imprudens, uage, dicere fata, Properti?
>   non sunt a dextro condita fila colo.
> accersis lacrimas cantans, auersus Apollo:
>   poscis ab inuita uerba pigenda lyra.

> Where are you rushing, Propertius you fool, to utter the fates? These threads were not set up on a favorable distaff. You are inviting tears by your singing: Apollo is against it. You seek words from your unwilling lyre that you will regret. (4.1.71–74)

Condere is a word of building, and also of weaving; we saw above how these lines attach Propertius' poetic project to his urban project. Yet these lines also bring into play the relationship between building a city (and weaving poetry) and understanding one's place in a wider universe, by speaking the will of the gods (*dicere fata*, 4.1.70). Propertius' project of understanding Roman identity simply via the *sacra diesque* and *cognomina prisca locorum* is, to Horos, foolish, off-task, and unsanctioned by the gods. In fact, the explicit absence of divine sanction for Propertius' project, seen in the phrases *non . . . a dextro . . . colo* and *auersus Apollo*, frustrates the hopes of the poet who just five lines earlier hoped for favorable portents (*candida omina*) and an auspicious (*dextera*) bird of omen (4.1.67–68). In Horos' opinion, the omens did not appear.[33]

In contrast, Horos claims to speak for the god Apollo, even to be his proxy—or at least to be privy to the god's thoughts. He breaks into the poem just as Apollo had in Callimachus' *Aitia* 1.23–24, with a warning and with some advice about what sort of poetry is appropriate (τὸ μὲν θύος ὅττι πάχιστον θρέψαι, τὴν Μοῦσαν δ' ὠγαθὲ λεπταλέην; feed the victim to be as fat as possible, but keep your Muse slender). Horos twice voices Apollo's displeasure with Propertius' intended theme of topographical poems: at 4.1.73 (*auersus Apollo*) and again at 4.1.133 (*Apollo . . . uetat insano uerba tonare Foro*). Horos' access to the god's will is a byproduct of his acquaintance with the heavens: he is a bona fide astronomer/astrologer, and takes every chance to offer his credentials as such. Indeed, he asserts the reliability—*fides*—of his craft four times in the poem (4.1.80, 92, 98, and 108), and traces his roots to the likes of the famous Hellenistic astronomers Conon and Archytas (4.1.77–78). He is thus an expert not only at the stars, but at the sort of erudite art Propertius has promised.[34] Horos is skilled in the movement of the stars (4.1.75–76) and poses the value of knowing the topography of the heavens:

> aspicienda uia est caeli uerusque per astra
> trames, et ab zonis quinque petenda fides.

> You must pay attention to the path of the sky, and the true corridor through the stars; seek assurance from the sky's five zones. (4.1.107–8)

Though he extols such astrological knowledge as an alternative to oracles, hepatoscopy, haruspicy, and necromancy—all of which failed to foretell the fates in the particular case Horos is describing (4.1.103–6)—his description emphasizes the spatial layout of the sky: its paths and passageways (*uia, trames*), and its neighborhoods (*zonis*).

With his expertise in the stellar topography that allows him to sing the fates, Horos redirects Propertius' gaze to individuals as inhabitants of the city. From this perspective, Rome's existence and growth rests on such events as the sacrifice of Iphigeneia, the lost innocence of Cassandra, and the death of Arria's two sons.[35] The astrologer brings the point home by reading Propertius' own stars, concentrating on the profoundly sad effect Rome has had on his own life. As it was then, so it is now:

> hactenus historiae: nunc ad tua deuehar astra;
> incipe tu lacrimis aequus adesse novis . . .
> ossaque legisti non illa aetate legenda
> patris et in tenuis cogeris ipse lares:
> nam tua cum multi uersarent rura iuuenci,
> abstulit excultas pertica tristis opes.

> Enough of ancient history: now let me proceed to your stars; you, be ready to deal with renewed tears. . . . And you collected the bones of your father, which should not have been collected at such a young age, and you are forced into a lowly estate. For although many bulls used to turn over the soil in your fields, a grim surveyor's rod took away the riches you had cultivated. (4.1.119–20, 127–30)

Propertius, Horos argues, can never view the city unprejudiced by his sad past; thus he should abandon his project and keep to personal elegies. The city can never be divorced from the individuals who inhabit it; a fall must accompany the rise, and thus Horos can only promise to sing of tombs:

> dicam: "Troia cades, et Troica Roma resurges";
>   et maris et terrae longa sepulcra canam.

> I shall say: "Troy, you will fall, and Trojan Rome, you will rise anew";
> and I shall sing of the tombs widespread on land and sea.[36] (4.1.87–88)

CONCLUSION

Propertius' introductory poem, then, while promising to explain Rome's monuments in the book to come, does so by offering many ways, often contradictory, of explaining them. The multiple perspectives on Rome's places offered in elegy 4.1 raise the possibility that Rome's monuments are not monolithic in their meaning, but rather mean different things to different people or to the same people at different times or in different contexts. With this open program in place, the poet turns his pen to individual places and monuments, the first of which—the statue of Vertumnus—offers a test case for the flexibility embodied in elegy 4.1. The rest of the topographical elegies in Book 4 also respond to the nuances and questions raised in this programmatic elegy, exploring Rome's change and continuity over time (elegies 4.4, 4.9, 4.10); the diverse faces it offers to insiders and outsiders (4.2, 4.10); the city as a monument of words rather than stone (4.6, 4.10); how Rome differs when seen through a variety of generic lenses— elegy, epic, didactic, and the like (4.2, 4.9, 4.10); the gulf between the Rome inhabited by men and that inhabited by women (4.2, 4.4, 4.9, 4.10); and the tension between individual and institutional Romes (4.4, 4.10).

CHAPTER 2

Shifting Vertumnus

PLURALITY, POLYSEMY, AND AUGUSTAN
ROME IN ELEGY 4.2

IN ELEGY 4.2 Propertius adopts the voice of a statue of Vertumnus, an Etruscan god established at Rome in the archaic period. The god revels in his shifting identity and sets the tone for the poem in its opening couplet:

> qui mirare meas tot in uno corpore formas,
>   accipe Vertumni signa paterna dei.

> Passerby, do you marvel that I have so many figures in one body? Learn the ancestral signs of the god Vertumnus. (4.2.1–2)

He proceeds to describe how mutable these ancestral signs are, as various people clothe his statue in different costumes—female, male, agricultural, military, and political—according to their desire. Because of this mutability, many readers have understood Vertumnus as a mouthpiece for the poet, who thus demonstrates with brio the flexibility of his own elegiac poetry.[1] Indeed, Book 4 is a catalogue of Vertumnian flexibility, assuming sometimes male and sometimes female perspectives, sometimes amatory and sometimes epic themes.

I believe this poem celebrates not just the variety possible in elegiac poetry, but the variety inherent in Roman identity itself, particularly in regard to ethnic identity. The god Vertumnus has Etruscan origins and resides in Rome, where he was brought at the time of the Sabine assimilation into Roman culture. According to Propertius, moreover, his statue was crafted by an artisan with Oscan connections. In this way the statue is a witness to and result of the Roman melting pot. The location and setting of Vertumnus' statue support this interpretation. Vertumnus was worshipped at two sites in Rome: a temple on the Aventine, built after the Roman conquest of Volsinii in 264 BCE, and a statue adjacent to the Forum on the Vicus Tuscus. Propertius' Vertumnus, though he alludes to the former monument at 4.2.4, speaks from the latter location and draws attention to this part of Rome as its most diverse quarter. It is Rome's most bustling entry point on the banks of the Tiber river, a place that preserves in its name (Vicus Tuscus) and its activity the newcomer's delicate balance between foreign and Roman —i.e., a place where foreigners begin to become Romans.

Propertius' Vertumnus highlights the fact that he prefers his place at the edge of—not within—the Roman forum (4.2.6). Though resident in Rome for hundreds of years, he still considers himself an outsider looking in. Indeed, at the poem's beginning, Vertumnus speaks of his ancestral—i.e., Etruscan—marks (*signa paterna*, 4.2.2). Near its end he speaks of his ancestral—i.e., Roman—language (*patria lingua*, 4.2.48). Which is his *patria*—Volsinii or Rome? In this respect, too, Vertumnus is much like Propertius himself, who, as we saw above, reveals his own hybrid identity in the introductory poem to Book 4, identifying both with his native *patria* Assisi (4.1.64) and with his adopted *patria* Rome (4.1.60). Following on the heels of the multiple perspectives delineated in 4.1, Propertius' mutable Vertumnus draws attention to the instability of the construction of Roman identity. What is it to be Roman? Are all Romans Roman in the same way?

At the same time, Vertumnus invites questions as to the meaning of Roman monuments. As his statue adapts itself to each diverse and individual passerby Vertumnus demonstrates that his monument—any monument—may be viewed in different ways by different viewers. As with poem 4.1, Vertumnus draws attention to a polysemy of Rome's monuments that matches the variety of Roman viewers. In a bold statement about the meaning of his own and other Roman monuments, Propertius' Vertumnus effectively says, "Read me any way you want."

VERTUMNUS IN ROME: TOPOGRAPHICAL ALTERITY

Vertumnus' presence in Rome is a perfect example of the city's integration of other peoples and their gods. Both Vertumnus' Roman monuments were understood as commemorations of Rome's assimilation of another Italic people; and both lay in places resonant with Rome's "other" Romans—that is, outsiders who became insiders. As such, both these monuments contemplated Roman identity, as they reminded all Romans, old and new, about the plurality of their community. What is more, both monuments suggested to outsiders visiting Rome the possibility of themselves becoming Roman. Though these two monuments both dealt with *Romanitas*, they differed in one important respect: one suggests a peaceful, the other a violent assimilation into Roman identity.

Vertumnus' origins and heritage were as obscure then as they are now. The Romans believed he was an Etruscan deity absorbed into Roman religion early in the city's development. Varro calls Vertumnus *deus Etruriae princeps* (*Ling.* 5.46), but this statement is difficult to assess; does Varro mean that Vertumnus is the foremost Etruscan god, or the oldest, or (like Janus) the first to be celebrated in the new year?[2] The widespread appearance of Etruscan inscriptions to the god Velthune supports the first interpretation of Varro's words, as does the fact that this god was venerated as Voltumnus at Volsinii, meeting point of an Etruscan federation; Livy 4.22.5 speaks of an Etruscan League that met *ad Voltumnae fanum* (at the shrine of Voltumna/us). As the patron of an Etruscan federation, this god also appears on an Etruscan mirror, presiding over an instance of hepatoscopy.[3]

Nevertheless, even though the consonant clusters -*th*-, -*lt*-, and -*mn*- are common features in Etruscan words, the god's name also evokes Indo-European roots. Roman poets and antiquarians linked the name to the verb *uertere*, to turn.[4] Modern Etruscologists and linguists have also seen in the god's name traces of a proto-Latin (and Greek-flavored) syncopated participle *uert-omenos* from *uertere* (similar to *alumnus*, from *alomenos*/*alere*),[5] or traces of various other Indo-European —i.e., not Etruscan—roots.[6] The question remains: was Vertumnus originally an Etruscan god adopted by the Romans, or an Italic god adopted by the Etruscans and then re-appropriated by the Romans? Whatever the god's origins in the Italian peninsula, it is important to note that the Romans themselves blended Vertumnus' identity, considering him an Etruscan original but assigning him an etymologically Roman past. For the Romans, therefore, the god is both Etruscan and Roman. Propertius will have much to say about this elasticity of Vertumnus' origins and identity, but we must first understand the Roman monuments to which his poem responds.

Vertumnus' earliest monument in Rome (and the one whose voice Propertius adopts) was a statue of the god, known as the Signum Vortumni (= Vertumni), located at the edge of the Velabrum near the crescent of the Tiber river. In one source it is called a *sacellum*, but this need not imply a building around the statue—simply a sacred spot.[7] The monument was most likely a statue on a base, a description supported by an inscription dating from the tetrarchy: *Vortumnus temporibus Diocletiani et Maximiani.*[8] The monument may predate the Forum and the Cloaca Maxima, which bends around it, seemingly to accommodate it.[9] Propertius' elegy 4.2, to be discussed below, reveals that it was frequently the recipient of offerings of various kinds, including fruit, flowers, clothing, and grain.[10]

Both the *signum Vortumni* itself and the area surrounding it have a strong Etruscan resonance. According to Varro and Propertius (probably following Varro), this statue was erected to commemorate the aid given by the Etruscans to Rome during Rome's conflict with Titus Tatius and his Sabines.[11] These same Etruscans who aided Rome are supposed to have given their name to the Vicus Tuscus, the street that starts at the Signum Vortumni and runs from the statue between the Capitoline and Palatine hills toward the Forum Boarium. Alternative traditions name either settlers left by Porsenna after his treaty with Rome or Tarquinius Priscus' supporters as the eponymous group for the Vicus Tuscus.[12] One modern scholar even plausibly suggests that the street was so named because it was the quickest path from the Forum Romanum to Etruscan territory on the opposite side of the river.[13] The accommodation of the Tarquin-channeled Cloaca Maxima to Vertumnus' existing monument suggests Etruscan respect for, if not veneration of, the god.

The stories about the monument's foundation and its location indicate that, for the Romans, the god Vertumnus was a totem for their relations with the Etruscans. Indeed the founding of his statue as recorded by Propertius and Varro was a gesture of cooperation between Romans and Etruscans, and all three versions of the origin of the Vicus Tuscus chronicle friendly relations.[14] At the end of the Vicus Tuscus, Vertumnus' statue marks the edge of the area that was once the Velabrum marsh—a shallow but navigable area in archaic times that would welcome visitors from the north who arrived on the Tiber. It is not surprising that, once drained, this area (the future Vicus Tuscus) became a cosmopolitan commercial district for fine clothing, jewelry, books, and other goods traded between Romans and their rich northern neighbors.[15] The huge Horrea Agrippiana, warehouse complexes

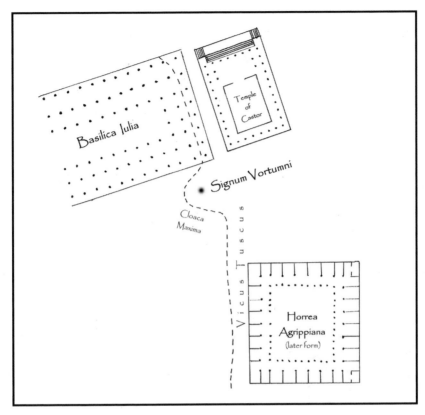

FIGURE 2. Plan of the Vicus Tuscus, depicting the Signum Vortumni, around which bends the Cloaca Maxima. The statue marks the transition from the ordered Forum Romanum on the north to the more densely built commercial district to the south. After Colonna 1987: 60.

of the Augustan age erected in *opus reticulatum* with travertine additions, also testify to this area's commercial nature.[16] The Signum Vortumni, standing watch over this district and separating it from the Forum Romanum, was, at the same time, both a beacon of the friendship between the Romans and their neighbors the Etruscans, and a reminder of Roman diversity—indeed, a reminder of Rome's dependence on others in times of need.[17]

This diversity, however, had its negative side. So many things were traded there—including the flesh of prostitutes—that the Vicus Tuscus suffered from a rather unsavory reputation throughout the Republican era. Plautus and Horace both speak of the area with sardonic scorn, labeling it as a place unsuitable for upstanding people.[18] This feature of the Vicus Tuscus area poses some interesting questions about Roman assimilation of other peoples: were immigrants consigned to low-status roles in the city, indicating that Vertumnus served as a strong boundary between the area for newcomers and that reserved for more established Romans? Was assimilation quicker politically than economically, suggesting a Vertumnus who stood as a point of transition? Or rather, since Romans seem to have been eager participants in the Velabrum's commerce, does the area suggest a meeting place of cultural values, pointing to a Vertumnus who promoted cultural traffic in both directions? A glance at a map of the area (Figure 2) reveals Vertumnus' position as both boundary and mediator between diverse segments of the Roman landscape.

Vertumnus' other monument in Rome also speaks to Rome's assimilation of other peoples, but the message is less welcoming. Vertumnus was venerated at a temple on the Aventine, called the *aedes Vortumni*, every August 13, the temple's *dies natalis* according to several Fasti.[19] Inside this temple a painting of Marcus Fulvius Flaccus in triumphal garb indicated that the temple was dedicated after Flaccus' conquest of the Volsinians in 264 BCE.[20] It is possible that Vertumnus was brought officially to Rome by *euocatio*—a process whereby Romans in times of war invited their enemies' gods to switch their loyalties to Rome, under the promise of better temples and more assiduous worship.[21]

Like its counterpart in the Vicus Tuscus, this Vertumnus also spoke to Rome's plurality and invited its onlookers to reflect on what it was to be Roman. Its message about Roman plurality, however, was quite different from its partner monument in the Velabrum. Unlike the Velabrum's Vertumnus, which monumentalized peaceful and gradual absorption of foreigners into Roman culture, the Aventine temple symbolized Rome's violent assimilation of other peoples and their gods into Roman culture. The Roman victory over Volsinii was particularly thorough, and even sparked anti-Roman propaganda about Roman abuse of this rich town—namely, that Romans had conquered Volsinii merely to confiscate its artworks (Pliny *HN* 34.34). While booty might have added further incentive to soldiers and commanders, Rome's violent intervention into Volsinian internal affairs (strife between social classes) and its relocation of survivors suggest a desire to eliminate Volsinii as a political force and to expand Rome's dominion into Etruria.[22] Not only does the Aventine Vertumnus thus bear witness to his own defeat and assimilation, but, from his location on that hill, he would also observe other conquered peoples led into Rome in future triumphs. From his perspective, to be Roman means to have been conquered by Romans. In this context, the god's supposed *euocatio* is particularly interesting. The *euocatio,* signaling as it does the god's acceptance of defeat and willingness to abandon his hometown in favor of Rome, provides a powerful model for other conquered peoples to behave likewise. The fact that throughout the Republic the Roman army depended increasingly on Italian manpower lends weight to the importance of violent assimilation in Roman culture.

Like the Aventine itself, the *aedes Vortumni* thus commemorated outsiders who, though assimilated, were still somehow marginalized, still somehow not Roman.[23] The relative absence of Volsinian families from Senatorial records of the last century of the Republic reveals their continued marginality in Rome.[24] The location of the *aedes Vortumni* on the Aventine is telling. Like the Velabrum, the Aventine was an area for commerce and attracted both foreign and local tradesmen.[25] Also like the Velabrum, the Aventine held negative connotations for some Romans. From its earliest use as Remus's base in his contest with Romulus, this hill was considered a place for outsiders or for others not central in Roman ideology. Excluded from Rome by the course of the *pomerium,* the Aventine became the favored hill of the plebeians, who settled there when they wanted to secede from Rome—i.e., when they wanted, in a sense, no longer to be Romans. The *lex Icilia* of c. 456 BCE even gave the Aventine over to the plebeians for them to distribute among themselves.[26]

It was also a hill favored by other outsiders in Rome. Diana, chief goddess of the Latin league, had her temple on the Aventine and shared Aventine Vertumnus' birthday. Though the importation of this pan-Latin goddess was touted as a unifying move on the Romans' parts, Livy reveals that Servius' foundation of this cult in Rome was a crafty attempt to wrest power from the Latin people by appropriating their chief god.[27] Diana's temple was thus a mark of Roman superiority over the Latin League—another example of Rome's aggressive assimilation.[28] Add to this Aventine hub the nearby temple to Juno Regina, evoked in 396 BCE just before Camillus' final destruction of Etruscan Veii,[29] and the tenor of the hill becomes clear: the Aventine is a place for Romans at odds with being Roman—either because (like Rome's defeated neighbors) they were made Roman or because (like the plebs) they were not made Roman enough.

While Vertumnus' temple on the Aventine surely evoked feelings of pride or ambivalence for Romans and for those they conquered, the Velabrum monument's meaning is harder to pin down. As an ancient statue of an ancient god, a playful monument situated at the juncture between the bustling Vicus Tuscus and the stunning Forum Romanum, Vertumnus' monument was a bit of a mystery for those who passed by. With its changes of clothing and the variety of offerings left to it, the statue may have been an amusing conversation piece and a curious tourist destination, much like Brussels' Manneken Pis today. Like its ancient counterpart, the Brussels statue boasts many myths of its origin and meaning, and overshadows in popularity many more venerable and grand monuments.[30] It is this mysterious Vertumnus who speaks in elegy 4.2.

READING VERTUMNUS' POEM

Propertius' poem on Vertumnus has more than once been omitted in treatments of Book 4 as a whole.[31] Several possible reasons suggest themselves. First, the statue of Vertumnus is a small and relatively unimportant monument in Augustan Rome, and, unlike the other topographical foci in the book, this monument lacks a known Augustan intervention. Second, the subject himself is quite elusive; not much is known about the god Vertumnus or his shrine beyond the tantalizing details presented in this poem. Third, the poem, though imbued with details important in understanding Roman constructions of gender, can be overshadowed by other poems with similar themes (4.3's wife Arethusa, 4.8's martial Cynthia, 4.9's gender-bending Hercules, 4.10's male-only cast, and 4.11's *uniuira* Cornelia). Fourth, the poem has no obvious Vergilian or Livian analogue, and does not lend itself easily to other types of *Quellenforschung*.

Nevertheless, Vertumnus occupies a prominent place in the book, as an inauguration into the sort of poetry Propertius promises in elegy 4.1. Elegy 4.2 may be read in a metapoetic light: Vertumnus masks the poet, and his speech elucidates the elegies that follow. The strong affinities between Vertumnus and Propertius point to an alignment of the god and the poet. Both celebrate their Tuscan origins. At 4.2.3 Vertumnus boldly states his ethnic heritage: *Tuscus ego <et> Tuscis orior* (I am Tuscan and I spring from Tuscan roots), a heritage Propertius himself celebrates at 4.1.64: *Umbria Romani patria Callimachi* (Umbria, the fatherland of the Roman Callimachus).[32] Likewise, Vertumnus connects himself to Apollo and to Bacchus, the twin divine sources of Propertius' inspiration:[33]

cinge caput mitra, speciem furabor Iacchi;
furabor Phoebi, si modo plectra dabis.

Bind my head with a turban, and I shall commandeer the appearance of
Bacchus. I'll commandeer Phoebus', if you will give me a plectrum.
(4.2.31–32)

Moreover, the poem is replete with self-conscious literary puns that
cast Vertumnus as a poet discussing his book.[34] If Vertumnus masks the
poet, then his speech of self-revelation is easily understood as a commentary on Propertius' poetry. Vertumnus begins his poem by
expressing his aptitude for variety:

qui mirare meas tot in uno corpore formas,
    accipe Vertumni signa paterna dei.

Passerby, do you marvel that I have so many figures in one·body? Learn
the ancestral signs of the god Vertumnus. (4.2.1–2)

As I mentioned above, this variety of form embodies the *poikilia* sought
after by the self-proclaimed Roman Callimachus.[35] It exists within the
poem itself, as Vertumnus dazzles us with his ability to assume diverse
guises. This *poikilia* is also a feature of Book 4 as a whole, and this poem
acts as a sort of "second proem" to the book that follows. Various scholars have discussed this function of the poem. For Shea, the solution to
the poem's opening riddle ("what am I?") is "Propertius' apostrophe to
Book IV."[36] The poem's curious denouement (*sex superant uersus,*
4.2.57)—itself a veiled etymology for the god's name—connects the
god's/poet's verses with the six transformations (*uersus*) into other
characters later in the book (Arethusa, Tarpeia, Acanthis, Cynthia,
Hercules, and Cornelia). Wyke and DeBrohun both read Vertumnus'
"turnings" as evidence of the "bipolar poetics" of Book 4, which alter-
nates between opposite discourses such as the amatory and the patriotic, the private and the public, or the elegiac and the aetiological.[37]

Vertumnus is certainly a mouthpiece for Propertius' elegiac poetry.
Given the poem's metapoetic content, the fact that the poem is an
aetion for a monument becomes especially provocative. O'Neill, in a
highly suggestive article, has connected Vertumnus' generic play with
the topography of the poem.[38] Adducing evidence from a variety of literary texts, O'Neill reveals the seamier side of the Vicus Tuscus. A hub

of commercial activity in Rome, the Vicus Tuscus was one of the city's bookselling districts as well as a center for prostitution. The god's choice of this location over the more respectable *aedes Vortumni*, with its connotations of triumph, is a strong statement of his generic preferences: the Vicus Tuscus connects Vertumnus with amatory and with literary themes. The odd god therefore overcomes elegy 4.1's apparent schism between amatory and aetiological poetry.

While I agree that this poem connects Propertius' choice of genre with the cityscape he celebrates in Book 4, I believe the connection between genre and city is even more pervasive than O'Neill suggests. Roman elegiac poetry constructs itself as oppositional—not by its opposition to any moral code, Augustan or otherwise, but rather by its systematic refusal to conform to any code through the contradictions inherent in its moral and discursive positions.[39] So, too, Vertumnus' monument resists categorization or easy identification. As the god describes himself in Propertius' poem, he is himself an amalgam of various ethnic contributions to Rome, who enjoys a marginal perspective on Rome and is self-conscious about his marginality. What is more, Vertumnus' identity changes with every viewer (who dresses the god according to his desire) and every reader (who provides any etymology he likes). The monument's meaning is deliberately difficult to pin down. Vertumnus' self-presentation in this poem invites the reader to question Roman identity and to regard it not as something stable or monolithic but rather as something flexible and plural. Furthermore, the poem invites the reader, by this example, to question the meaning of Roman monuments in general, and to regard them, too, not as monolithic in their meaning but as subject to individual interpretations. The poem therefore introduces the reader to the various perspectives on Roman monuments that will appear in the poems to follow, and prepares the reader to read those monuments with an open mind.

WHOSE READING? VERTUMNUS AND PLURAL IDENTITY

Vertumnus begins his poem with a promise to reveal the signs of his fatherland. From his first lines he introduces his own plurality and his Tuscan origins:

qui mirare meas tot in uno corpore formas,
  accipe Vertumni signa paterna dei.
Tuscus ego <et> Tuscis orior nec paenitet inter
  proelia Volsinios deseruisse focos.
haec me turba iuuat, nec templo laetor eburno:
  Romanum satis est posse uidere Forum.

Passerby, do you marvel that I have so many figures in one body? Learn
the ancestral signs of the god Vertumnus. I am Tuscan and sprung from
Tuscan origins, nor am I grieved to have deserted the hearths of Volsinii
in the heat of battle. This crowd pleases me, and I do not delight in an
ivory temple. It is enough to be able to see the Forum Romanum.
(4.2.1–6)

If his body contains many forms, so too does his ancestry, and in the
course of the poem's sixty-four lines Vertumnus invokes the Etruscans,
Romans, and Sabines (and maybe Oscans) as participants in his own
creation and, indeed, in Rome's history. In this way he is a strong symbol of Rome's religious diversity and a fitting prelude to the diversity
of poems to follow.[40]

Of his many ancestors Vertumnus begins with his Tuscan origins,
but he is careful to define which Etruscans are not part of his background: he is not one of the Etruscans defeated by the Romans at
Volsinii in 264 BCE.[41] The way of becoming Roman that relies on imperialism and expansion is not that of Propertius' Vertumnus: he is not
grieved to have become Roman through violent aggression, nor does
he require triumphal temples such as the one on the Aventine.[42] Rather,
he stresses his location on the Vicus Tuscus, the bustling commercial
district discussed above as a cosmopolitan place that hosted many visitors to Rome. Indeed, at 4.2.6 Vertumnus emphasizes the fact that he is
not in the Roman Forum (the symbolic center of Roman hegemony)
but rather on its margins. His perspective on *Romanitas*, therefore,
comes not from the center but from the periphery.

Later in the poem Vertumnus returns to his Tuscan origins, this time
stressing the fact that he was assimilated as a friend and ally to Rome
rather than as a conquered enemy:

et tu, Roma, meis tribuisti praemia Tuscis,
  (unde hodie Vicus nomina Tuscus habet),

tempore quo sociis uenit Lycomedius armis
    atque Sabina feri contudit arma Tati.
uidi ego labentis acies et tela caduca,
    atque hostis turpi terga dedisse fugae.

And you, Rome, provided rewards for my fellow Etruscans (from whom
the present-day Vicus Tuscus has its name), back when Lycomedius
arrived with allies and crushed the Sabine forces commanded by cruel
Tatius. I saw the crumbling battles and the weapons falling, and enemies
who turned their back in shameful flight. (4.2.49–54)

Vertumnus stresses that his entry into Roman culture fell at the time of
the Sabine wars, a tradition shared by Varro but not by Livy, Dionysius,
Tacitus, or Festus.[43] The god's lingering description of this event suggests the idea of Roman plurality; the Sabine wars would lead to the
assimilation of Sabines and Romans into one community, and Titus
Tatius would eventually share Rome's monarchy with Romulus.[44] The
Sabines were thus indirectly responsible for Vertumnus' arrival at
Rome. Pursuing this thought, Vertumnus again evokes the Sabine presence in the city:

stipes acernus eram, properanti falce dolatus,
    ante Numam grata pauper in urbe deus.
at tibi, Mamurri, formae caelator aenae,
    tellus artifices ne terat Osca manus,
qui me tam docilis potuisti fundere in usus.

I was a maple stump, hewn by the quick blade, a poor god in a pleasing
city before Numa. But, Mamurrius, engraver of my bronze form, may
the Oscan earth not wear away your artist's hands, since you were able
to cast me into so many pliant uses. (4.2.59–63)

The Sabine Numa, Rome's second king and one legendary for devel-
oping and codifying religious practices in Rome, contributed to
Vertumnus' presence in Rome. During Numa's reign, as the text
implies—and perhaps even at the king's commission—the legendary
artisan Mamurrius Veturius crafted a more permanent statue of the
god. The fact that Propertius' Mamurrius was buried in Oscan territory adds perhaps another ethnic dimension to Vertumnus' identity. If

Mamurrius was of Oscan descent (a possibility), or had other strong ties to the Oscans (guaranteed by his burial in Oscan soil), then his work on Vertumnus' statue marks yet another ethnic contributor to the god's identity. Vertumnus begins by promising to reveal his *signa paterna*, the signs of his fatherland; at the end of the poem he reveals that there are many clues to his fatherland, or, to put it another way, that his *patria* includes many parts of Italy.

Vertumnus' celebration of Italian identity manifests itself elsewhere in the poem as well. To explain one of his (suspect) etymologies, i.e., that his name has an agricultural origin and derives from *uert-annus*, the god launches into a description of the countryside under his purview, and later describes the agricultural roles he can assume:

> seu, quia uertentis fructum praecepimus anni,
> Vertumni rursus credis id esse sacrum.[45]
> prima mihi uariat liuentibus uua racemis,
> et coma lactenti spicea fruge tumet;
> hic dulcis cerasos, hic autumnalia pruna
> cernis et aestiuo mora rubere die;
> insitor hic soluit pomosa uota corona,
> cum pirus inuito stipite mala tulit.
>
> . . . .
>
> pastor me ad baculum possum curuare uel idem
> sirpiculis medio puluere ferre rosam.
> nam quid ego adiciam, de quo mihi maxima fama est,
> hortorum in manibus dona probata meis?
> caeruleus cucumis tumidoque cucurbita uentre
> me notat et iunco brassica uincta leui;
> nec flos ullus hiat pratis, quin ille decenter
> impositus fronti langueat ante meae.

Or, because I receive offerings of the first fruits of the turning year, you believe in turn that mine is the rite of *Vert-annus*. For me the early grape changes color on the purple cluster, and the coarse corn swells with milky fruit. Here you see sweet cherries, here you see plums in autumn, here you see the blackberries blush on a summer day. The grafter fulfills his vows by placing a crown of fruit on my head, after his pear tree has borne apples on its unwilling branch.

. . . .

> Like a shepherd I can bend myself to the shepherd's crook, or I can like-
> wise carry a rose in baskets amidst the dust. For what will I say about the
> thing for which I am most famous, that choice gifts from gardens are
> presented in my hands? The green cucumber, and the squash with its
> swollen belly mark me out, and the cabbage bound with a light rush; no
> flower ever blooms in the meadow, which, when placed on my forehead,
> does not droop modestly. (4.2.11–18, 39–46)

These two passages constitute a lovely miniature of Vergil's *laudes Italiae*, a highlight of the *Georgics* (2.136–76), and they are replete with direct allusions to that text. Dee, who traces all these allusions, sees Propertius' "Georgics" as an opportunity for the poet to combine poetic and rustic language, producing the Callimachean effect of *uariatio*.[46] Shea also sees a literary-critical subtext to these allusions, as Propertius appropriates one of the forms of Augustan poetry.[47] The evocation of Vergil's Italy has a cultural dimension as well. The *Georgics*, especially the *laudes Italiae*, is a text of Italian nationalism, reorienting Roman identity from a Rome-centered perspective to a perspective that includes all Italy. The poem's production and publication coincided closely with the oath of Italy, sworn to Octavian on the eve of his last civil war.[48] The Roman countryside had been praised before; Vergil's innovation in the *laudes Italiae* was to connect that countryside to Rome's own greatness. Italy participates in every aspect of Rome's growth: Italy provides food to sustain Rome, soldiers to expand its dominion, and beasts with which to celebrate Roman triumphs (2.148–50). While critics disagree to what extent Vergil's *laudes* are encomiastic or censorious of Rome's mission, they agree that at the heart of this question is the contribution—be it begrudging or enthusiastic—made by Italy and its peoples to Rome.[49] In the context of Italianization it is telling that Vertumnus is venerated with the fruits of a hybrid tree, one grafted unwillingly (*inuito*, 4.2.18). If the hybrid crop is a double for Vertumnus, then the adjective *inuito*, like the mention of Volsinii's conquest in 4.2.4, hints at violent or unwelcome ways of becoming Roman. In the spirit of Vergil's *laudes* Vertumnus' poem not only makes precious the sublime, but also admits of several perspectives on *Romanitas*.

Vertumnus' mini-*laudes* likewise outline the contributions of Italy to Rome, but the god takes it one step further. As god of the turning year, Vertumnus is responsible for Italy's fecundity and, as recipient of dedicatory offerings, he is a conduit for the fruits of Italy to come to Rome.

Being himself an ethnic hybrid, Vertumnus is also a symbol not so much of Roman Italy, but rather of Italian Rome. Despite his pan-Italian characteristics, Vertumnus resides in Rome. He mentions the city three times during the poem:

Romanum satis est posse uidere Forum.

. . . .

et tu, Roma, meis tribuisti praemia Tuscis,
    (unde hodie Vicus nomina Tuscus habet) . . .

. . . .

sed facias, diuum Sator, ut Romana per aeuum
    transeat ante meos turba togata pedes.

It is enough to be able to see the Forum Romanum.

. . . .

And you, Rome, provided rewards for my fellow Etruscans (from whom the present-day Vicus Tuscus has its name) . . .

. . . .

But, divine Parent of the gods, may you grant that the toga-clad Roman crowd passes before my feet forever. (4.2.6, 49–50, 55–56)

Despite his Italian roots Vertumnus is now Roman, or Romanized. The *princeps Etruriae* subordinates himself to a higher god (*diuum Sator*). As his capstone (and self-preferred) etymology Vertumnus states that it is precisely his ability to change from one thing (Italian) to another (Roman) that explains his name:

at mihi, quod formas unus uertebar in omnis,
    nomen ab euentu patria lingua dedit.

But because I was able to convert my singular self into any form, from this capacity my native tongue gave to me the name *Vert-omnis*. (4.2.47–48)

These words baffle for several reasons. First of all, they confound understanding of Vertumnus' name. Linguists link Vertumnus' name to the Etruscan Veltune/Velthune.[50] Yet the name also acts as a syncopated present passive participle along the lines of *alumnus*. This would be proto-Latin and Indo-European, i.e., not Etruscan. What, then, does Vertumnus mean by "native tongue"? This phrase is complicated by its resonance with the opening couplet:

> qui mirare meas tot in uno corpore formas,
>   accipe Vertumni signa paterna dei.

> Passerby, do you marvel that I have so many figures in one body? Learn the ancestral signs of the god Vertumnus. (4.2.1–2)

The word *paterna* in this opening couplet clearly refers to Etruria, but the word *patria* in the later couplet (*patria lingua*, 4.2.48) refers to Rome itself. What is Vertumnus' *patria?* The resonance between these two couplets reinforces Vertumnus' assertion of himself as Romanized. Latin is his *patria lingua* because he has become Roman. His hint recalls Cicero's statement that every Roman citizen has two *patriae:* his native land, and Rome.[51]

Vertumnus' amalgamated identity raises interesting problems for the poem and for Roman identity. Johnson, exploring the crux of mixed identity in Vergil's *Aeneid,* poses this challenge: "The dialectics of hybridity function variously. Some immigrants become wholly assimilated (the massive purity of the recent convert), but some remain, in some degree, émigrés. What we need is a history of Roman literature that searches for traces of such conflictedness, such indeterminate feelings, in all the Roman writers who are émigrés (which means, most of them)."[52]

Traces of such an ambivalent outlook can be found in Vertumnus' poem, as the god voices the perspective of the outsider who has become an insider. First of all, his exact position in Rome is telling. At the tip of the Velabrum and the entrance to the Forum Romanum, Vertumnus' statue was a beacon for newcomers who arrived by the Tiber, like the newcomer, not fully assimilated into his Roman setting but on the verge of being so. He lacks Johnson's "massive purity of the recent convert" and occupies a marginal position at the edge of the Forum, with a marginal perspective vis-à-vis Rome:

> haec me turba iuuat, nec templo laetor eburno:
>   Romanum satis est posse uidere Forum.
> hac quondam Tiberinus iter faciebat, et aiunt
>   remorum auditos per uada pulsa sonos:

at postquam ille suis tantum concessit alumnis,
  Vertumnus uerso dicor ab amne deus.

This crowd pleases me, and I do not delight in an ivory temple. It is enough to be able to see the Roman Forum. The Tiber river once made his path here, and they say the sound of oars could be heard as they struck the shallows. But after he granted so much to his foster-children, I am called *Vert-amnis* from the withdrawal of the river. (4.2.5–10)

As we saw above, Vertumnus' rejection of a triumphal temple is a rejection of Roman assimilation through conquest. His position at the edge of the Forum is telling; he is not a part of the civic and symbolic center of Rome, but rather enjoys a perspective on it from the margins. The Tiber river, a very Roman figure which was all the same a conduit to Rome for so many émigrés, Vertumnus casts as a foster parent to his adopted children—that is, to the non-Roman Romans. The word *alumnis* in 4.2.9, or foster-children, is striking after Vertumnus' reference to his natal background, or *signa paterna*, in 4.2.2 (*accipe Vertumni signa paterna dei*, learn the ancestral marks of the god Vertumnus). This combination of natal and adopted fatherlands finds its analogue in the dynamics of the Roman family, in which adoption was common, yet adopted children still traded on their natal heritage.[53] Vertumnus has (at least) two perspectives on Rome.

The word *alumnis* also resonates strongly with Propertius' introduction to Book 4, a poem that purports to introduce Rome to an outsider (*hospes*, 4.1.1):

nil patrium nisi nomen habet Romanus alumnus:
  sanguinis altricem non putet esse lupam

The Roman foster child has nothing from his ancestors except the name: he would not wish to believe that a she-wolf nursed his bloodline. (4.1.37–38)

Johnson makes much, but not overmuch, of this couplet's comment on assimilated inhabitants of Rome. It is worth quoting him at length:

Propertius and his contemporaries (whom, in this volume, he offers to escort through the city and its histories) are Romans in name only because they have become, caught between two sign systems, the monkey in the middle. The small rustic village that was the seed of the huge

metropolis they live in, now the hub of a world empire's wheel, is so
remote from them in time, is, in the paucity of its physical remains, so
hidden from them, that they cannot "connect with" their founding myths.
Therefore, they need the help of a Roman Callimachus to reveal to them
Rome's *aetia* (its causes) by expounding the significance of the extant
monuments that they see about them every day as they go about their
business in the old/new city . . . in short, the Romans too are *alumni.*[54]

These are the *alumni* whom the Tiber fosters, who, like Vertumnus, are
both Roman and not Roman. Perhaps this is the reason the singular
Signum Vortumni boasts about his plural *signa paterna. Signa* is more
than a poetic plural, as some commentators suggest; and it is more
than a synonym for *indicia,* as others suggest.[55] Rather, it is a powerful
indication of the plurality of sign systems that inform Roman identity,
or, more precisely, of the polysemy of Roman signs.

READING VERTUMNUS' STATUE

Having introduced the ideas of polysemy and Roman identity in the
poem's opening lines, Vertumnus goes on to demonstrate with spirit
his own polysemy—i.e., his ability to assume various guises. One concrete expression of his polysemy is the number of variant etymologies
he offers for his name: there are at least three ways to understand it. It
is useful here to recall these etymological possibilities Vertumnus
offers:

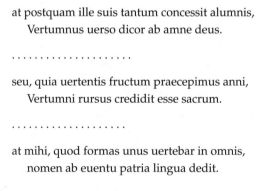

at postquam ille suis tantum concessit alumnis,
        Vertumnus uerso dicor ab amne deus.

. . . .

seu, quia uertentis fructum praecepimus anni,
        Vertumni rursus credidit esse sacrum.

. . . .

at mihi, quod formas unus uertebar in omnis,
        nomen ab euentu patria lingua dedit.

But after he [Tiber] granted so much to his foster-children, I am called
Vert-amnis from the withdrawal of the river.

. . . .

Or, because I receive offerings of the first fruits of the turning year, you believe again that mine is the rite of *Vert-annus*.

. . . .

But because I was able to convert my singular self into any form, from this capacity my native tongue gave to me the name *Vert-omnis*. (4.2.9–10, 11–12, 47–48)

Though Vertumnus seems to endorse the last of these three etymologies, assigning it an active verb and distinguishing it with *at*, the others make sense to his suppliants. His name means different things to different visitors, according to their needs and their relationship to him. One of the sign systems at play in this poem is language, as Vertumnus draws attention to the mutability of words. With this sort of wordplay Vertumnus (and Propertius behind him) situates himself within the Varronian tradition of etymologizing. As Wallace-Hadrill has pointed out, this tradition is far from politically neutral.[56] As the semantic field of words became an ideological battleground during the fall of the Republic, etymology arose as a way to validate meaning via a "neutral" history. Vertumnus' multiple etymologies defy any attempts to assign fixed meaning to these signs. In fact, I would add a fourth etymologizing example that drives home the point of his polysemic name:

opportuna mea est cunctis natura figuris:
   in quamcumque uoles uerte, decorus ero.

My nature is fitting for all formulations: con-*vert* me into whichever you wish, and I'll be appropriate to it. (4.2.21–22)

Make whatever etymology you like, Vertumnus says, and you will be right. Vertumnus plays here on the etymology of *figura* (figure) from *fingo* (to devise or fashion).[57] An extension on the poem's interplay of linguistic sign systems is its insistence on evoking many literary genres, from epic (*arma tuli quondam*, 4.2.27) to pastoral (*pastor me ad baculum possum curuare*, 4.2.39) to epigram (*te, qui ad uadimonia curris,* / *non moror*, 4.2.57–58) to Priapea (*tumido . . . uentre*, 4.2.43),[58] to traditional love elegy (*indue me Cois, fiam non dura puella*, 4.2.23). This variety is more than *poikilia*; it is a statement about the lightning ability of words to blur the boundaries of sign systems.

As Vertumnus' etymologies and literary registers shift, so too can the Signum Vortumni, in this poem, shape-shift into any and all *signa* (4.2.2). Vertumnus adapts himself and can be adapted to any sort of passerby, and adopts no fewer than fifteen personae, each with its own accouterment. For DeBrohun these changes signal a "rhetoric of fashion" through which elegiac poetry tries on different costumes.[59] For me, Vertumnus' changing fashion blurs into his changing identity, as he becomes whatever his audience wants him to become. As Hardie points out, " . . . the long catalogue of metamorphoses has been uttered by a motionless statue: the principle of mutability frozen in the perfection of a work of art."[60]

The monument has no fixed identity independent of the viewer's desire. The meaning of the monument lies with the viewer as much as the maker.

CONCLUSION

At 4.1.69 Propertius promised to unfold the meaning of Roman monuments: *sacra diesque canam et cognomina prisca locorum* (I shall sing of the rites and festivals of Rome, and of the hallowed names of its places). Poised at the opening of this book, Vertumnus provides a powerful lesson to Propertius' audience about reading monuments: they may be read in many ways. Indeed Vertumnus' own polysemy paves the way for Propertius' unconventional interpretations of monuments in the rest of the book. Just as elegiac poetry espouses the rejection of conventional morality and social roles, Vertumnus' poem urges us to resist the received wisdom on any given monument. After a decade of focused and thematic urban renovation by the Princeps, Vertumnus' defiance is strong: though the Signum Vortumni was of no particular interest to Augustus in his urban renovation, the mutability that Vertumnus imparts to all Roman monuments militates against the broader *imprimatur* of the emperor on the gentrified city. In this way, the poem is intimately connected not only with the topographical poems that follow and their aetiological program, but also with the majesty of the Augustan city.

It is connected with its immediate neighbors in the book as well. By standing on the edge of the Forum, Vertumnus follows Horos' injunction to avoid that central urban node at 4.1.134 as a place antithetical to his generic—and cultural—identity. Arethusa, in the next poem, will draw new attention to the interplay of marginality and centrality. In a letter expressing her longing for her husband, Lycotas, who is away on military service, Arethusa promises to dedicate a votive offering of thanks at the city's Colline gate (4.3.71–72), the exact point on the city's threshold where it is permeable, and where Lycotas may repatriate himself after his tour abroad. Arethusa contrasts nicely with Vertmnus: whereas Vertumnus offers an outsider's perspective on Rome, Arethusa, imagining the far-off places where Lycotas serves, reveals a Roman perspective on other parts of the world.

It is ironic that this poem about marginality is central to reading both Propertius' fourth book and Augustan Rome. More important, though, is the way Propertius links the Signum Vortumni with a variable Roman identity. His poem reminds us that Rome's splendors appeared differently to different audiences. As Vertumnus signifies something unique for women and men, for soldiers and statesmen, for shepherds and suppliants, this poem admits of perspectives other than that of the elite Roman man—whose own perspective is by no means rigid or circumscribed. This poem, then, goes some small distance toward redressing the balance of Roman texts by recuperating perspectives that are lost or silenced in our literary sources. In a culture masterful at incorporating others into itself, a culture proud of its hybridity, a culture destined, as it thought, to civilize the rest of the world, Vertumnus' multiplicity stubbornly reasserts an awareness of the other within the Roman self. Propertius thus invites us to go beyond our narrow (and imperialist) view of Roman identity, and to consider if not further voices, then at least further eyes.

CHAPTER 3

Amor vs. Roma

CITY AND INDIVIDUAL IN ELEGY 4.4

IN THE POPULAR version of her myth, found in Varro, Livy, Dionysius of Halicarnassus, Ovid, Valerius Maximus, and Plutarch, and reflected in all extant visual representations of her story, Tarpeia is a Roman maiden who betrays the Capitol to Titus Tatius, commander of the Sabine forces besieging Rome in response to the rape of the Sabine Women.[1] Her motivation in all these versions, whenever expressed, is greed; in return for her betrayal she demands what the Sabines wear on their arms. She means, of course, their bracelets and rings, but the Sabines reward her instead by crushing her with their shields, which they also wear on their arms. As a grim reminder of Tarpeia's betrayal, the Romans christened the Tarpeian rock on the Capitol, a particularly nasty crag from which, as tradition holds, traitors were thrown to their deaths.[2] Tarpeia's story, and the rock named for her, came to represent the threat posed to the state by the selfish pursuit of private goals over public needs.

To be sure, Tarpeia's myth was not uncomplicated, and variations appear in other versions of her story.[3] Like the mutable identity of Vertumnus, these variations in Tarpeia's myth point to tensions in Roman ideology. Though her betrayal was memorialized in the Tarpeian rock, for example, Tarpeia was also venerated at her tomb in the city, which is no longer extant.[4] These two Roman places—Tarpeia's rock and her altar—create an ideological contradiction: her betrayal of Rome is to be condemned (the symbolism of the rock), while her contribution to Roman pluralism is to be commended (via worship at the tomb). Similar tensions arise from her status in Rome: Tarpeia was either daughter of the Roman commander with no other known social role, or a Vestal Virgin. If the former, as in most versions, her transgression was a private act, while if the latter, as in Varro's telling, it was sacrilege that tainted the state's public institutions and required public expiation.[5] She may not even have been Roman.[6] Another variant, preserved in Simylus' elegy of unknown date, has Tarpeia betray Rome to the Gauls rather than the Sabines; in this case, there is no resulting assimilation of the invader to palliate her guilt.[7] Another oddity appears in Simylus' version: the girl acts out of love, not greed. This variant raises questions about the extent to which these two motives are interchangeable in the threat they pose to the state.[8]

In this chapter I explore the tensions in Roman identity that are exposed by Propertius' particular combination of variant details, and his intricate use of Roman topography to emphasize these tensions. Propertius' telling veers sharply from the popular version. First, the elegist follows Varro in making Tarpeia a Vestal Virgin, a public role that emphasizes her duty to the state and raises the heinousness of her treason. Second, innovating if Simylus' elegy postdates his own, Propertius motivates Tarpeia not with greed but with love for Tatius—a motive she elaborates in the long monologue she delivers at the heart of the poem (4.4.31–66). This detail changes the conflict of her story from private gain against the state, as it is in the version given by Livy et al., to emotion against the state, or *amor* vs. *Roma*. Tarpeia in love, and the dilemma she faces because of this love, reveal an elegist's perspective on Roman history. Her emotional motivation generates sympathy for Tarpeia, and we see her in this poem searching for a way to reconcile the irreconcilable: her private passion and the needs of the state.

Propertius makes Tarpeia's predicament even more vivid by his careful placement of her in the Roman landscape. Though Propertius' poem is ostensibly an *aetion* of the Tarpeian grove and tomb (4.4.1–2), the spatial scope of the poem's action is much wider, ranging across the Capitol and the Forum valley, two areas rich with patriotic timbre. In the poem Tarpeia spends most of her time between these two areas, comfortable in neither and ultimately unwelcome in each. I argue that Tarpeia's confinement to this liminal area, a place precipitous and rugged in Propertius' poem, mirrors her confinement to a chaste and loyal life in the service of Rome. The elegist's mapping of Tarpeia's struggle onto Rome's most symbolic locales thus emphasizes her predicament as a feeling individual within a state that subsumes all to itself, and draws attention to Tarpeia's alterity and its confrontation with (and contribution to) Roman ideology. As we shall see, the elegist's combination of Tarpeia and the city comments not only on Tarpeia's unfortunate situation, but on the city's threatening power as well.

TARPEIA IN AUGUSTAN ROME

Tarpeia's myth was told not only through words such as in the texts mentioned above, but also through images and places. Tarpeia's rock and her altar had been visual reminders of her story and her demise since the third century BCE at least, but the end of the Repubic saw three new visual tellings of her story: two coin types and a monumental sculpture. The first coin, a silver denarius minted by L. Titurius Sabinus in 89 BCE, shows Titus Tatius on the obverse, with or without a laurel victory branch near his chin.[9] The reverse shows Tarpeia about to be crushed by Sabine shields; a crescent moon appears over the girl's head, suggesting perhaps the nocturnal setting of her treachery or indicating some of her cult associations. Titurius issued his coin during the Social War, a crisis that, like the legend of the original Sabine synoikism, brought ethnic identity to bear on Rome's understanding of itself. Depending on the holder, it could mark hope for a renewed Sabine synoikism, a call to a stronger (and perhaps anti-Roman) current of Sabine nationalism; or, from a Roman perspective, a promise of Rome's supremacy over threats to her hegemony.[10]

More dramatically, Tarpeia's legend was enshrined in the sculptural program of the Forum Romanum. The Basilica Aemilia had been a focal point in the Forum since its erection in c.200 BCE. It was restored between 54 and 34 BCE by L. Aemilius Paullus and then his son L. Aemilius Lepidus Paullus; the restoration was financed by Julius Caesar.[11] The Julian restoration boasted a sculpted frieze of scenes from Rome's foundation, of which several fragments survive. Among reliefs of Romulus and the *spolia opima*, the building of the first walls, and Romulus and Remus' departure from Alba Longa for Rome are depictions of the punishment of Tarpeia and the rape of the Sabine women.[12] In the Julian context, the frieze of Rome's foundation sets Rome's new dynast in the context of her first monarchic founders— Romulus (here building walls) and Numa alike, since Tarpeia's *felix*

FIGURE 3: Coin of P. Petronius Turpilianus links a monarchic image with the Principate. Photo courtesy of the American Numismatic Society.

culpa led to the Sabine partnership in Rome that made Numa's kingship possible, and Numa is an ancestor to Julius Caesar via the latter's grandmother Marcia.[13]

Augustus thus inherited a myth of Tarpeia that was becoming increasingly meaningful in the changing order, and her myth took on further nuances under his rule. In 19 BCE, the moneyer P. Petronius Turpilianus issued another coin featuring the doomed maiden's punishment—again a silver denarius, showing Augustus on the obverse and Tarpeia buried under shields on the reverse (Figure 3).[14]

Turpilianus' coin, like his other coins that feature Liber and Feronia, attests his own Sabine background and connects him to Tarpeia by punning on their names, Tarpeia and Turpilianus.[15] With the influx of new peoples added to the Roman citizenship during the civil wars, the Tarpeia coin sends a message to its holders: that the elite *gens Petronia Turpiliana* had been a part of Rome since the very birth of the city. More to the point, the combination on this coin of a monarchic image with Augustus' image, as well as the celebration of Princeps and moneyer alike, both speak to the evolving sense of the Augustan regime, ready to use the imagery of kingship in its visual program of tradition and innovation.[16] By associating Augustus with Tarpeia, the coin draws attention to the Sabine, and specifically Numan, strain of Augustus' Julian ancestry. As Grimal suggests, Tarpeia's act contributed to (and was indeed necessary for) Augustus' pedigree.[17]

A few years later, Augustus' name would again be associated with Tarpeia. In 14 BCE, Augustus paid to restore the Basilica after a fire and added a portico to his grandsons and heirs Gaius and Lucius (Figure 4).

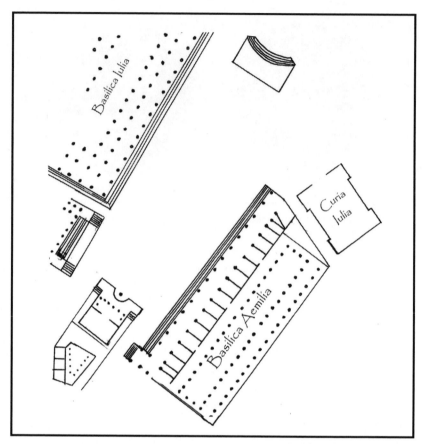

FIGURE 4. Plan of the Basilica Aemilia (bottom right) with portico to Gaius and Lucius. Situated between the Regia (left) and the Curia (above), this building, like Turpilianus' coin, bridges the monarchy and the Republic. Augustus' renovation adds the Principate to this historical semantic. After Favro 1996: 197.

Augustus' restoration of the building served many purposes.[18] First of all, it associated the Princeps and his restoration of Rome with the foundation and building of the original city—an association already palpable in the restoration of cults and temples around Rome, and soon to be further monumentalized on the Ara Pacis and in the Forum of Augustus. Second, the restored Basilica strengthened his dynastic claims to Roman rule by associating his own urban activity with Caesar's, and by extension with Caesar's ancestor Numa as described above. Third, it built Augustus' heirs Gaius and Lucius, honorees of the new entrance hall, into the legends of Rome's urban founders.[19]

Yet even before the fire of 14 BCE, the building, and the frieze in particular, spoke in subtle and more overt ways to the concerns of the

FIGURE 5. Tarpeia relief from the Basilica Aemilia. The panel's visual narrative stresses the acts of viewing and judging—lessons for viewers outside the sculpture? Photo courtesy of the Fototeca Unione.

new order—foremost among them the role of women. The Sabine women and Tarpeia are two of the very few examples of women on civic monumental art in the Augustan age. Their presence at the heart of the Forum, in a place marked by many kinds of public traffic, is striking. Augustus' legislation on marriage and adultery, passed in 18 BCE, spoke to the ability of women to undermine proper relationships between men.[20] The laws on marriage and adultery sought to stabilize families via children, social classes via restricted intermarriage, and female conduct via the punishment of adultery. They also established a new relationship between the individual and the state, subordinating private desires and personal liberties to public needs and state authority.[21] In this context, the reliefs of the Sabine Women and Tarpeia instructed Romans as to the benefits of proper female behavior. When they behaved appropriately as wives, daughters, and mothers, Roman women acted as social mediators between men and even facilitated Roman expansion. Tarpeia's perfidy, on the other hand, represented the danger of unregulated female conduct.

On the Tarpeia relief, the girl stands framed by billowing drapery, with a heap of shields at her feet (Figure 5). Like an Amazon, her left breast is bared, a mark of her marginality and of her hostility to the natural order. There is a soldier on either side of her adding his shield to the heap. These three characters are flanked by two men who contemplate the scene, variously identified as Mars/Romulus and Titus Tatius. The man on Tarpeia's far right, most probably Tatius, is in a position of repose and looks upon the girl with what Warden calls "the sternness of the incorruptible judge."[22] His pose, however, is also that of the lover gazing upon his beloved. Tatius' gaze at once casts him as desiring subject of the object Tarpeia (and, as such, master of her narrative) and as

object of the lesson she imparts, transfixed by his sight of her.[23] These
contemplative men also constitute a paradigm for the male viewer of
the relief. Like the sculpted onlookers, men visiting the Basilica after 18
BCE were to look upon Tarpeia's punishment and contemplate its
meaning, both interpreting her story and being interpreted by it. Seeing
Tarpeia as the other, as a woman, an Amazon, an outsider, a traitoress,
the male viewer reinforces the construction of his own identity as the
self, male, Roman, insider, and loyal. The female viewer, on the other
hand, sees in Tarpeia an extreme and dangerous version of herself: on
the margins, not quite fully Roman but potentially so, if she does not
act as Tarpeia does. It is no coincidence that adjoining Tarpeia's scene
on the frieze is a proper marriage scene;[24] the pair encapsulates the
scene lesson succinctly: the *matrona*, not Tarpeia, is the model women
should choose.[25] As Miller says, "The Augustan Symbolic quintessen-
tially operated to recuperate the alien, through a complex movement of
dialectical synthesis. . . . Augustus from the perspective of these works
(sc. the coin and the frieze) is portrayed as both the scourge of treason,
who recuperates and incorporates the transgressive, and the direct
beneficiary of Tarpeia's act."[26]

   Given the themes of Tarpeia's legend—gender, patriotism, assimilation—it is not surprising that her story became popular in the last century of the Republic, when the role of the individual in the state was in
flux, and when traditional paths to success gave way to new models of
power. As Romans struggled to define themselves and their public and
private roles against this changing backdrop, the new Princeps used
Tarpeia's myth to encourage deference toward the state. For Romans
of the Augustan age, Tarpeia's legend spoke to the new Roman identity or, rather, to Roman nonidentity.

THE ELEGIAC TARPEIA: *AMOR* VS. *ROMA*

Thus Propertius inherited the mythic tradition of Tarpeia in the first
century BCE. To be sure, Book 4 in all likelihood predates the Augustan
restoration of the Basilica; the last datable reference in Book 4 is the consulship of Scipio in 16 BCE (4.11.65–66), and no more notice of
Propertius or his poetry is given until 2 BCE, when Ovid mentions his
death using the past tense (*Rem. Am.* 764). Nevertheless, there is no
doubt that Tarpeia's presence was pervasive in the cityscape as a negative example, and that the new demands of the new order had already

pressed the moral of her story to further heights when Propertius turned his pen to it.

Propertius disagrees with the use of Tarpeia as a negative example. He exonerates her from the greed named in other sources by changing her motive to love. In good Alexandrian fashion, the elegist lends Tarpeia extra sympathy by granting her a subjectivity lacking in other sources. Focusing the narrative through Tarpeia's perspective, Propertius portrays Tarpeia's love as compelling and her concerns real.[27] Like Ovid's heroines who are in part patterned after her, Tarpeia tells her own story, and the reader is allowed a glimpse into her feelings and motivations. His Tarpeia is not greedy, nor does she think only of herself, nor is she naively blind to the implications of her passion.[28] Rather, in her long monologue—more than a third of the poem—Tarpeia demonstrates that she is aware of the potential consequences of her desire, and loath to do harm to the state. Her oscillation between desire and duty gives her a moral dimension she lacks in other sources.

Throughout Tarpeia's speech her mind flickers back and forth, between following her desires (marked as *'amor'* below) and noting the costs of these desires to herself and the state (marked *'Roma'*):[29]

ignes castrorum et Tatiae praetoria turmae	AMOR
et formosa oculis arma Sabina meis,	
o utinam ad uestros sedeam captiua Penatis,	ROMA
dum captiua mei conspicer ora Tati![30]	AMOR
Romani montes, et montibus addita Roma,	
et ualeat probro Vesta pudenda meo:	ROMA
ille equus, ille meos in castra reponet amores,	AMOR
cui Tatius dextras collocat ipse iubas!	
quid mirum in patrios Scyllam saeuisse capillos,	
candidaque in saeuos inguina uersa canis?	ROMA
prodita quid mirum fraterni cornua monstri,	AMOR
cum patuit lecto stamine torta uia?	
quantum ego sum Ausoniis crimen factura puellis,	ROMA
improba uirgineo lecta ministra foco!	
Pallados exstinctos si quis mirabitur ignis,	
ignoscat: lacrimis spargitur ara meis.	AMOR

O fires of the camp, and headquarters of Tatius' squadron, and Sabine weapons lovely to my eyes, O would that I might sit at your hearth as a captive, as long as I might gaze upon the face of my Tatius in captivity!

Roman hills, and upon the hills, Rome, and you, Vesta, who must be shamed by my sin, fare well: that horse, that horse will carry my passions back into his camp, that horse whose mane Tatius himself smoothes to the right. Why wonder that Scylla violated her father's hair, and her shining loins were changed into vicious dogs? Why wonder that the monstrous brother's horns were betrayed, when the twisted path lay revealed by a gathered thread? How great a crime am I about to commit for Italian girls, I, a sinful girl chosen to be minister to a virgin's hearth! If someone should wonder that the fires of Pallas have gone out, let him forgive me: the altar is wet with my tears. (4.4.31–46)

As quickly as a new line unfolds Tarpeia's thoughts shift; she is searching for solutions to her dilemma, and finding none so far. For example, she first expresses her desire to be a member of Tatius' household (a testament to her *amor*), but realizes that she can only do so as a captive (a capitulation to *Roma*). Even in her choice of mythical *exempla* Tarpeia sees tensions: both Scylla and Ariadne choose love over fatherland (*amor;* 4.4.39, 41–42), but not without punishment (*Roma,* 4.4.40). At 4.4.43–46, she recognizes not only a general danger posed by her desire (*quantum . . . crimen*) but even the specific transgressions caused by that desire: she violates the virginal chastity of her priesthood (*improba . . . ministra*, 4.4.44) and lets the sacred fire go out (*exstinctos . . . ignis,* 4.4.45). Her tears reveal Tarpeia's perplexity at her impasse: with her mind searching for explanations and solutions, she realizes she is caught in an irreconcilable situation. Her very pain is a sacrifice at Vesta's altar.

At 4.4.53, her mind takes a sudden turn. With a balanced case for *amor* and *Roma,* Tarpeia instead justifies her transgression by condemning Rome:

> te toga picta decet, non quem, sine matris honore
> nutrit inhumanae dura papilla lupae.

> It is you the *toga picta* befits, not that one whom, without the honor of a mother, the harsh nipple of a wolf-bitch nursed. (4.4.53–54)

Tatius, she says, is more worthy of her loyalty than wolf-suckled Romulus, who is unaccustomed even to a mother's love. Tarpeia questions the loveless state that she serves. However, this resentment toward Rome does not last long, as her flickering mind soon seizes upon a solution that would benefit the city, the Sabines, and herself: namely, that her marriage to Tatius would bind Romans to Sabines:

hic, hospes, patria metuar regina sub aula?
   dos tibi non humilis prodita Roma uenit.
si minus, at raptae ne sint impune Sabinae
   me rape et alterna lege repende uices!
commissas acies ego possum soluere nupta:[31]
   uos medium palla foedus inite mea.
adde, Hymenaee, modos: tubicen, fera murmura conde:
   credite, uestra meus molliet arma torus.

Here, stranger, will I be revered as queen in your country's palace? Rome betrayed comes as no humble dowry to you. Or, as punishment for the rape of the Sabine women, take me and settle the score by the law of retribution! I, as a bride, am able to resolve the battles that have begun. Enter into a compromise through my wedding gown! Hymenaeus, add your strains! Trumpeter, stop your wild sounds! Believe me, my marriage bed will soften your weapons. (4.4.55–62)

Like the Sabine women, Tarpeia envisions herself combining marriage and peacemaking. Her mention of dowry, the Hymenaeus, wedding dress, marriage-bed, the reference to herself as *nupta* and her sexual pun in *molliet* all reveal Tarpeia's hope for a marriage with the Sabine king.[32] Indeed, she sees the solution that eventually does bring peace— the reconciliation brought about by the Sabine women through their marriage. Tarpeia wants to facilitate, not undermine, this process, an interesting comment since Tarpeia and the Sabine women are so often foils for each other in the sources, such as Livy's history and the relief sculptures in the Basilica Aemilia. Tarpeia's hopes for a treaty with the Sabines and an end to the war, seen in *soluere* and *foedus*, and encapsulated in the chiastic *arma torus* (4.4.59, 60, and 62, respectively), embody a hope of all Roman marriages: namely, that marriages blur the distinctions between families and strengthen the community, rather than sever community ties.[33] Tarpeia's hopes are noble. In envisioning a winning situation for all parties, the elegist's Tarpeia would become a positive example for all time.

The extended moral debate she has with herself, in which she tries to reconcile her private desires with her public duty, makes Tarpeia human, and therefore sympathetic to us. Propertius further complicates her situation by making her a Vestal Virgin. In no other version of

her story is Tarpeia so torn by conflicting forces; Propertius alone combines Tarpeia's ritual chastity and her desire. For some interpreters,
Tarpeia's status as a Vestal Virgin only serves to increase her shame.[34] In
this view, as a girl whose ritual chastity was so beneficial to the state,
Tarpeia's love constitutes an especially selfish and heinous crime. The
combination of chastity and love in the poem and the resultant erotic
frisson would therefore produce a more rousing condemnation of the
girl than had appeared in earlier versions of her legend. On the contrary: this combination highlights the barrenness imposed on Tarpeia's
life by the cult of Vesta and throws into high relief the conflict between
Tarpeia's private desires and her public duty. This conflict aligns her
with the elegiac poet and lover, who disdains public institutions, especially those that mandate or limit sexual activity.[35] Tarpeia recognizes
the tension inherent in her situation: her criticism of unmothered
Romulus at 4.4.53–54 hints that, for her, love is incompatible with the
Roman state. Indeed, her mention of the wolf recalls the story of another Vestal Virgin, Rhea Silvia, whose sexuality was activated (albeit by a
god) and who was punished for it.[36] Like Tarpeia, Rhea Silvia was performing her Vestal duties when she was caught by *amor*.[37]

This tension between *amor* and *Roma* is emphasized by Vesta's dis-
concerting appearance in the poem:

> . . . et incerto permisit bracchia somno,
>   nescia se furiis accubuisse nouis.
> nam Vesta, Iliacae felix tutela fauillae,
>   culpam alit et plures condit in ossa faces.

> And she gave her arms to fitful sleep, not knowing that she was going to
> bed with new demons. For Vesta, propitious keeper of the torch from
> Troy, feeds her sin and plants more fires in her bones. (4.4.67–70)

Vesta is thus the goddess who mandates Tarpeia's chastity as a Vestal
Virgin, and makes that chastity impossible by fanning the flames of her
love. Some editors, at a loss to explain Vesta's perplexing behavior,
emend this line to read "Venus."[38] As one editor states, "the fires of
torches and love are the province of Venus and Amor, and for Vesta to
arrogate them to herself to compass so cruel a purpose as the further
undoing of her votary is monstrous."[39] Indeed it is, but in my view the
reading stands: the poem's malicious Vesta is a distilled and potent
image of Tarpeia's own predicament.[40] As Vesta is the focus for
Tarpeia's public duties, this goddess's intervention makes all the more

problematic the tension between *amor* and *Roma* that Tarpeia feels: the very state the maiden serves fosters her transgression against it. The problem is not only Tarpeia's, and this poem dramatizes the contradictions inherent in the broader cult of Vesta. This goddess's priestesses guaranteed Rome's growth and fertility via their own unfruitfulness, an ideological conundrum manifest in the ambiguous sexual status of Vestal Virgins in Roman thought.[41] Such contradictions indicate a Roman attempt to negotiate sexual identity and to tease out permutations of gender. Tarpeia's elegiac story, therefore, speaks not only to the difficulties of her own situation but also to deeper fissures in Roman ideology, "fault lines . . . in the larger architectonics of Roman ideology."[42]

Propertius' Tarpeia is thus stuck, confined in her public role and confounded in her desire. Tarpeia rejects her priestly virginity, and convinces herself that proper service to Rome requires that women be married. She envisions a solution that would restore her fertility and serve the state: a marriage with Tatius that would unite the two peoples. By exposing her tormented inner thoughts and by emphasizing the contradictions in her priesthood, Propertius causes the Roman reader to question both the suppositions behind Tarpeia's negative legend and the urban monuments that are its legacy, such as the rock named for her and the Basilica Aemilia reliefs. Tarpeia's love therefore constitutes a subtle challenge to the contemporary status and use of her legend.

CAUGHT IN THE MIDDLE
Tarpeia and the Capitol

Tarpeia's monologue reveals to the reader that she is fully aware of the conflict she suffers and of the ramifications of her decision. She is pulled in opposite directions by two forces: her loyalty to the state of Rome, and her love for the Sabine king Tatius. This tug of war between state and love is played out in her movements in the city as well, as she is pulled toward the Capitol on the one hand, the temporary location of Rome's forces, and the Forum on the other hand, the site of Tatius' Sabine encampment. Tarpeia's emotional struggle takes place in sites of strong Roman ideological signification.

As we have seen, putting Tarpeia in the city center was not new. The Tarpeian rock on the Capitol eternalized her betrayal, and Caesar (and later Augustus) chose the Forum as a fitting place to commemorate her punishment. Propertius rewrites the girl's relationship to the city center, repositioning Tarpeia within the cityscape so that she is an example not of how the individual threatens the state, but rather how the state threatens the individual. Stahl, a critic concerned with the tension between public and private in this and all Propertius' poems, touches on this locality of Tarpeia's situation: "Thus her conflict, expressed in local terms, is that, though physically on her state's territory (in the neighborhood of Iuppiter Optimus Maximus), she emotionally longs to be in the enemy's camp. It is worth noting how once more Propertius chooses the scenic as a vehicle for the emotional."[43]

It is important to realize that Propertius' topographical tableau is decidedly not an accurate, or even plausible, representation of the city at war with the Sabines. As Richardson indicates, the Sabines would have come to Rome on the Via Salaria and encamped near the Comitium.[44] The Romans would have fortified the Palatine and perhaps the Temple of Vesta. Nothing as yet existed on the Capitol to warrant the Romans' encampment there. Propertius' placement of Tarpeia on the Capitol may be the result of a tradition confused by many centuries of lapsed time and by many variations in her legend, including the fact that the Tarpeian Rock is located on that hill rather than the Palatine and is often called Mons Tarpeius. We must admit that the legend grew and changed as Rome did. What is more to the point, historical accuracy is not the point of the elegist's aetiological poem. Rather, his ancient Rome is an imaginative prototype of the imposing city it would become, a forerunner of the *urbs aeterna* that is believable without being either archaeologically sound or even internally consistent from poem to poem or within a single poem. The malleability of Rome's early landscape is, indeed, a conclusion Propertius' poetry encourages.

We begin, as does Propertius, with the Capitol, the temporary home for Tarpeia and the Roman state. Each day Tarpeia descends the Capitol to fetch water, and to gaze upon her Tatius. Evenings she ascends again, scratched by brambles, into the Roman camp. She delivers her monologue while sitting on the edge of the hill, overlooking Tatius' camp. This hill was the religious and ideological head of the Roman empire.[45] Rome's most important temple, that of Jupiter Optimus Maximus, stood at its crest, as did its oldest, the temple of Jupiter Feretrius. Both these temples figured prominently as symbols of Rome's imperial domain. The triumphal ceremony, a splendid celebration of Roman military victory, reached its climax atop the Capitol in the great Temple to Jupiter. Regalia from these ceremonies were dedicated in the temple and displayed permanently along the triumphal route up the hill, making it a permanent museum of Rome's dominion. The Temple to Jupiter Feretrius housed *spolia opima*, the state's rarest and highest possible military honors. Finally, the Capitol testified to Rome's eternity.[46] The Capitol was so fully considered a symbol of Roman dominion that most colonial outposts, even those built on flat land, featured a Capitolium.[47] To revise the popular maxim, as long as the Capitol stood, so would Rome stand.

   With these associations, the Capitoline Hill forms a pointed setting for Tarpeia's unhappy situation. Tarpeia's crime is multifaceted. She violates the city religiously by transgressing the rules of her priesthood; by violating the sacred fire, a crime she mentions in 4.4.45, she opens Rome to possible disaster. She violates the city militarily by opening its defenses to the enemy, literally opening a path for the enemy to enter. Finally, she violates Rome symbolically by betraying the Capitol, Rome's strongest symbol of itself. Her final journey down the Capitol, in a sense, reverses the Roman triumph in which victorious generals would bring foreign resources into the city. Tarpeia, exiting the Capitol, leads those very resources out of the city, away from its head.[48] These layers of her betrayal heighten the notion of the damage she does to the state.

   Tarpeia's final departure from the Capitol emphasizes her rejection of Rome's public realm. In choosing Tatius she rejects cult, state, and urban center, fleeing the pervasive public presence in her life in order to achieve her private desires. In short, her private desires cannot be met on the Capitol, a place where her actions are interpreted as treason and permanently enshrined as such in the establishment of the Tarpeian rock. Propertius has expressed Tarpeia's crime against the community in topographical terms that raise the stakes for both betrayed and traitor, a point he underscores in the poem's introductory lines:

Tarpeium nemus et Tarpeiae turpe sepulchrum
   fabor et antiqui limina capta Iouis.

I shall tell of Tarpeia's grove, and Tarpeia's shameful grave, and how the
threshold of ancient Jove was captured. (4.4.1–2)

The Temple of Jupiter gets captured, and Tarpeia gets a grave.[49]

CAUGHT IN THE MIDDLE
Tarpeia and the Forum

Tarpeia violates the Capitol to achieve her love with Tatius, who is encamped in the Forum valley below. In so doing she hopes to escape the restrictions placed on her by Rome and by her public role as a Vestal Virgin. However, in her escape she rushes into another urban area loaded with symbolic meaning about Rome's political dominion. Tatius has stationed his troops in the Forum Romanum, the area that would become the political, commercial, and social center of Rome. Though she imagines otherwise, Tarpeia's fate in this urban sector will be no better than it was on the Capitol under Rome's jurisdiction.

Tatius is encamped in the northern portion of the Forum Romanum, in an area stretching from the Tullian Spring (his water source) to the Curia (4.4.13). This whole area was visible from the southwestern edge of the Capitol.[50] Propertius pays careful attention to his description of this locale:

> Tarpeium nemus et Tarpeiae turpe sepulchrum
> fabor et antiqui limina capta Iouis.
> lucus erat felix hederoso conditus antro
> multaque natiuis obstrepit arbor aquis,
> Siluani ramosa domus, quo dulcis ab aestu
> fistula poturas ire iubebat ouis.
> hunc Tatius fontem uallo praecingit acerno,
> fidaque suggesta castra coronat humo.
> quid tum Roma fuit, tubicen vicina Curetis
> cum quateret lento murmure saxa Iouis?
> atque ubi nunc terris dicuntur iura subactis,
> stabant Romano pila Sabina Foro.
> murus erat montes: ubi nunc est Curia saepta,
> bellicus ex illo fonte bibebat equus.

I shall tell of Tarpeia's grove, and Tarpeia's shameful grave, and how the threshold of ancient Jove was captured. There was a lush copse, hidden by an ivy-clad overhang, and many a tree rustled by the local spring. It was the wooded home of Silvanus, where the sweet pipe used to bid sheep to come out of the summer heat and drink. Tatius surrounded the spring with a maple palisade, and he ringed his trusty camp with heaped-up earth. What was Rome then, when the nearby trumpeter of the Sabines shook the stones of Jove with a low rumbling? And where now laws are pronounced for conquered peoples, Sabine javelins used to stand in the Roman Forum. Their walls were hills: where now the Curia lies, there used to be sheep-pens, and the warhorse used to drink from that fountain. (4.4.1–14)

Propertius begins his poem with a mention of Tarpeia's grove (*nemus*, 4.4.1). This reading is contested, however, and some editors emend *nemus* to *scelus*.[51] Though *scelus* is attested in no manuscripts, the primary problem these editors find with *nemus* is that there is no monument known that was Tarpeia's grove. I believe *nemus* should remain, for four reasons. First, the action on the Capitol's slopes suggests a grove; Livy describes the asylum of Romulus as situated in the saddle between the hill's two peaks, *inter duos lucos* (between two groves, 1.8.5). Second, the poem spends much time describing proto-Rome's natural, undeveloped landscape. Springs, trees, plants, and flowers abound on Tarpeia's path, and these seem as grove-like as any such description. Third, the juxtaposition of nature and the built environment is prominent in elegy 4.4, emphasizing the various Romes on the spot; in the lines above, the natural (*nemus*) stands in sharp contrast with the constructed (*sepulcrum*). Fourth, and most importantly, the lack of a formally attested "Tarpeia's grove" in the cityscape—indeed, its replacement by the Tarpeian rock—testifies to the city's ability to organize its myths according to its need. The Tarpeian rock, like the Basilica Aemilia and the tomb mentioned in 4.4.1, focuses attention on Tarpeia's punishment rather than her motivations or intentions. Propertius' Tarpeian grove, on the other hand, painted in pastoral terms, focuses attention on the girl's predicament. Tarpeia's grove can be seen as a " . . . topographical crystallization point from which . . . Tatius and Tarpeia can now be measured . . . by reference to their attitude towards peaceful pastoral landscape."[52] In short, Tatius makes the *lucus* a *locus* for warfare, while Tarpeia makes it a *locus* for her love.

Tatius' camp is a perversion of the pastoral landscape, as he turns a *locus amoenus* into a military locale. Trees appear not as a source of pleasant shade (as in Vergil *Ecl.* 1.1) but rather as a military barricade. The hills, too, are defenses, rather than pleasant places to relax and sing (Vergil *Ecl.* 1.82–83). Tatius' camp disrupts the normal sounds of the pastoral world as well; instead of singing shepherds and piping goatherds who pass peaceful days (as in Vergil *Ecl.* 1.10), we hear the trumpeter call Sabines to war. Even the animals in Tatius' realm are militarized: the fountain sates not sheep but the warhorse (cf. Vergil

Ecl. 7.11–13). The first half of poem 4.1 similarly blends a pastoral proto-Roman landscape with its future monuments of military might, and with the men who made Rome great.[53] In that portrait of early Rome, the poet adopts what Stahl calls the Palatine viewpoint—not only focalization from the Palatine, but also evaluation according to the values of the Augustan state.[54] Tatius adopts this same viewpoint, seeing the grove not as Tarpeia's *locus amoenus* but as a place where he may prepare for war.

Propertius, moreover, identifies the Forum Romanum for his Roman audience as a place where laws are pronounced for conquered lands (4.4.11–12), but at the narrative time of the poem as an area for Sabine weapons. This identifies the Forum as the nucleus for the exercise of military power—whether Roman or Sabine does not really matter, since this war will unite the two into a single military force. The poet also brings before our eyes the Senate House (*Curia,* 4.4.13), the seat of Republican political power and the site where Roman foreign policy was formulated until it was superseded by Augustus' Forum several years after Propertius' poem appeared.[55] The war-horse mentioned in 4.4.14, though certainly referring to the Sabine horse, hints at the future Lacus Iuturnus, a monument to the great Roman victory at Lake Regillus in 496 BCE. As Grimal notes, Propertius' readers would also "see" in this area the Forum Iulium, which abuts the Curia—dedicated as the Curia Iulia in 29 BCE.[56]

With these details (the laws for the conquered, the Curia, and the war-horse) Propertius draws attention to the Forum as a place symbolic of Rome's manifest destiny, more particularly, of that destiny as fulfilled by Caesar and his heir Augustus. Tarpeia seeks out this locale in order to escape the pressure put on her by the state; yet like Vertumnus in elegy 4.2, she stands outside the Forum looking in (curiously, too, both characters predate the Forum proper). Tarpeia's perspective on the proto-Forum landscape from its sidelines is much softer than what it would later be; it is not Stahl's "Palatine viewpoint." For her, the place is a playground for Tatius' erotic sport and for her desiring gaze:

> uidit harenosis Tatium proludere campis
>   pictaque per flauas arma leuare iubas:
> obstipuit regis facie et regalibus armis,
>   interque oblitas excidit urna manus.
> saepe illa immeritae causata est omina lunae,
>   et sibi tingendas dixit in amne comas:
> saepe tulit blandis argentea lilia Nymphis,

Romula ne faciem laederet hasta Tati:
dumque subit primo Capitolia nubila fumo,
rettulit hirsutis bracchia secta rubis,
et sua Tarpeia residens ita fleuit ab arce
uulnera, uicino non patienda Iovi.

She saw Tatius exercise on the sandy fields and raise his painted
weapons above his golden crests. She stood fast, struck by the face of the
king and by his royal arms, and her urn fell through her forgetful hands.
Often using omens of the blameless moon as a pretext, she said she had
to wash her hair in the river. Often she carried silver-white lilies to the
softhearted Nymphs, praying that Romulus' spear not scar Tatius' face.
When she ascended the Capitol hazy with the first smoke of night's fires,
she returned with arms cut by bristling thorns, and Tarpeia thus sitting
down wept for her wounds from the citadel, wounds that nearby Jove
would not tolerate. (4.4.19–30)

Looking at Tatius' activities Tarpeia sees not military exercises, the
technical meaning of *proludere*,[57] but rather hints of the poetic and
amatory activity that is the hallmark of elegiac poetry: *pro-ludere*.[58] She
pays attention to Tatius' adornment (*picta arma, flauas iubas*) and to his
face (*facie*), and she prays to pastoral rather than patriotic or martial
gods to preserve her beloved's face (*Nymphis*). She temporarily forgets
her duties as a priestess, and even drops the urn with which she was
carrying out her duties.[59] She is transfixed by her gaze, and, like the
Propertian lover of 1.3 before her, her perception of the landscape
matches her erotic fantasies.[60] Also, like that lover, Tarpeia's vision is
proven to be illusory. Just as the sleeping Cynthia awakens and shatters
the lover's fantasy, so, too, Tarpeia finds not love but rather death in the
Roman landscape. She escapes the Capitol, sure that with Tatius her
private desires will be fulfilled and the good of the state will be served
by reconciliation between the two peoples, accomplished by her:

commissas acies ego possum soluere nupta[61]
uos medium palla foedus inite mea.

I, as a bride, am able to resolve the battles that have begun. Enter into a
compromise through my wedding gown! (4.4.59–60)

However, in joining the Sabine commander she enters into an arena
equally marked for Roman public life, equally resonant with Roman

public institutions, successes, and policies. There she finds herself in a predicament similar to that she faced on the Capitol—faced with a military leader unwilling to sanction her love. Like the Capitol, Tatius' encampment is an unsafe place for her personal goals: the Sabine king kills her on the spot (4.4.91–92), reinforcing the Roman values that mandated her public service, and eventually leading to a pact between the two people, a pact entered not by Tarpeia's love but by her death. Tarpeia's grove thus becomes not a nostalgic glance that privileges the "lost—and irretrievable—natural innocence of the unpopulated pre-urban community," as has been suggested.[62] Rather, her grove forebodes the meaning and power of the future city.

Though Tarpeia believes she is acting in Rome's interest and her own, combining love and state in a way ominously resonant with the new state Augustus was trying to create, her actions are, to the Roman eye, criminal and doomed to fail.[63] Her departure from one site of Roman power, the Capitol, enacting as it does the reverse of a triumph, nevertheless leads her to the other urban axis of Roman dominion, the Forum Romanum. She departs from one center of Roman ideology to rush into another in which she is equally bent to the will of the state—in which, indeed, her story would be enshrined as a negative example in the Basilica Aemilia. She has nowhere to go.

THE PERILS OF THE THRESHOLD

Tarpeia, as we have seen, spends most of her time moving between the Capitol and the Forum, from the edge of the precinct of Jupiter Optimus Maximus to the edge of Tatius' camp below.[64] Each day she descends the hill on the pretext of washing her hair, drawing water, gathering lilies, or expiating omens (4.4.15 and 23–25), and each night she climbs the hill again: *subit primo Capitolia nubila fumo* (she ascends the Capitol hazy at the first smoke of night's fires, 4.4.27). Her exact path is of little concern; all approaches to the Capitol are abrupt, even with modern paving. More important is the way Propertius presents the area through which she moves. It is dark and threatening.

Tarpeia describes in her soliloquy the path that she travels, the very path that she eventually reveals to Tatius:

> tu cape spinosi rorida terga iugi.
> lubrica tota uia est et perfida: quippe tacentis

fallaci celat limite semper aquas.

You, seize the dewy back of the thorny ridge. The whole path is treacherous and slippery, for always it hides silent waters along its deceptive track. (4.4.48–50)

She does not describe a pleasant locale, but one difficult to maneuver, beset with hidden dangers, and perilously wet. The poet later confirms her evaluation: *mons erat ascensu dubius festoque remissus* (the mountain was difficult to climb and neglected for a holiday, 4.4.83); this is one reason Romulus left it unmanned during the celebration of the Parilia. Tarpeia, moreover, is wounded by thorns and brambles along the way:

dumque subit primo Capitolia nubila fumo,
　　rettulit hirsutis bracchia secta rubis,
et sua Tarpeia residens ita fleuit ab arce
　　uulnera, uicino non patienda Ioui.

When she ascended the Capitol hazy with the first smoke of night's fires, she returned with arms cut by bristling thorns, and Tarpeia thus sitting down wept for her wounds from the citadel, wounds that nearby Jove would not tolerate. (4.4.27–30)

Indeed, her dangerous path is similar to that negotiated by Ariadne, who also, Tarpeia argues, used her womanly resources (thread, the implements of weaving) to help a man travel a tricky route:

prodita quid mirum fraterni cornua monstri,
　　cum patuit lecto stamine torta uia?

Why wonder that the monstrous brother's horns were betrayed, when the twisted path lay revealed by a gathered thread? (4.4.41–42)

Both Tarpeia and Ariadne betray their families for the sake of love, by making accessible to men the contorted, dangerous paths they themselves have maneuvered. The women are masters of paths neither straight nor straightforward.[65] At either end of Tarpeia's travels, where men dwell, the ground is habitable—the Forum valley below and the crest of the hill above.[66] Her in-between area, the slope of the hill where she treads daily and where she sits nightly, is steep and hazardous.

Tarpeia's literal marginality echoes her emotional marginality. She is threatened on both sides; on the one side—the top of the hill—she is constrained to be unnaturally barren as a Vestal Virgin; on the other— the bottom—she expresses her desire but is killed for it. Propertius has presented Tarpeia's internal emotional struggle between *amor* and *Roma* in topographical terms, using the physical to convey the emotional. Yet his landscape invites us to consider Tarpeia's social situation as well, i.e., her position in society with respect to others. We have seen how the areas between which Tarpeia travels are ideologically charged, urban shorthand for Rome's power and glory, and its favor by the gods. Tarpeia's assigned area is empty, liminal, un-urban and untamed in its lack of future monuments to Rome's glory.[67] To be sure, two "monuments" were located on the slopes of the Capitol, but both of them are testimonials of marginality, of exclusion from the Roman state: the Tarpeian rock and the Carcer Tullianum. Like the Carcer's detainees and criminals and those condemned to the Tarpeian rock, Tarpeia is confined to Rome's "no-man's land."

This liminal area is the only place in which she can speak. Tarpeia's entire soliloquy is delivered from the threshold of the hill (*fleuit ab arce*, 4.4.29). On either side of her liminal space she is muted by indirect discourse. Furthermore, at the top of the hill she must lie, inventing pretexts for her visits to Tatius' camp: *saepe illa immeritae causata est omina lunae* (often using omens of the blameless moon as a pretext, 4.4.23) and at the bottom she is silenced by death: *ingestis comitum super obruit armis* (he overwhelmed her with the heaped-up weapons of his comrades, 4.4.91). Her confinement is replayed in the structure of the poem. Tarpeia's soliloquy lies in the middle of the elegy between the descriptions of her situation and of her demise. Her subjectivity, therefore, is poetically bracketed by the voice of the omniscient narrator, just as she is bracketed by the urban axes of Rome's dominion.

CONCLUSION

Tarpeia's topographical confinement is more than a metaphor for her situation. By making her liminality central—Tarpeia has the poem's most extensive voice, speaking thirty-six of its ninety-four lines (4.4.31–66)—the poet invites us to consider her point of view. The reader is led to sympathize with Tarpeia. From this space in the margin between two dominant urban centers, her perspective is drawn, and it proves to be unlike the snapshot of her in the Basilica Aemilia. Though appointment as a Vestal Virgin was a high honor in Rome, in Propertius' poem Tarpeia disagrees with the state's appropriation of her sexuality for its own benefit, and this is expressed in her desire to marry Tatius and in her negative evaluation of Romulus, child of another Vestal Virgin whose sexuality had been activated (Rhea Silvia was raped by Mars). From the margin, Propertius' Tarpeia also dreams of the best effects of personal affection: her affection would close off the margin between warring states, increasing Rome's greatness. From the margin, however, Tarpeia can only ascend into one area of public, masculine control and values, or descend into another.

Yet Propertius has allowed Tarpeia to voice dissent against Rome's mandates and leaves the reader with a sense of shock at her quick dispatch. The poet thereby creates a space for recovering women's perspective. Gold has spoken of Propertius as opening up a space where the woman's voice can be heard. She argues that having a woman (Cynthia) as anchor for his text destabilizes the gender roles; Cynthia's multiple roles (as lover, topic, literary critic, and friend) further destabilize the *status quo* between men and women, opening up a space for consideration of the asymmetry of gender roles.[68] Tarpeia's complicated gender perspective is underlined by the situation of this poem between elegy 4.3, in which a woman physically confined within the city comments on the mobility of men and the locations available to them alone (see, e.g., 4.3.35–40 and 45), and elegy 4.5, in which an angry man (the poet?) seeks to confine a threatening woman (a *lena*) in the ultimately controlled, marginalized, and circumscribed space: a tomb under the earth itself (4.5.1–5). Like Tarpeia, the *lena* resists her confinement via an inset speech.

In elegy 4.4 Propertius creates an actual physical space for Tarpeia's voice, a location where she may speak, though one riddled with problems, interstitial, and apart from the areas claimed by men. The fact that Tarpeia's space lies between those that men have claimed for themselves draws attention to the imbalance of power with respect to gender in Rome. The characterization of Tarpeia's liminal space as dangerous and treacherous destabilizes the construction of Roman gender relations that prizes traditional masculinity, for it reveals the cost of this construction for anyone who is "other."

Propertius was one such other, and in this he shares a great affinity with Tarpeia.[69] Both poet and *puella* are pressured by the state to abandon their love affairs. Both try to reinterpret their own and others' social roles within the state. Both are accomplished elegiac poets; Tarpeia's monologue reenacts the traditional *paraklausithyron*, complete with weeping and complaining. Her song-before-the-gates employs the learned mythical exempla and rapid shifts of thought that are the hallmark of elegiac poetry.[70] She performs it in a setting strongly resonant of Callimachean aesthetics.[71] Indeed both Propertius' poetry and Tarpeia's poem look to the model of Parthenius, whose Ἐρωτικὰ παθήματα presents the psychological torment of love through first-person narrative in elegiac verse.[72]

Given the displacement of the poet's subjective voice onto the *puella*, it is tempting to see in Tarpeia's situation a commentary on the relationship between elegiac poetry and the Roman cityscape. Elegy, like Tarpeia, dwells in Rome's margins and is vulnerable to the city. By attaching Tarpeia's story to Rome's urban places, Propertius works a double purpose. First, he underlines some problems of Tarpeia's particular situation, torn as she is between public and private duties. The second and subtler point is that, through Tarpeia's punishment, the poet comments with foreboding on the physical areas of Roman identity and power. Threatened by the disorder Tarpeia represents, the city crushes her.

CHAPTER 4

Ars gratia Martis

ART, WAR, AND
PALATINE APOLLO IN ELEGY 4.6

Musa, Palatini referemus Apollinis aedem:
  res est, Calliope, digna fauore tuo.

Muse, I shall present the temple of Palatine Apollo: a task that is worthy of
your favor, Calliope. (4.6.11–12)

THUS PROPERTIUS introduces his extended treatment of the battle of
Actium in one of the strangest and most contested poems in his poetic corpus. Scholars have found in elegy 4.6 a round endorsement of the
new Princeps and his victory over Cleopatra (Grimal, Cairns, Fedeli);
a grudging capitulation to imperial pressures to compose encomiastic
court poetry (Stahl); a subtle parody of the victor and his achievements
(Johnson, Janan) or of the subject position of the self (P. A. Miller); or a
bitter commentary on the origins of the new regime (Connor, Gurval,
Nethercut).[1] Alternately, focusing on poetics, some critics have found a
failed attempt at the high style (Williams); or a clever adaptation of
grand themes to the delicate Callimachean aesthetic (Sweet, Arkins, J.
F. Miller).[2] While all these responses to the poem are appropriate, and
together they help map the poem's complexity, I shall focus on one
aspect of the poem—the fact that it is an *aetion* for a Roman monument.
It is an easy theme to pass over, since it seems hardly important to the
poet himself: Propertius says virtually nothing about the monument
itself and concentrates instead on the event that Romans of his day
considered integral to the temple's genesis.

In this chapter I confront the discrepancy between what the poem
promises explicitly to discuss (the temple of Palatine Apollo) and what

it actually delivers (nothing concrete about the temple). The discrepancy leaves the reader with an unsettling sense of something missing, and raises questions about the meaning behind the monument. In this way, even though the elegy fails to describe the temple of Palatine Apollo, it does not fail to interpret it. Throughout this elegy Propertius draws attention to the fact that the conflict associated with the temple complex is incommensurate with the temple itself, its artistic result. In this poem, as in others, Propertius makes a strong statement of his preference for art over war and, moreover, asserts the power of his poetry to interpret and give meaning to a Roman cityscape that increasingly evoked the Princeps' achievements.

The severance of temple from poem is emphasized by the poem's evocation of elegy 2.31, Propertius' polished description of the temple at its dedication in 28 BCE. An interpretive dilemma confronts those who would understand this poem's relationship to the temple of Palatine Apollo; it functions both as a source for the temple's decorative program (indeed, our primary and fullest literary source) and a response to that monument. We are lucky to have three recourses in this dilemma: that almost every detail Propertius gives about the temple in elegy 2.31 is confirmed by other sources both literary and archaeological; that these other sources differ enough from Propertius' description to point to the ways his poem is a selective description of the temple, that is, an interpretation of it; and that Propertius himself uses language and imagery to describe the temple that he has used in other contexts, thus layering it with meaning drawn from within his poetry.[3] In elegy 2.31, Propertius describes the temple as an elegant and peaceful place in the same delicate terms he uses to describe his art and his love. Ignoring any imperial connotations of the Palatine complex, whether it commemorates Naulochus or Actium, this sophisticated elegy employs all the power and nuance of ekphrasis, raising questions about the relative viability of verbal and visual arts and dramatizing the act of a subjective reading/viewing of an artwork. Propertius' verbal art describes, or rather constructs for the reader, a work of visual art that surpasses in beauty its real models. Propertius' refined elegy thus makes a statement about the poet's ability to resist an imperial agenda and to rival the Princeps in defining and creating meaning in Rome's urban landscape.

In describing the events of Actium in elegy 4.6, Propertius alludes to his earlier poem on the temple in order to draw attention to the dissimilarity between the fierce god who directed the battle in 4.6 and the stylish one on display at the temple in 2.31. We shall see that in various ways he undermines our respect for the battle behind the temple. At the end of elegy 4.6 warrior Apollo exchanges bow for lyre (4.6.69–70) and becomes again the artistic god of poem 2.31, leading Propertius and other poets in a sympotic evening of song. The language of this poetic denouement links the happy symposium with the poem's introduction, in which the poet as *uates* prepares for his song by invoking his Alexandrian poetic predecessors. Beginning and end thus provide a contrasting tableau by which the inset battle may be assessed: Propertius' poetic celebration, much like elegy 2.31, is far preferable to and more pleasant than the hostile reality behind the temple. In this finale, moreover, the poet recuperates key images from his battle narrative, transforming them into peaceful, happy elements of his celebration. Like elegy 2.31, these transformations testify to the poet's ability to create an artistic reality that is more appealing than reality itself.

THE TEMPLE OF PALATINE APOLLO
Becoming Augustus in Rome

The temple of Palatine Apollo was by any standard one of the gems of the Augustan building program. Vowed at Naulochus in 36 BCE and dedicated in 28 BCE, it remained a favorite of the Princeps, who mentions it in his *Res Gestae* (4.1).[4] Precious little survives of the temple and the complex that surrounded it, but the site is well attested by ancient authors, and archaeology has provided tantalizing and beautiful remains.[5] Though the temple was conceived as a thanksgiving offering to the god for Octavian's success against Sextus Pompeius, by the time it was dedicated the battle against Antony at Actium was considered the deciding battle of the civil wars, and the temple soon took on an Actian color. In his study of Roman responses to the battle of Actium, Gurval urges a cautious approach to interpreting the monument. Arguing that the complex was conceived, planned, and built mostly before the battle, that the temple's dedication lacked connection to the Actian battle or its triumph, and that its decorations are ambiguous, Gurval concludes that the temple complex was neither an attempt to assimilate the victor at Actium with Apollo, nor a propagandistic celebration of that victory.[6]

While I agree with Gurval's caution against seeing a focused propagandistic machine at work behind the temple and its decorative

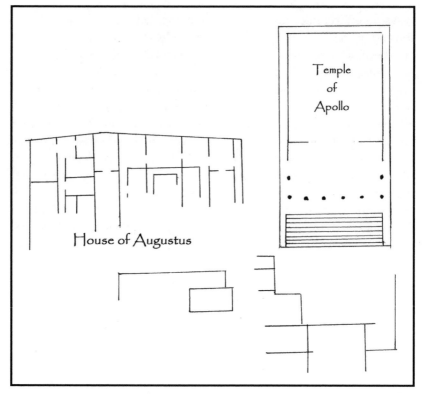

FIGURE 6. Plan of the Temple of Palatine Apollo, whose visitors might also catch a glimpse of the Princeps, Apollo's neighbor. After P. Zanker 1988: 52.

program, I disagree that it lacks an Actian nuance. Rather, I believe, following P. Zanker, that the temple complex brilliantly combines several threads, among which is the victory at Actium.[7] The organization of the compound, its surroundings, its materials, the iconography and symbolism of its decorations, and its contents all contributed to a monument with multifaceted associations; a monument that shows well the experimentation in imagery that marks the young building program of the new Princeps and admits of the polysemy that Gurval rightly prefers to see in place of a propaganda machine.

One such association is with Hellenistic monarchy.[8] The temple of Palatine Apollo was the centerpiece of an elaborate and unified compound that abutted Augustus' own house (Figure 6). This combination of domestic and sacred space is highly suggestive. The temple itself was framed by a portico that was populated with sculpture. Propertius and other authors tell us about the sculptural decorations in this portico: Danaids facing their unfortunate bridegrooms between the portico's columns, and a central altar group with an image of Apollo and four sculpted cows.[9] Adjacent to the portico, though exactly where or how large is yet unknown, was a library with sections for Greek and Roman authors, and clipeate portraits of famous authors.[10] The temple and portico were connected via a ramp to the new house of the Princeps, and somewhere nearby was a park.[11] This combination of various types of spaces within one multipurpose complex, made harmonious by design elements and structure, recalls the great sanctuaries of the Hellenistic dynasts such as those at Pergamum and Alexandria.[12] Such Hellenistic structures served to aggrandize the builder by setting him in the context of his chosen divine patron; to insinuate him into the variety of activities taking place at the complex, such as worship, research, and performance; and to blur the distinction between what is private and what is public.[13] In the Palatine complex these effects were heightened by the connection between house and temple mentioned above: the new Princeps could appear suddenly at the temple's pronaos as a sort of *deus ex machina*, a marvelous way to inch toward the image of the divine ruler.

These features appealed to the ever more powerful dynasts in Rome in the last century of the Republic, and the multipurpose complex became an increasingly popular architectural form in the decades before the battle at Actium. The Sullan sanctuary of Jupiter Anxur at Terracina and the theater of Pompey belong in this tradition, as do Caesar's Forum, complete with temple, portico, and adjacent library. The danger of flirting too closely with the model of a Hellenistic ruler-king was tempered by the combination of Hellenistic and distinctly Roman architectural features in these complexes at Rome. All four late Republican complexes—Anxur, Pompey's theater, Caesar's Forum, and Palatine Apollo—feature traditional Roman frontal temples upon high podia. By 28 BCE, the megacomplex had become a way for Octavian to signal both his conformity with Roman tradition and the novelty of his political situation.[14]

If evocation of the Hellenistic ruler-king was one feature of the Palatine Apollo complex, a general philhellenism was another. Not only did Greek literature constitute part of the temple's library, but Greek artworks were visible everywhere one turned. The Danaids and their fiancés that decorated the portico were surely Greek in style if not in craftsmanship.[15] The altar group in front of the temple consisted of four cows and a statue of Apollo holding a lyre; according to Propertius 2.31.5–8, the cows, at least, were by Myron, a late-Classical sculptor.[16] Pliny the Elder speaks of sculptures by Bupalos and Athenis, two

FIGURE 7. The Sorrento base preserves the composition of the temple's cult images and suggests not so much the fame of the Greek originals as that of their Roman arrangement. Photo courtesy of the Deutsches Archäologisches Institut.

sixth-century artists, on the temple's roof (36.9–13). He also describes the cult statues inside the temple as the work of Greek artists of the fourth century BCE: an Apollo *citharoedus* by Skopas, Diana by Thimotheus, and Latona by Kephisodotus (36.32). Though none of these cult figures survive, the famous Sorrento base reproduces their form and arrangement (Figure 7).[17]

These works of Greek art reflect Rome's increasing philhellenism in the late Republic and testify to Rome's struggle to negotiate its own cultural identity in the wake of Greece's older and more sophisticated culture. Like Horace's famous dictum *Graecia capta ferum uictorem cepit et artis / intulit agresti Latio* (Greece the captive took its savage victor captive, and brought the arts into rustic Latium, *Epist.* 2.1.156–57), the works in the temple complex simultaneously reveal Rome's own sense of indebtedness to the Greeks, as well as its anxiety about cultural inferiority.[18] They boast Rome's ability to compete with Greece in terms of cultural sophistication while they demonstrate Rome's hegemony over Greece. Given Romans' tendency to inscribe ethics into the rhetorical and visual arts, these Greek pieces in the temple complex also send their own "moral message."[19] Two of the works depict artists in the process of creating art (the courtyard image of Apollo with his lyre, Apollo *citharoedus* again in the temple), suggesting an interesting specific "moral message" for this set of works: that Rome, and more specifically Octavian, rehabilitates and re-enables the Greek arts. The resurrection of religious images (the cows at the altar, the cult images of Diana and Latona) suggests Rome's (Octavian's) rehabilitation of a failing piety.

The temple complex worked the rehabilitation of a Roman tradition as well. The *casa Romuli* was located on the Palatine, near the site of the new temple. By situating himself and his temple there, Octavian strengthened an association between himself and the city's legendary founder that grew throughout the years of civil war. The *casa Romuli* was a small and simple place whose humility was admired by ancient authors. Octavian's house was not overly elaborate either. This modest choice not only set Octavian in the context of Rome's founder and his rustic humility, but it repositioned Romulus within the context of a Greek god whose temple was adorned by the most splendid tokens of Greek cultural achievement.

Within this intricate framework we can put into perspective those aspects of the temple complex that resonate with the Actian victory. The Romans were accustomed to temples that commemorated military victory; such manubial temples had long lined the route of the triumphal procession and had spilled over into other parts of town. The very materials of the temple complex on the Palatine boasted Rome's access to foreign resources: while the temple itself was Italian Carrara marble, columns of Numidian marble and statues of Egyptian basalt adorned the portico, the temple doors were African ivory, and its cult statues were Greek marble. The preponderance of African materials used in the temple complex invites us to consider it in the context of Octavian's use of imported obelisks as urban focal points.[20] These imperialist features are not Actian *per se*, but they do set the temple into a triumphal context, and it is important to recognize how common

FIGURE 8. Coin of Antistius Vetus links Princeps and temple for those who could not visit in person. Photo courtesy of the British Museum.

such use of materials was in evoking conquest. In this case, the African materials surely hint at Rome's mastery of Egypt and Cleopatra.

It is easier to see an Actian theme in the subjects chosen to adorn the temple complex. Upon entering the portico a visitor was met with sculptures of the fifty Danaids holding their jars, set between the portico's columns, facing their fifty fiancés on horseback; nearby was Danaus with his sword.[21] In the context of this temple the Danaids, African maidens who followed their father's injunction and killed their fiancés on their wedding night, have been understood as nods to Cleopatra, another tricky African woman who spelled destruction for her fiancé.[22] The fact that the statues were carved out of exotic black stone adds to the evocation of Africa.[23] Carrying their leaky jars, the Danaids signal eternal punishment for their heinous crime; the monument thus dramatizes Cleopatra's eternal shame. The Danaids' crime and punishment in the underworld might also serve as an analog for Antony's crime and his punishment by the Romans at war. The reverse of this interpretation has been suggested as well: that the Danaids stand for the Romans, while the sons of Aegyptus evoke Antony and Cleopatra; the Danaids punish Aegyptus' sons just as the Romans punish Antony and Cleopatra.[24] A more general interpretation has also been put forth: the myth of the Danaids involves a sort of civil war, since the girls' quarrel with their fiancés was simply an extension of the feud between their fathers, who were brothers.[25]

Like the rest of the complex, the Danaid portico resists a stable interpretation. We must be careful, therefore, to recall that while the monument may have "meant" many things to its builder, it must also have been "read" in many ways by its visitors. Nevertheless, very little in the myth of the Danaids connects them to Apollo, and so their presence in this god's temple complex invites speculation that they were chosen as decorative motifs precisely for their potential Actian nuance.[26] The African materials used in the portico would support an Actian interpretation, as would the possibility that the figure of Apollo in the portico of the Danaids was styled "Apollo of Actium." A coin of Antistius Vetus issued in 16 BCE shows an Apollo with lyre and *patera* standing on a podium decorated with rostra; the legend reads *"Apollini Actio"* (Figure 8).[27]

In his ekphrastic poem on the temple, Propertius describes a statue of Apollo with lyre in the portico (2.31.5–6), which P. Zanker has plausibly identified with the image on the coin.[28] Though Propertius mentions no rostra in 2.31 and omits the detail of the *patera* at that point, this does not preclude the identification;[29] as I hope to demonstrate, Propertius' choice of details in elegy 2.31 is highly selective. The presence of an explicitly Actian Apollo in the portico of the Danaids would lend ominous nuance to an already suggestive tale.

The doors to the temple have also been interpreted as evocative of Actium. According to Propertius, they were inlaid with carved ivory relief sculptures of scenes of Apollo's successes. Though these doors do not survive, Propertius describes them in detail (2.31.12–14). One door was decorated with relief sculptures of Apollo's punishment of the Niobids. The other depicted Apollo successfully defending Delphi from invading Gauls. The theme of righteous vengeance comes through in these reliefs—a theme applicable both to Octavian's vengeance upon Caesar's assassins, and to the conclusion of the civil wars.

Some terracotta reliefs from the temple have survived, the so-called Campana reliefs, on which it is possible to see an Actian element.[30] One relief, for example, shows Perseus and Athena with the Gorgon's head; another shows maidens with the *betyl* (a stone totem of a god, usually the sun god), and a third type shows Hercules and Apollo in a struggle over the Delphic tripod. These reliefs may be interpreted as mythological stand-ins for the struggle between Octavian and Antony. Perseus and Medusa evoke the triumph over tricky barbarian women; the *betyl*, a symbol the new emperor found appealing, adorns one of the prominent rooms in Octavian's house adjacent to the temple. Most significantly, though, Apollo defending Delphi's tripod against Hercules' attack easily symbolizes (Apolline) Octavian's triumph over (Herculean) Antony (Figure 9).

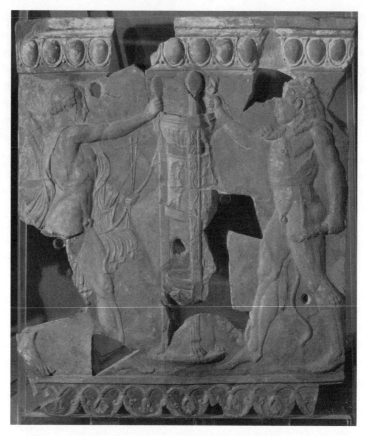

FIGURE 9. The archaizing terracotta relief of Hercules and Apollo comments on Antony and Octavian but also links their conflict to the mythic past. Photo courtesy of Scala via Art Resource.

The balance and symmetry of the composition of Apollo and Hercules hint at the recuperation of Antonian imagery by his conqueror. What is more, all these reliefs are framed by moldings of lotus flowers and elephants, and *simae* (water spouts) in the shape of Isis flanked by sphinxes—unabashedly Egyptianizing images. Nevertheless, it is important to note that the terracotta decorations also include elements that do not seem particularly to evoke Actium (such as celebrants carrying candelabra or incense holders), and that even the Actian decorations admit of multiple resonances (the gorgoneion, for example, also evokes Hellenistic authority).[31]

Octavian's complex thereby produced a series of thematic associations: between Greece and Rome, past and present, Princeps and founder, Princeps and god, history and myth, private and public, self and state. The use of imagery from Greek myth likewise inserts Octavian's Actian victory into a larger tableau, promoting an idea of continuity rather than disruption. Roman visitors thus saw in the temple's decorations and design a visual reunification of east and west after the schism of the civil wars. Rather than interpreting the monument primarily as an Actian celebration, it is more prudent instead to see thematic complexity in this monument. As Fowler notes, we would do the same for any work of literature.[32]

ARS GRATIA ARTIS
Propertius' Palatine Apollo in Elegy 2.31

Elegy 2.31 was written just after the temple of Palatine Apollo had been opened to the public. The opening inspired Horace also, and like the elegist the lyric poet turned the dedication to his own poetic use (*Carm.* 1.31). As Gurval has shown, these early poetic responses to the temple do not emphasize its possible connection to the battle of Actium; that connection was to await the hindsight of another decade of the Principate.[33] Rather, the temple served as a set-piece in which each poet might elaborate the themes of his chosen genre. In Horace *Carmina* 1.31, the poet prays to Apollo for health, contentment, and song (17–20), the fruits of the peaceful and simple existence that permeates the *Carmina*.[34] The public place, for Horace, is an invitation to contemplate the private pleasures of the lyric life.

Likewise, in his first response to the new temple, Propertius neglects the martial or triumphal aspects of the temple and concentrates on the usual themes of his early elegiac poetry: desire and art, and the connection between them. In describing the elaborate and polished complex, Propertius has written an elaborate and polished poem that resonates strongly with Callimachean tastes. Rather than dwelling on conflict or glory, Propertius focuses his attention and ours on the complex's layout, materials, and decorative program:

> quaeris, cur ueniam tibi tardior? aurea Phoebi
>   porticus a magno Caesare aperta fuit.
> tantam erat in speciem Poenis digesta columnis,
>   inter quas Danai femina turba senis.

hic equidem Phoebo uisus mihi pulchrior ipso
    marmoreus tacita carmen hiare lyra;
atque aram circum steterant armenta Myronis,
    quattuor artificis, uiuida signa, boues.
tum medium claro surgebat marmore templum,
    et patria Phoebo carius Ortygia:
in quo Solis erat supra fastigia currus,
    et ualuae, Libyci nobile dentis opus;
altera deiectos Parnasi uertice Gallos,
    altera maerebat funera Tantalidos.
deinde inter matrem deus ipse interque sororem
    Pythius in longa carmina ueste sonat.

You ask why I come to you a little late? The golden sanctuary of Apollo was opened by great Caesar. It was arranged in remarkable splendor with Punic columns, between which were statues of the female brood of old Danaus. Here a marble statue seemed to me surely to be more beautiful than Phoebus himself, and gave the impression of performing its verses even though its lyre was silent. And around the altar stood the artist Myron's herd, four fashioned cows, lifelike images. Then the temple soared in the middle out of shining marble, dearer to Phoebus even than his own homeland Ortygia: atop this temple above the pediment was a chariot of the Sun, and its doors were refined craftsmanship of Libyan ivory. One door lamented the Gauls cast down from the peak of Parnassus, while the other mourned the deaths of the children of Tantalus' daughter. Then inside the Pythian god himself, standing between his mother and his sister, wearing his long robe, recites his verses. (2.31.1–16)

Propertius immediately depoliticizes the temple by setting it in an erotic context. His visit to it is the reason he is delayed for a rendezvous with Cynthia: *quaeris cur ueniam tibi tardior?* (2.31.1).[35] This opening dramatizes a typical elegiac response to the cityscape as the setting for love affairs. Indeed, in Propertius' poetry when one lover or the other leaves Rome the implication is that infidelity is involved and the affair jeopardized (e.g., 1.6, 1.11). Ovid would take this trope even further in his treatises on love, in which public events and Augustan monuments, including this one, become simply venues for flirtation (*Ars am.* 1.67ff.) and travel abroad is the best prescription for getting over lovesickness (*Rem. Am.* 213). The fact that this poem adjoins elegy 2.32 in the manuscript tradition draws attention to its erotic, not political, nuances. The poet's description of the temple serves to justify his tardiness to his waiting lover. The opening phrase of this description, *tantam erat in speciem,* validates his delay: the temple was *such* a beautiful site that it inspired him to linger there.

As with any ekphrasis, Propertius' description involves focalization (i.e., presentation from a particular point of view) and all the questions inherent in focalization, notably how shifts in perception or point of view color the description.[36] In this respect, the poet imposes on the reader a sequence of "viewing" the temple. His ekphrasis mimics a visit to the temple, taking the reader from the outer portico to the altar to the temple doors to the cult figure within. Richardson emphasizes this movement in Propertius' poem:

> [H]is description is a minor masterpiece, with all the freshness of a first visit, and the best description that has come down to us. It is as if the poet were exploring the complex; each part comes in its proper sequence: first the colonnade of the Danaids, then the statue of Apollo in the court, the altar, the temple itself, the temple doors, and finally the cult images. We move with him along the main axis, drawn along in the experience of the architect's conception and development, the ritual of architecture that is supremely Roman.[37]

The sequence of viewing that Propertius imposes is reinforced by temporal words in his description: then (*tum,* 2.31.9) the temple towered, next (*deinde,* 2.31.15) the god appeared inside. With this movement Propertius gives the reader the impression of space and layout; he heightens the effect by some instances of creative word order. At 2.31.3 the phrase *Poenis digesta columnis* enacts the intercolumniation of the porticus, with the word *digesta* spacing out the Numidian columns; an ekphrastic double-play, *digesta* simultaneously indicates physical and poetic layout. Line 2.31.9 mimics a temple's pediment: the verb *surgebat* forms a pinnacle for the line, and is the center of an ABCBA structure, with mirrored pairs of words on either side of the central verb like the sloping roof of a pediment.[38] The line describing the temple in the middle of the complex also falls right at the middle of the poem (in line 9 out of sixteen). Word order adds to the effect at 2.31.15 as well; here Propertius describes the arrangement of cult images inside the temple: Apollo in the middle, flanked by his sister and mother. *Deus ipse* appears at the center of the line, flanked by the words *inter matrem* and *interque sororem.* With such devices Propertius gives the reader experiential access—or an experiential axis—to the complex's layout.

As Fowler observes, "when we describe in words a scene, we have to decide the order in which we are to present the details and the duration—which may be zero—of the description of each of them."[39] Propertius omits the detail of the plinth of the statue in the courtyard, which the coin of Antistius Vetus depicted as adorned with Actian *rostra*. He omits the connection to the Princeps' house. He omits the archaizing terracotta reliefs of Hercules, Perseus, and Victory. He omits mentioning that one of the Apollo statues in the temple complex bore likeness to Augustus (or, more accurately, depicted Augustus with Apollo's attributes).[40] Finally, and curiously, he omits the Greek and Latin libraries adjacent to the complex. Whether his reader has seen the temple yet or not, Propertius' guided tour suggests a (new) way of viewing and interpreting the monument. His omission of Octavian from the complex, as well as his concentration on the vivacity of the images he does describe, invite the reader to see in the temple complex a celebration not of the Princeps, his victory, and his new grand status, but rather of the power and beauty of art—naturally enough, since his addressee in this poem is Cynthia.

As we move further into the ekphrasis and the temple, the art we see is ever more lifelike, ever a better rival to the real figures it models. Propertius characterizes the Danaid statues in the portico as a womanly throng (*femina turba*, 2.31.4); he elsewhere uses this term to refer to a crowd of real people (e.g., 2.32.8), and his choice of words here emphasizes how lifelike they are.[41] Likewise, Propertius vivifies Danaus with the adjective "old" (*Danai . . . senis*, 2.31.4); the adjective suggests both moral and physical experience.[42] The sculpture of Apollo in the courtyard, his mouth open in song, seemed more beautiful than the god himself (2.31.5)—art has surpassed its living model. This same statue comes alive for Propertius and his reader; sculpted Apollo was seen singing, even though his lyre was silent (*uisus . . . tacita carmen hiare lyra*, 2.31.5–6). The *apo koinou* construction of *uisus* with both *pulchrior ipso* and *hiare* emphasizes the tension between being seen and seeming, between witnessing and interpreting, and between reality (what is seen) and art (what seems).

This tension persists. Sculpted cows around the altar are living images (*uiuida signa*, 2.31.8); the apposition or, more accurately, the absence of an overt simile with a comparison word such as *ut*, blurs the distinction between what they are and what they are like: the cows *are* living images. The word *artificis* emphasizes the comparison of art to reality, and Myron was renowned for the naturalism of his animals.[43]

Perhaps this is why Propertius mentions this artist by name. This couplet also evokes the famous ekphrastic proem to the third book of Vergil's *Georgics*, in which Vergil builds a temple with his words.[44] In it will stand Greek statues: *Parii lapides, spirantia signa* (*G.* 3.34). As Vergil's temple is full of Greek art, his description of it looks also to Greek literary models for inspiration.[45] Propertius' Greek cows likewise evoke the Greek literary tradition; the Palatine Anthology contains dozens of epigrams on a famous cow of Myron that predate Propertius (*Anth. Pal.* 9.713–42, 793–98), all of which stress the sculpted work's vividness. The two words used most frequently in these epigrams to describe the cow are ἔμπνους (living, breathing) and πλάττειν (to mold, craft); it is easy to see in Propertius' *uiuida signa* an awareness of and nod to this body of elegiac poems.

In the next couplet, we find that the temple is dearer to the god than his very place of birth (*patria . . . carius Ortygia,* 2.31.10). Apollo, like Vertumnus, is happy to have found his way to Rome, but the poet is even more specific: his temple, a work of architecture, is more pleasing to the god himself than is his actual homeland. Propertius then moves to the doors—which, too, rival living models. In a striking pathetic fallacy, the poet tells us the doors themselves mourn the images of defeat and downfall depicted on them. This testifies both to the power of the art to evoke emotions, and to the vividness of the works themselves—a classic case of ekphrastic *enargeia*.[46] It is interesting to note also that here for the first time in the poem Propertius applies active, transitive verbs to the works of art. Where earlier Apollo seemed to sing, the bulls stood, the temple towered, and there was a chariot, here the artwork described has a direct and active effect on some object. Finally, the cult image within the temple sings as if it were alive (another transitive verb, *sonat,* 2.31.16). Propertius' descriptions mark a range of interpretations, from art that is like its living models (*femina turba, Danai senis, uiuida signa,* 2.31.4, 4, and 8) to art that seems to surpass its models (*pulchrior ipso, carius Ortygia,* 2.31.5 and 10) to art that is, for all intents and purposes, alive (*maerebat, sonat* 2.31.14 and 16).

All this emphasis on the impact of art vis-à-vis its model fits squarely in the tradition of ekphrasis. It invites the reader not only to share a perspective with the internal viewer and to evaluate his reactions, but also to explore the relative merits of the verbal and visual arts. Propertius here credits art and artifice above reality; the statue improves upon the real Phoebus, and Propertius' poem improves upon the statue. The temple does not exalt Octavian's achievements, or even Apollo's, but rather poetic artistry and its effect on our reception of the things that surround us. It is no accident that the poem ends with a snapshot of Apollo reciting his poems (*carmina . . . sonat*, 2.31.16). Propertius' temple is a victory monument for poetry, and the poem's climax is a triumph of song. In this respect the temple parallels Cynthia, who provides Propertius poetic inspiration (cf. 2.30.40), and on whom the poet confers beauty even beyond the real.[47]

The connections between this elegy and the next reinforce the effect of describing and creating beauty, and of their complements viewing and desiring. In elegy 2.32 the poet complains about Cynthia's desire to leave Rome as a pretext for infidelity, laments that infidelity, and then exonerates her because women have ever been untrustworthy and because her beauty excuses her. Elegies 2.31 and 2.32 are connected in the best manuscripts; though editors almost always separate the two poems and/or transpose some couplets in order to facilitate the transition between the poems,[48] I believe the text as transmitted makes a powerful statement about art and beauty, and that the two poems are meant as a diptych.

Elegy 2.32 begins famously:

> qui uidet, is peccat: qui te non uiderit ergo,
>   non cupiet: facti lumina crimen habent.

> He who sees you sins: he who hasn't seen you will not desire you: the eyes cause the transgression. (2.32.1–2)

Until the clarification in the third line, where Propertius names Cynthia in the vocative, these lines might just as easily refer to the cult image of Apollo in the temple, the last image Propertius brought before his and our minds' eyes in 2.31. This suggestion finds support in the fact that the connection between viewing and status is drawn from Callimachus' *Hymn to Apollo*.[49] In that poem, the narrator, introducing the rites of Apollo before he takes up the god's accomplishments, advises participants that he who sees the god is great; who doesn't see him is lowly (ὅς μιν ἴδῃ, μέγας οὗτος, ὅς οὐκ ἴδε, λιτὸς ἐκεῖνος, *Hymn* 2.10). Like the unspecified *te* at 2.32.1, this verbal echo of Apollo's hymn is further indication that elegy 2.32 is also, to a degree, about Apollo and his temple.

Propertius proceeds to list the places that entice Cynthia away from Rome, and argues that when she has leisure (*uacabis*) she should stay in this place, *hoc . . . loco* (2.32.7)—referring, surely, to the temple of Apollo, which he has just described in such detail. She may, he explains, find other places in Rome too shabby for her leisure time, such as the portico of Pompey, an arboretum, and some fountains:

> scilicet umbrosis sordet Pompeia columnis
> porticus, aulaeis nobilis Attalicis,
> et platanis creber pariter surgentibus ordo,
> flumina sopito quaeque Marone cadunt,
> et leuiter lymphis tota crepitantibus urbe
> cum subito Triton ore recondit aquam.

> Maybe the portico of Pompey with its shady columns is too shabby for you, posh with its Asian tapestries, and the thick row of pruned plane trees towering above, and the fountain that flows while Maro sleeps, and the one whose gentle splashing can be heard through the whole city where Triton gulps back water. (2.32.11–16)

Here Propertius repeats some of the words he had used in 2.31: *columnis* (2.31.3 and 2.32.11, in the same *sedes*), *porticus* (2.31.2, 2.32.12), *nobilis* (2.31.12, 2.32.12, both referring to resplendent materials), and *surgo* (2.31.9, 2.32.13). The repetition of these words brings again before our mind's eye the temple of Palatine Apollo, which Cynthia could hardly find shabby after the poet's description in the previous poem. Moreover, if Cynthia does spend her free time in Apollo's temple, the god will be able to attest that she has remained faithful: *testis eris puras, Phoebe, uidere manus* ("You will be a witness, Phoebus, that you saw her hands were pure" [2.32.28]).

Yet the poet knows that Cynthia does not seek to escape Rome's monuments, even Apollo's, but rather to escape his scrutiny (2.32.17–20). Public opinion tells him so (*sed tibi me credere turba uetat*, 2.32.8), but malicious rumor is the curse of the beautiful (2.32.21–27). As in the opening of 2.31 (*quaeris, cur ueniam tibi tardior?*), these details and the correspondences between poems eroticize the temple of Palatine Apollo and our visit to it through the poet's eyes. A visit to it is a justifiable delay to a pressing erotic engagement, and a guarantor of fidelity while apart: the temple is a fitting and trustworthy substitute for the elegiac lover. These twin poems thus celebrate the inspiration to be found in beauty of any sort, the power of artifice to confer fame, and the ability of poetry to determine reception. So long as Propertius' poetry swells Cynthia's beauty, so long as his poetry enhances the beauty of Apollo's temple and its decoration, he who sees this beauty—or reads it—sins, and becomes great.

❧

MARS GRATIA ARTIS
Apollo and his Temple in Elegy 4.6

The Actium elegy remains one of Propertius' most puzzling poems. Standing at the center of Book 4, elegy 4.6 defies the poet's earlier promise to sing about the ancient names of places: *canam et cognomina prisca locorum* (4.1.69): the temple of Palatine Apollo is brand-new. It also repudiates the poet's earlier explicit claims that he would avoid encomiastic poetry and epic themes, such as the battle of Actium; at 4.6.11–12 Propertius prays to Calliope, the muse of epic poetry, for her favor in this great task (*res est, Calliope, digna fauore tuo*, 4.6.12).[50] Then the poem ignores epic adventures and revels in mannerist details. This poem does indeed praise Caesar; it overpraises him, in fact, and thus straddles the edge between encomium and *ridiculum*. What is more, the poem sits uncomfortably between the two elegies that flank it; 4.5 offers a *lena*'s advice to the elegiac *puella* who is her protégée, and 4.7 resurrects Cynthia for one last heated argument with Propertius. What is Actian Apollo doing here?

For these reasons and others, many recent readers and critics have found the poem's "patriotism" problematic to say the least.[51] Whether their doubts arise from the Callimachean and mannerist details that obscure the glory of the victory, from Octavian's non-role in the victory as compared to Apollo's hyperbolic success in battle, from the poem's peaceful denouement, or from the sort of palinode that follows it in elegy 4.7, I agree with their general assessment of the poem: it is not sincerely encomiastic, nor does it celebrate the Roman victory. But partisanship on this interpretive crux clouds a deeper matter that runs throughout Book 4: the evolution of Roman national myths and their adaptation to the new circumstances. Propertius' exploration of the rites, festivals, and ancient names of its places is really an examination of Roman identity at this crucial time, and of the changing ways Romans identified and understood themselves, e.g., myth, history, literary heritage, images, and physical monuments. While the other topographical poems in the book re-craft existing myths and the places they inform, the Actium elegy examines the creation of a new myth and the ways that myth is communicated.

By 16 BCE, when Propertius published elegy 4.6, the political, social, and artistic cultures in Rome had begun to adjust to the new regime and to understand its durability. External and internal threats such as the constitutional crises of 27 and 23 BCE and the emperor's own failing health had been handled successfully; Augustus' heirs were preparing for their future role in the state; and the very landscape of the city had been dramatically transformed. Hindsight saw the battle of Actium ever more clearly as the pivot between Republic and Principate.[52] Vergil's *Aeneid* in particular had established the temple of Palatine Apollo as the locus—literally as well as figuratively—of the Princeps' triumph over Rome's dissident forces (*Aen.* 8.720–23). Propertius' Actium elegy responds to what the temple of Palatine Apollo had become by 16 BCE: a talisman and monument of the Princeps' authority.

If the temple of Palatine Apollo in elegy 2.31 had nothing to do with the battle of Actium, the battle in elegy 4.6 has little to do with the temple of Palatine Apollo, even though the temple is the poem's professed subject. Propertius' silence on the temple undermines its status as a token of the emperor's authority, and, as we shall see, when the poet does explicitly mention the Palatine, it is to cast doubt on the new complex atop the hill. The hymnic frame of the poem likewise separates the victory from the temple. At the poem's opening and closing, Propertius employs language that links him with the artistic Apollo who appears to celebrate the victory with wine and song, the artistic Apollo he had described in the temple in 2.31. Instead of interpreting the temple and its god as a ratification of the Princeps' authority, therefore, Propertius uses them to endorse his own choices of poetry and lifestyle. Though I focus on the topographical aspect of the poem and not on its patriotism *per se*, my approach is heavily indebted to those critics who have tried to tease out the broader relationship this elegy presents between the poet and the Princeps.

After the poem's hymnic introduction, Propertius promises to sing the temple of Palatine Apollo. Thus begins his battle narrative:

> Musa, Palatini referemus Apollinis aedem:
> res est, Calliope, digna fauore tuo.
> Caesaris in nomen ducuntur carmina: Caesar
> dum canitur, quaeso, Iuppiter ipse uaces.
> est Phoebi fugiens Athamana ad litora portus,

> qua sinus Ioniae murmura condit aquae,
> Actia Iuleae pelagus monumenta carinae,
>   nautarum uotis non operosa uia.

> Muse, I shall present the temple of Palatine Apollo: a task that is worthy
> of your favor, Calliope. Songs are being composed in the name of Caesar:
> while Caesar is celebrated in song, I pray you too, Jupiter, make room in
> your schedule. There is a port of Phoebus that recedes toward the shores
> of Athamas, where the bay lays to rest the murmur of the Ionian
> waters—an Actian monument to the Iulian fleet, this bay does not over-
> burden the prayers of sailors. (4.6.11–18)

After promising to discuss Palatine Apollo, Propertius instead
describes a different monument: the sea where Octavian based his fleet
(4.6.17). The line is awkward.[53] Whatever the *pelagus* is (if different
from the port or bay), what does it mean that it is itself a monument?
Perhaps the poet intends *monumenta* in its root sense: something that
brings to mind (*moneo*) the fleet that once stood there—oddly so, however, since the bay as described is a calm place not feared by sailors
(*murmura condit*, 4.6.16 and *non operosa uia*, 4.6.18). Or, he is referring to
the naval trophy Octavian dedicated at Actium when he founded
Nicopolis, a trophy of ten ships captured from Antony's fleet.[54] This
interpretation, too, is perplexing, since the trophy did not yet exist.
This mannered and playful description belies the battle about to be
fought there.[55] The lines therefore raise many questions: what sort of
monument could the waters be? How is this calm location a monument of the battle? What can this sea-monument mean, given the fact
that the site of Actium boasted another monument to the battle—the
newly restored temple of Apollo on the overlook? However we understand the *monumenta* of line 17, it is certainly not the temple Propertius
promised to discuss.

Having set the scene for the battle, the poet proceeds to describe
Apollo's epiphany. His description serves to jeopardize the connection
between the battle and the Palatine temple even further, for Apollo
appears very unlike his representation in the temple. Recall the poet's
earlier description of the god in the temple's forecourt, as an artist in
mid-composition:

> hic equidem Phoebo uisus mihi pulchrior ipso
>   marmoreus tacita carmen hiare lyra.

Here a marble statue seemed to me surely more beautiful than Phoebus himself, and gave the impression of performing its verses even though its lyre was silent. (2.31.5–6)

Apollo in battle in elegy 4.6 presents an entirely different mien:

tandem aciem geminos Nereus lunarat in arcus,
    armorum et radiis picta tremebat aqua,
cum Phoebus linquens stantem se uindice Delon
    (nam tulit iratos mobilis una Notos)
astitit Augusti puppim super, et noua flamma
    luxit in obliquam ter sinuata facem.
non ille attulerat crinis in colla solutos
    aut testudineae carmen inerme lyrae,
sed quali aspexit Pelopeum Agamemnona uultu,
    egessitque auidis Dorica castra rogis,
aut qualis flexos soluit Pythona per orbis
    serpentem, imbelles quem timuere lyrae.

Finally Nereus had bent the battle lines into twin crescents, and the water trembled as it reflected the shining armor, when Phoebus, leaving behind Delos now stationary under his protection (for this island alone had been nomadic as it suffered the angry gusts of the winds), stood atop the prow of Augustus' ship, and a strange flame shone three times, bent into a jagged flash. He did not wear his hair loose on his neck, nor did he bring with him the song of peace that belongs to the tortoise-shell lyre, but he appeared with the same sort of face with which he looked upon Pelops' descendant Agamemnon, and when he emptied the Greek camps onto greedy funeral pyres, or as he looked when he destroyed the Python's twined coils, abhorred by the peaceful lyre. (4.6.25–36)

For Mader, this set of similes is linked firmly to the battle narrative that follows.[56] Apollo of the similes is defender against hubris (*Pelopeum Agamemnona*) and chaos (*Pythona serpentem*, whose enjambment reenacts his flexed coils). *Apollo heroicus* thus appears in order to restore a world in which *Apollo doctus* can thrive. Since Apollo stands on Augustus' side in battle, according to Mader the god's restoration of cosmic order lends praise to the Augustan victory and the order that followed; the poem is panegyrical.

To be sure, Apollo's intervention restores order. But rather than simply say how this vengeful Apollo looked as he did so, Propertius takes pains to point out how he did *not* look: Apollo in battle is nothing like Apollo in his temple as described in elegy 2.31.[57] Fighting Apollo does not carry his lyre, the instrument of unarmed poetry (*carmen inerme lyrae*, 4.6.32), and the instrument that marked him in the temple's court. The fact that the cult image inside the temple intones poetry suggests that both Apollos in the temple complex were musicians, not warriors; at least, in Propertius' description to Cynthia they are (2.31.16).[58] Other details in the description of warrior Apollo contrast with Propertius' earlier description: he leaves Delos not out of a preference for his new temple at Rome, as in 2.31.10, but to stand on the stern of Augustus' ship, while guarding Delos from afar as its protector (*se uindice*, 4.6.27). Apollo in battle appears poised to punish hubris, as he had in the Trojan War when Agamemnon scorned his priest Chryses (*Pelopeum Agamemnona*, 4.6.33–34). Contrast the doors of the temple as described in 2.31, which presented a mournful, not righteous, account of the deaths of other descendants of Tantalus (2.31.14). Finally, Apollo in battle looks as he did when he slew the Python, whom unwarlike lyres feared (*imbelles quem timuere lyrae*, 4.6.36). He was not a poet at the time.

The discrepancy between Apollos described in 2.31 and 4.6 destabilizes the connection between the event and its commemorative monument, and raises questions about the authorship of the myth that is enshrined in the city. If his first elegy on the temple of Palatine Apollo demonstrates the poet's power to construct our impression of the temple, Propertius' later elegy shows what the Princeps glossed over in decorating his temple: an Apollo fit for battle, with angry and vengeful aspect, warlike, and unpoetic. The narrative of the battle itself unsettles the creation of the myth in other ways as well. For one thing, Propertius consistently refers to the Actian victor anachronistically as Augustus (4.6.29, 4.6.38), a name he did not adopt until the settlement of 27 BCE, four years after the battle and one year after the temple complex was dedicated. The poet further alludes to the emperor's new name (*augur*, 4.6.43) and the title he chose for himself in 27 BCE (*Principe*, 4.6.46). Perhaps instead of carelessness Propertius exercised care in choosing his terminology, for just as his description of Apollo draws attention to the transformation of the god from warrior in the battle to artist in the temple, so, too, his inaccurate use of the name and title of the Actian victor draws attention to the transformation of Octavian into Princeps Augustus.

Having refused so far to discuss the temple in his poem, Propertius finally does mention the Palatine explicitly at 4.6.44. Apollo, exhorting Augustus to toughen up and fight for his country, likens his protégé to Rome's first founder:

> quam nisi defendes, murorum Romulus augur
>   ire Palatinas non bene uidit auis.
> et nimium remis audent prope: turpe Latinis
>   Principe[59] te fluctus regia uela pati.

> Unless you defend your fatherland, it meant nothing good that Romulus, the augur of the city, saw the birds fly over the Palatine. And now they dare to come too close with their oars; it is shameful for Latins that the waves suffer royal sails while you are Princeps. (4.6.43–46)

Here Augustus' actions are seen as validating Rome's history.[60] The adjective *augur* and the phrase *te Principe* confirm the connection between Romulus and Augustus, but Propertius hints at the connection's unflattering aspects. *Augur* recalls the contest between Romulus and Remus for rule in the new Roman state; Romulus, in station on the Palatine, either saw or pretended to see more birds than Remus, stationed on the Aventine. Romulus' subsequent murder of Remus left him sole claimant to the Roman throne. The name "Romulus" was, of course, rejected by Rome's new leader because of the specter of fratricide that it conjured, and Romulus' murder of Remus was uncomfortably similar to Octavian's defeat of Roman Antony.[61] Propertius is explicit that the site of Romulus' victory was the Palatine hill. His use of the adjective *Palatinas* in 4.6.44 recalls its prior appearance in the poem, in the promise of 4.6.11: *Musa, Palatini referemus Apollinis aedem.* Augur Romulus and Roman Augustus share the Palatine connection, and the uncomfortable stigma of civil conflict.

Propertius, looking askance at the new regime, seems to take pleasure in reminding his Roman readers of Remus.[62] This poem is no exception. In addition to the overt reference to the myth of Remus via the Palatine birds and the epithet *augur*, Propertius drives the point home with a thinly veiled wordplay on the name Remus at 4.6.45: they dared to come too close with their oars (*et nimium remis audent prope*), or, suggestively to the ear, Remus dared to come too close. While *Remus* (the brother) differs from *remis* (the oars) in vowel quantity—itself not uncommon in Latin poetry—[63] the combination of Romulus, birds, and *remis* in the passage cleverly recalls Romulus' dubious victory in the contest of augury and his violent behavior in its aftermath, and colors the reader's approach to the temple subliminally as well as out loud. This pun may seem a bit far-fetched at first glance; however, Propertius repeats it elsewhere in the poem. At 4.6.19–22, he describes the opposing forces in the battle:

> hunc mundi coiere manus: stetit aequore moles
>   pinea, nec remis aequa fauebat avis.
> altera classis erat Teucro damnata Quirino,
>   pilaque feminea turpiter acta manu.

> Here the armies of the world came together. A mass of pine stood on the sea, and the augural bird did not favor each set of oars equally. The second fleet had been condemned to fall to Trojan Romulus, and the pikes driven shamefully by a woman's hand. (4.6.19–22)

Here the epithet *Teucro* connects Romulus (= Quirinus) to Aeneas; the connection was a recent but already canonical innovation in Rome's foundation myths. Through this legend Augustus claimed descent both from Rome's human founders, i.e., Romulus and Aeneas, and from its divine parents Venus and Mars. As in Romulus' other appearance in the poem, here Augustus and Romulus are linked by an augural image, and Remus lurks nearby, again in a pun across vowel quantity. This time heaven's bird does not favor Remus (or the oars) equally (*nec remis aeque fauebat auis*, 4.6.20), and the fleet was condemned to fall to Trojan Romulus. Though the poem's nominal enemy is Cleopatra, with Antony conspicuously absent, these puns serve to point to Antony and civil wars as the conflict behind the myth.[64] Once again the association between Augustus and Romulus is darkened by the hint of fratricide, and with it darken also the Palatine quarters that they share.

Without saying a word about the temple itself, Propertius thus manages nevertheless to comment obliquely on it. In contrasting Apollo in battle with Apollo in song, he exposes the grim reality behind Palatine Apollo; the god is not always an artist, and it was not the artistic Apollo, Propertius' Apollo, who guided Octavian to victory against Antony. The temple complex that Octavian built masks the violence of the god and his war. Elegy 4.6 exposes the fiction of the temple, namely, the

discrepancy between what happened at Actium and how it was represented in the city. Romulus' presence in the poem also lends a sense of
foreboding to the temple complex, by hinting that the connection
between Rome's founders is not always flattering. Propertius' poem
makes evident what the temple's author left out, and reveals what the
temple itself—and the myth it supports—elides.

The elegist ends his battle narrative with the flight of Cleopatra and
the prospect of a dubious triumph:

> illa petit Nilum cumba male nixa fugaci,
>> hoc unum, iusso non moritura die.
> di melius! quantus mulier foret una triumphus,
>> ductus erat per quas ante Iugurtha uias!
> Actius hinc traxit Phoebus monumenta, quod eius
>> una decem uicit missa sagitta ratis.

She seeks the Nile, barely clinging to her skiff, achieving only this: that
she would not die on the appointed day. Thank the great gods above!
How paltry a triumph would one woman have been, led through the
same streets through which Jugurtha was led in earlier times! Actian
Phoebus has his monument because each of his arrows shot took out ten
ships. (4.6.63–68)

As with *Teucro Romulo* above, it is tempting to see in these lines a parallel between Augustus and Aeneas; the former fails to kill Cleopatra
on her bidden day (*iusso non moritura die*, 4.6.64); the latter hastens
Dido's death, which is unmerited and before her fated time (*nam quia
nec fato, merita nec morte peribat, / sed misera ante diem*, Aen. 4.696–97).[65]

Here again Propertius mentions a monument at 4.6.67. As in the
previous use of this word at 4.6.17, this monument is curiously undefined. Does it refer to the temple of Apollo on the Actian shores? Or the
temple on the Palatine? Or to the trophy of ten ships Octavian dedicated on the spot of the battle?[66] Does it differ from the monumental sea
mentioned earlier in 4.6.17? The word appears in the same *sedes* in each
case (as does the adjective *Actiae/Actius*), reinforcing the connection
with the site of Actium and undermining further the connection
between the battle narrative and the Palatine temple. Propertius' *aetion*
thus destabilizes the connection between cause and effect, between the
battle and its monument, between the victor and the builder.

PROPERTIUS AND APOLLO

The battle narrative shows that the victor's patron god is different
from the one represented in the temple, and that the temple does not
reflect the battle. In contrast, the hymnic frame of the poem presents an
Apollo *Musagetes* closely aligned with the poet's goals and means. The
elegy opens and closes with a picture of the *uates* in action, performing
rites and songs for the god he honors. The poet ends his battle narrative with a note of relief: *bella satis cecini,* I have sung about war enough
(4.6.69). He seems to prefer musical Apollo to Apollo the warrior, and
this preference alone says something about the temple Octavian built.
But the elegist goes even further in reinterpreting the meaning behind
it: he appropriates the temple to serve his own poetic goals. In the
poem's opening, Propertius clearly capitulates to the pressures to sing
patriotic themes, but he will do so only on his own poetic terms. In the
poem's closing lines Propertius describes his bibulous reverie with
language that recalls both the poem's opening and its battle narrative.
These correspondences liken him to the god and victor of the battle.
Propertius triumphs, and the temple pays tribute to his poetry.

The poem opens with the poet in mid-sacrifice, and immediately
launches into an endorsement for Alexandrian and elegiac poetics:

> sacra facit uates: sint ora fauentia sacris,
> et cadat ante meos icta iuuenca focos.
> serta Philiteis certet Romana corymbis,
> et Cyrenaeas urna ministret aquas.
> costum molle date et blandi mihi turis honores,
> terque focum circa laneus orbis eat.
> spargite me lymphis, carmenque recentibus aris
> tibia Mygdoniis libet eburna cadis.
> ite procul fraudes, alio sint aere noxae:
> pura nouum uati laurea mollit iter.
> Musa, Palatini referemus Apollinis aedem:
> res est, Calliope, digna fauore tuo.

The celebrant performs the rites: let every mouth favor the ceremony,
and let the heifer fall stricken before my hearth. Let Roman garlands vie
with the ivy clusters of Philetas, and let the urn decant the waters of
Cyrene. Give me the soft balsam and the honors of mellow incense, and
let the skein circle three times the holy fire. Sprinkle me with waters, and

let the ivory pipe make a libation of song from Mygdonian wine on fresh altars. Deceit, stay far away, offenses, may you stay under another sky. Pure laurel softens the unfamiliar path for the priest. Muse, I shall present the temple of Palatine Apollo: a task that is worthy of your favor, Calliope. (4.6.1–12)

The Alexandrian programmatics of these opening verses are apparent:[67] the mention of Philetas and Callimachus, Alexandria's two greatest poetic practitioners; the learned allusion to elegy's origins in *Mygdoniis . . . cadis* (4.6.8); the reference to the metapoetic water of Callimachus; words that couch Alexandrian literary values, such as *pura, molle, blandi, mollit,* and *nouum;* and emphasis on the private and personal in *meos, mihi, me.*

This opening, moreover, clearly recalls Callimachus' own *Hymn to Apollo* with several specific verbal echoes and with broader similarities.[68] Both poets urge reverent silence (4.6.1 and cf. *Hymn* 2.17, εὐφημεῖτ' αἴντες ἐπ 'Απόλλωνος ἀοιδῇ), playfully exhorting even Jupiter or the sea to pay attention (*Iuppiter ipse uaces,* 4.6.14, and cf. *Hymn* 2.18, εὐφημεῖ καὶ πόντος); and both banish whatever is false from the ceremony (*ite procul fraudes,* 4.6.9 and cf. *Hymn* 2.2: ἑκὰς, ἑκὰς ὅστις ἀιτρός). In both poems, celebration of the god frames narration of his deeds, and the ritual that comprises the celebration is more a literary than a religious exercise.[69] Indeed, the similarities between the two texts, combined with the preponderance of personal pronouns mentioned above, suggests that Propertius' poem is not to be read as part of a public observance of the temple, or group hymn, as Cairns believes, but rather as a private affair or, more accurately, a private fiction.[70] Finally, Propertius' and Callimachus' poems both contain a strong metapoetic content. Callimachus' second hymn manages to celebrate Apollo while also extolling the poet's own artistic choices; Apollo appears in a famous epiphany at the poem's end to endorse Callimachean poetics, arguing against Envy that small polished works outperform works of greater volume but less refinement (*Hymn* 2.108–12).

The elegist's Apollo likewise appears in an epiphany at the poem's end in a way that comments on poetic values. After the battle—one whose connection to the temple of Palatine Apollo the poet destabilizes—Apollo becomes again the artist he is in the temple complex:

bella satis cecini; citharam iam poscit Apollo
uictor et ad placidos exuit arma choros.

> I have sung enough about war; now Apollo the victor seeks the cithara
> and sheds his weapons in preference for the dance of peace. (4.6.69–70)

Apollo the artist, not the helper in battle, is the hero and climax of Propertius' poem.

To be sure, the trope of Apollo exchanging his bow for the cithara signals a celebration of victory. Yet as J. F. Miller demonstrates, this artistic Apollo serves two additional purposes.[71] The first is to bring before the reader's imagination Apollo *citharoedus* from the temple courtyard. Recall that this exchange comes on the heels of the poet's mention of the temple of Palatine Apollo (4.6.67–68). Two intertextual references support this association. Horace *Carmina* 1.31.1–2 celebrates the dedication of the temple with similar language: what should the poet ask of Apollo upon his dedication? (*quid dedicatum poscit Apollinem vates*). Vergil similarly follows the archer god Apollo, victorious at Actium, with Augustus' celebration of the victory from the threshold of the temple of Palatine Apollo (Vergil *Aen.* 8.704–22). Through Propertius' quick transition from battle to temple to lyre and through the passage's intertexts, Apollo the artist highlights the discrepancy between the god's demeanor in battle and his artistic representation in the temple. Apollo earned that monument with his bow, but he will decorate it with his lyre. The second purpose of the exchange is to conjoin Apollo with Propertius and his poetic aims.[72] As Miller points out, the phrase *bella satis cecini* can mean both "My story (is) done" and "Enough already"; the latter nuance reveals the limits both of elegy and the elegist that have been strained by the preceding battle narrative.[73]

It is the combination of these two purposes that interests me in this poem. The result of the combination is a rousing endorsement by Apollo for Propertian poetic exploits—an endorsement underscored by the self-casting of the poet as *vates,* sacred to and sanctioned by the god—and a tacit disapproval of the way Octavian had used that god in his urban program. Whereas Octavian's built Palatine Apollo does not reflect his association with the fierce god of the battle, Propertius' written Palatine Apollo reflects well the poet's aims and means. Propertius has claimed the temple for himself: it honors not so much Actium, or martial glory, but poetry itself. Apollo's arrival ushers in a night of revelry for Propertius and his poetic comrades:

> bella satis cecini: citharam iam poscit Apollo
>   uictor et ad placidos exuit arma choros.

candida nunc molli subeant conuiuia luco;
    blanditiaeque fluant per mea colla rosae,
uinaque fundantur prelis elisa Falernis,
    terque lauet nostras spica Cilissa comas.
ingenium positis irritet Musa poetis:
    Bacche, soles Phoebo fertilis esse tuo.
ille paludosos memoret seruire Sycambros,
    Cephean hic Meroen fuscaque regna canat,
hic referat sero confessum foedere Parthum:
    "Reddat signa Remi, mox dabit ipse sua:
siue aliquid pharetris Augustus parcet Eois,
    differat in pueros ista tropaea suos.
gaude, Crasse, nigras si quid sapis inter harenas:
    ire per Euphraten ad tua busta licet."
sic noctem patera, sic ducam carmine, donec
    iniciat radios in mea uina dies.

I have sung enough about war; now Apollo the victor seeks the cithara and sheds his weapons in preference for the dance of peace. Now let gleaming banquets be spread out in the lovely grove; and may fragrant roses tumble down my neck, and let wine be poured, wine pressed from Falernian wine presses. Let saffron powder anoint my hair three times. Let the Muse spark the talent of poets who are settled nearby: Bacchus, you are usually fruitful for your Phoebus. Let that one recount how the swamp-dwelling Sycambri were enslaved, let this one sing about the dark kingdoms of Meroe, Cepheus's island, and this other one recall how the Parthian surrendered with a late treaty: "Let him restore to Rome the standards of Remus; soon he will give up his own standards too: or if Augustus will spare the eastern archers for a time, let him defer those trophies until his grandsons can claim them. Rejoice, Crassus, if you can feel anything buried under the dark sand: now we may travel across the Euphrates to visit your tomb." Thus I shall pass the night with my cup, thus with my song, until the day casts its rays into my wine. (4.6.69–86)

Repeated words such as *molli* (line 71 and cf. *molle*, 5, and *mollit*, 10), *blanditiae* (72 and cf. *blandi*, 5), *terque* (74 and cf. 6),[74] and *Musa* (74 and cf. 11) serve to link this festivity with the rituals the poet performed with Alexandrian flair at the poem's opening. Yet his language also looks back to his battle narrative, and links Propertius' celebration to Apollo's deeds. In battle Apollo exhorts Octavian, *tempus adest, committe ratis; ego temporis auctor / ducam laurigera Iulia rostra manu*

("The time is near: engage your fleet. I am the author of the opportunity and I shall lead the Julian rostra with laurel in my hands"
[4.6.53–54]). As Apollo will lead the fleet (*ducam*) with laurel (*laurigera*),
Propertius will lead the night in wine and song (*ducam*, 4.6.85–86). The
opening is implicated as well: songs are sung in the name of Caesar
(*Caesaris in nomen ducuntur carmina*, 4.6.13), and Apollo's laurel softens
the new poetic path (*pura nouum uati laurea mollit iter*, 4.6.10). The final
image of the poem likewise recuperates imagery from the Actian battle. At the end of the poem Propertius promises to usher in the day with
his party; he will not stop his poetic celebration until the sun's rays are
reflected in his wine (*donec / iniciat radios in mea uina dies*, 4.6.85–86). The
poet had earlier described the battle lines in similar terms of rays of
light shimmering on a liquid surface:

> tandem aciem geminos Nereus lunarat in arcus,
> armorum et radiis picta tremebat aqua.

> Finally Nereus had bent the battle lines into twin crescents, and the
> water trembled as it reflected the shining armor. (4.6.25–26)

In repeating images and words from the battle, Propertius inserts himself into the action, and appropriates the terms of the battle for his own
ends: he leads with the laurel, framed by the sun's rays. Apollo now
shines for him, not for battle. Callimachus had done something similar in his *Hymn to Apollo*, weaving the same words throughout both
hymnic frame and aetiological tales (notably, forms of ἀείδω: *Hymn*
2.5, 17, 18, 28, 30, 31, 43, 44, 104, and 106).[75] The effect in that hymn is
a connection between Callimachus the singer and Apollo the god of
song, and an appropriation by the poet of the glory of the deeds of his
patron god: Callimachus singing about Apollo's accomplishments,
perpetuating their fame, defining their characteristics, is as much an
author of Apollo's deeds as the god himself was. Propertius' poem
functions in the same way, and in this respect the Roman elegist leaned
heavily on his Alexandrian model. Just as Callimachus makes himself
author of Apollo's deeds, Propertius makes himself author of Apollo's
temple. Spending the night with his *patera* and his song, the poet
becomes Apollo, standing in the courtyard and in the temple in a
salute to artistic skill.

Propertius' construction in poetry outshines Augustus' in marble: the poet's temple is consistent with his activities and lifestyle in a way Augustus' is not. Unlike the struggle between opposed forces in battle, in Propertius' celebration east and west come together; he uses the Mygdonian, or Phrygian mode in his ritual at the beginning of the poem, a mode popular in the worship of the Magna Mater (*tibia Mygdoniis libet eburna cadis*, 4.6.8), and the poem's end finds Bacchus in the service of Apollo (*Bacche, soles Phoebo fertilis esse tuo*, 4.6.76). Not only does Propertius unite the two divine sources of his own poetic inspiration in this line, but he also metaphorically reconciles Antony and Octavian, who had cultivated associations with Bacchus and Apollo, respectively. The Princeps, on the other hand, has not yet been able to reconcile east and west completely: a full Parthian settlement would have to await his descendants (4.6.81–82).

Given the achievement Propertius imagines his own Apollonian shrine to poetic art to be, the pointed use of the word *fides* in this poem merits attention. The word appears at 4.6.57, describing Apollo's contribution to the battle: *uincit Roma fide Phoebi* ("Rome wins because of the guarantee of Apollo"), and again a few lines later (4.6.60) in describing Julius Caesar's reaction to his apotheosis: *Sum deus; est nostri sanguinis ista fides*[76] ("I am a god; this is a guarantee of my divine bloodline"). A pun may be at play here: *fides* of course means "guarantee," which in Propertius' elegy connotes the trust between the lover and his mistress. Apollo's bond with Augustus and Augustus' with Caesar are just such bonds of trust.[77] But the word also can mean "lyrestring," and its appearance in this poem might therefore indicate that Rome won because of the music of Apollo, and that this music is the source of Caesar's divinity.

For this reason, namely, the primacy of Apollo's and Propertius' art over politics and warfare, time should be spent in Propertius' temple—i.e., in the cultivation of the elegiac lifestyle. Propertius had earlier urged his Cynthia to visit this place, the temple of Apollo, whenever she has free time (*hoc utinam spatiere loco, quodcumque uacabis*, 2.32.7). Jupiter himself should make time for Propertius' temple of Apollo: *Caesar / dum canitur, quaeso, Iuppiter ipse uaces* (while Caesar is being celebrated in song, I pray you too, Jupiter, make room in your schedule, 4.6.13–14). Propertius' song commands even Jupiter's respect.

CONCLUSION

In elegy 2.31 Propertius describes the new temple of Palatine Apollo in terms that elevate his own poetic artistry. In elegy 4.6 he elaborates on this theme. By dissociating the temple's images from the battle that was thought to be its inspiration, Propertius points to the discrepancy between the emperor's martial activity and his urban activity. Apollo in battle is not Apollo in song; Octavian in battle is not Augustus the builder. Propertius the poet, however, has much in common with the god of the temple—they share instruments, words, images, and talents, and the poet as *vates* is the god's voice on earth. Like Callimachus' *Hymn to Apollo,* Propertius' hymn to the god really becomes a paean for his own poetry. Indeed, it might be said that Propertius' poem owes as much inspiration to Callimachus' hymn as it does to Octavian's temple; the patent and subtle likenesses to Callimachus' poem highlight the textuality of the elegist's achievement.

To be sure, the temple of Palatine Apollo was not a simple monument—it may be interpreted and must have been interpreted in a number of ways by Romans and visitors. Nevertheless, by 16 BCE the temple was understood by Roman authors as a symbol of Octavian's victory at Actium. Propertius acknowledges this conventional wisdom only to reject it: the temple does not and cannot glorify the campaign, because of the dissonance between the battle and the temple's imagery. Likewise, Propertius calls into question the relationship of Augustus and Apollo that is enshrined in the temple complex. Within the poem the poet's assumption of the role of *vates,* too, redirects Apollo's energy away from Augustus' project to his own. The relationship between the Princeps and his Olympian patron is further destabilized by the context of elegy 4.6 within the book. Elegy 4.5, the curse of Acanthis, and elegy 4.7, Cynthia's ghost, both linger on magic and superstition in personal, not public, matters. Both highlight the various bonds and powers of elegiac love. These two poems thus enclose and contextualize the temple of Palatine Apollo's public, supernal content within private, infernal affairs.

In exploring the temple's tensions, Propertius raises questions not only about the temple's accepted "message," but more broadly about the meaning of the monuments, both new and restored, that now adorned the city. It is difficult to make sense of a topographical poem that has so little to say about topography. Since this is the one elegy in Book 4 that deals with a pointedly Augustan monument, I believe the poet's silence on the monument itself is condemnatory. Buildings cannot confer the sort of fame or reputation that poetry can; they are imperfect vehicles for ideology. Propertius repeatedly advises Cynthia of the power of his poetry to determine her reception. Now he speaks the same warning to Rome's first man. After all, the temple of Palatine Apollo no longer stands, but its memory and beauty remain enshrined forever in Propertius' poems about it.

CHAPTER 5

Masculinity and Monuments in Elegy 4.9

PROPERTIUS 4.9, an elegiac version of Hercules' visit in Rome, has enjoyed considerable scholarly attention in the past fifty years. Some critics read this poem in a political light. Since Augustus and his wife had revived ancient rituals and restored dilapidated shrines and temples, Propertius' celebration of religious *arcana* was seen to endorse and to congratulate the Princeps.[1] Other interpreters read the poem as a generic tour de force, whose dazzling and recondite details broadcast the poet's virtuosity and redefined elegiac poetry.[2] Recently many critics of this poem have focused on Hercules' alterity—particularly his transvestism—and how it unsettles the hero's place in the national canon.[3] Whether Hercules' transvestism confounds traditional gender categories (Janan 1998 and 2001) or reaffirms those categories (Cyrino 1998), whether it questions the very means for defining gender identity (Lindheim 1998), whether it calls into question Roman imperialism (Fox 1998) or historicism (Fox 1999), or whether it creates broader epistemological problems (Spencer 2001), these critics agree that Propertius' Hercules makes an important contribution to Rome's evolving sense of itself during the transition from Republic to Principate.

In this chapter I analyze Propertius' use of Roman monuments associated with Hercules. I ask what it means that Propertius connects the story of Hercules' transvestism and his re-emergent masculinity intimately with two of Rome's most ancient and venerable sites: the Ara Maxima, for which his poem is an *aetion*, and the sanctuary of the Bona Dea, at which most of its action takes place. Hercules differs from the

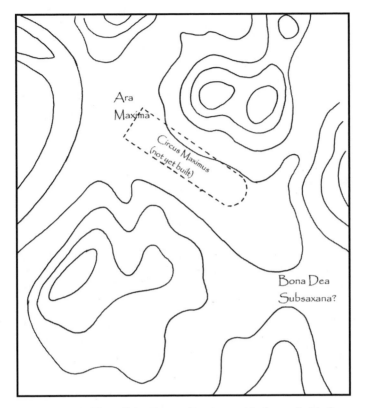

FIGURE 10. Plan of the Forum Boarium with the probable locations of the Ara Maxima and the sanctuary of the Bona Dea marked.
Note (as the poet does) the distance between the sites and their relative exposure to (Ara Maxima) or seclusion from (Bona Dea) public
traffic. After Favro 1996: 278.

feminized elegiac lover, whose ambiguous gender identity is ubiqui-
tous. In this poem, by contrast, Propertius locates Hercules' gender
play in specific Roman locations—locations that resonate both with
traditional gender roles and with the Augustan urban renovation.

Hercules, ridding Rome of the brutish thief Cacus, became a Roman
model of a civilizing agent. This legend, associated with the founding of
the Ara Maxima, proved a useful allegory for Augustus, who had
restored peace to Rome after decades of violent civil war. On August 12,
29 BCE, Augustus celebrated Hercules' rites at the Ara Maxima, or
Greatest Altar, the ancient shrine founded upon the hero's arrival at
Rome and his victory over the bandit Cacus. The next day Augustus
began a three-day triumphal celebration of his recent victories over

Dalmatia and Egypt and at Actium. The coincidence of rites and triumph forged a link between Augustus and the Ara Maxima, a bond that Vergil's *Aeneid* celebrated and elaborated in the next decade.

In elegy 4.9 Propertius minimizes the hero's dispatch of the local bandit, focusing instead on the aftermath of this heroic workout. Hercules seeks a drink at the sanctuary of the Bona Dea, tutelary goddess of Roman married women and a sanctuary that would become a favorite of Augustus' wife, Livia, who styled herself as Rome's "patron" of matrons. Propertius transforms Hercules from an epic-style hero to an elegiac-style lover, pleading for entry from a woman at her doorstep and abandoning traditional masculinity by boasting of his past experience as a cross-dresser. Likewise, this episode transforms the venerable priestess of the Bona Dea into a *lena* (the madam who controls access to elegiac girlfriends) and the goddess's sanctuary into a lover's bedroom. Refused entry to the all-female space, the elegist's Hercules breaks into the sanctuary and helps himself to its forbidden sacred waters. His thirst slaked, he establishes the Ara Maxima and forbids women ever to take part in its rites. In the poet's revised myth of the origins of the "Greatest Altar," Hercules' visit to Rome subverts the gender roles so important to Augustus and his wife, while the Ara Maxima itself commemorates a violent reassertion of those rigid roles.

MONUMENTS AND MORALITY:
The Princeps, Hercules, and the Ara Maxima

Elegy 4.9 is an *aetion* for the Ara Maxima, Hercules' most venerable Roman shrine, located in the Forum Boarium on the banks of the Tiber (Figure 10). The association of Hercules and the Princeps was forged on August 12, 29 BCE. On that day, the anniversary of Hercules' advent in Rome, Octavian celebrated Hercules' rites at the Ara Maxima.[4] The very next day Augustus began his triple triumph for his recent victories over the Damatians, the Egyptians, and over Antony's forces at Actium.[5] Hercules had long been a favorite of triumphators, and Octavian's scheduling was deliberate and shrewd.[6] Servius calls it εὐσύμβολον (= *feliciter, ad. Aen.* 8.102), and Donatus tells us that Octavian delayed his entry into Rome by lingering for four days in Atella while Vergil read him the *Georgics*.[7] The delay ensured that Octavian would repeat Hercules' advent into Rome. According to the prevailing tradition, the Ara Maxima commemorated Hercules' defeat of the outlaw Cacus and so solidified not only the hero's physical prowess but also his role as a civilizing agent in a time of lawlessness. This was a useful image for the Princeps, who had just restored peace to Rome after the civil wars. The association of triumphal Octavian with Hercules thus gave a veneer of legitimacy to Octavian's defeat of Antony. It also invited into Octavian's own personal pantheon of supporters the hero-god who had been Antony's favorite. The *gens Antonia* enjoyed an ancestral relationship with Hercules through Anton his son. Antony had especially cultivated this relationship, both to win prestige in Rome in the years after Caesar's death, and to develop his persona abroad. Hercules provided Antony with a linkage to Alexander, the East's great divinized king, who had himself cultivated an association with the hero who became a god.[8]

After the victory over Antony at Actium, the Princeps sought to recuperate Hercules for the Roman cause and for his own. Though not the most common god in the imagery of the Principate, Hercules' appearances are telling. He is featured prominently, for example, in the decorative program of the temple to Palatine Apollo, dedicated on October 9, 28 BCE, just a year after the triple triumph. The temple complex boasted representations of myths of vengeance mingled with notions of the dangerous foreigner—images that subtly reflected the Princeps' Actian victory.[9] Among them on the terracotta Campana-style plaques appears Hercules facing Apollo over the Delphic tripod (Figure 9, above). The calm posture of the two gods suggests not hostility but rather negotiation, the moment of reconciliation and resolution after the struggle for the tripod.[10] The symbolism is clear: like Apollo reconciled with Hercules, the Princeps' new order resolves the previous conflict between Roman forces.[11]

It should be noted also that while women seem to have worshiped Hercules freely elsewhere in Italy and even in Rome, his worship at the Ara Maxima was restricted to men only.[12] The exclusion of women from the Ara Maxima may have been linked to the fact that the cult was celebrated *ritu Graeco*, in the Greek fashion, and it may have been linked with the cult's original aristocratic flavor.[13] Augustus' activities at the Ara Maxima thus not only signal his new political role but also his participation in a club of elite Roman men. The coincidence of rites and triumphs in 29 BCE, celebrated in the public Fasti, marks a crux in imperial ideology. On the one hand, it looks back to the images of the civil wars and puts a symbolic end to the propaganda war against Antony. On the other hand, this event also looks forward to the tenor of

the new regime, in the way it links imperialism with the established
and traditional masculinity of Hercules' worship at the Ara Maxima.
This connection between imperialism and masculinity would appear
broadly in the Augustan architectural program for the next thirty years,
culminating in the sculptural program of the Forum of Augustus.[14]

However direct the Princeps was in cultivating a relationship with
Hercules, by 16 BCE, when Propertius' poem was published, the association would have been clear thanks to Vergil's *Aeneid*. In *Aeneid*
8.185–275, Evander tells Aeneas the story of Hercules and Cacus, and of
the subsequent foundation of the Ara Maxima. Vergil's narrative connects epic heroism, traditional masculinity, and Roman nationalism in
the figure of Hercules, locating this concentration of Roman virtue at
the Ara Maxima.[15] Vergil also makes clear that Aeneas repeats Hercules' advent into Rome, and that Augustus will be the next great hero
in the series of Rome's founders.[16] Vergil seems to have taken his cue
from the Princeps' activities in 29 BCE, for in Book 8 Augustus-as-Her-
cules appears at the climax of the shield ekphrasis, celebrating his
triple triumph. Hercules' victory and the Ara Maxima thus begin Book
8, and Augustus' triumph ends it.[17] Aeneas' partnership with Evander
throughout the episode and the conspicuous lack of women who participate in their encounter (the book's featured woman is Cleopatra on
the shield) make Book 8 into its own men-only club that repeats and
reinforces the restrictions of the Ara Maxima.

The connection between Augustus and Hercules also appears in
Livy's account of Rome's origins in 1.7. Though Livy's history does not
champion Augustus' cause, it is clear that the historian's national pride
lends emphasis to Rome's many founders. Each founder of Rome adds
something in Livy's account, and Rome is thus the product of combined, rather than individual, efforts.[18] Hercules' defeat of Cacus and
his subsequent apotheosis make him a fitting model for Romulus, himself destined to be deified for his achievements. Augustus is subtly
included in this Herculean nexus of foundation by the simple adjective
Livy uses to describe the hero: *formamque uiri aliquantum ampliorem
augustioremque humana intuens*, (seeing that the physique of the hero
was somewhat grander and more august than the human physique,
1.7.9).[19]

Horace, too, took inspiration from Octavian's activities in 29 BCE;
the lyric poet's association of Augustus and Hercules is prominent in
his work. *Carmina* 3.3 links Augustus with Hercules because they both
are reliable and righteous men (*iustum et tenacem propositi uirum*, 3.3.1),
who will enjoy the pleasures of eternal life (*quos inter Augustus recum-*

bens / purpureo bibet ore nectar, 3.3.9–12: reclining between them [Hercules and Pollux], Augustus will drink nectar with his purple-stained mouth). Again in *Carmina* 3.14 (*Herculis ritu* . . .) the poet explicitly compares Augustus' triumphant return from Spain to Hercules' arrival from Spain so long ago. Military conquest and victory over death align Horace's hero and the Princeps. Such was the climate of the decade after Actium. Sparked by the Princeps' own actions at the Ara Maxima, and fueled by the poets of the twenties, Propertius could rely on a firm and popular connection between Rome's first founding hero and its latest, a connection linking triumph and traditional masculinity and focused at the Ara Maxima.

MONUMENTS AND MORALITY
Livia, Womanhood, and the Bona Dea

Also featured in Propertius' elegy is the sanctuary of the Bona Dea at the foot of the Aventine (Figure 10, above), where Hercules takes his drink (*femineae loca clausa deae fontisque piandos*, 4.9.25).[20] Though many shrines to the Bona Dea have been identified in Rome by clusters of inscriptions, the sanctuary on the Aventine remained her most important and was the locus of her official urban cult. The Bona Dea's rites were celebrated twice annually in Rome. Calendars record a celebration to Bona Dea on May 1, the anniversary of Claudia Quinta's dedication of her Aventine sanctuary.[21] Little is known about this observance. More famous and better documented is the nocturnal celebration that took place each December at the home of the chief Roman magistrate or priest. These were state rites performed for the well-being of the Roman people as a whole, but they were done in secret by aristocratic women and were strictly forbidden to men.[22] The nocturnal mysteries were hosted by the wife or mother of the magistrate or priest and involved music, dancing, drinking, and revelry. The infamous Clodius scandal late in 62 BCE is particularly telling in this context. Clodius had dressed as a woman harpist and sneaked into the rites when they were being hosted by Caesar's wife Pompeia—an action that combined sacrilege, possible adultery, and sedition.[23] Cicero's repeated testimony against Clodius for his infiltration of the Bona Dea's rites and the interpretation of Caesar's resultant divorce of Pompeia reveal the ideological force of the Bona Dea's cult at Rome:

that proper female—and male—behavior was required for the proper working of the state.[24]

The sources for the cult of the Bona Dea are problematic; literary and material sources offer very different pictures about its appeal and practice. Inscriptions from all periods reveal that at Rome and elsewhere the Bona Dea welcomed celebrants of both sexes from all social classes.[25] The literary evidence for this goddess, however, reveals a strong ideological pull: she is a goddess for Roman aristocratic *matronae* of good standing in society and good morals. The discrepancy can be explained in a variety of ways: by a difference in her cult in Rome and outside,[26] the influence of Cicero's bias on the literary sources,[27] or a transition in the way she was worshiped and conceptualized in the first century BCE.[28] I believe the tension in the evidence for this cult is to be explained by the shifting positions of morality and identity at the crux between Republic and Principate. Cicero's invective against Clodius combines violation of gender roles with religious transgression and political insurrection. His comments betray deep and expanding fissures in Roman mores— especially those that govern gender roles.[29] The powerful feminine and aristocratic slant seen in Cicero's words about the Bona Dea mark an attempt by the orator to examine and understand this rupture of values, even to contain it. As Rome fell further under the control of dynasts at the Republic's end, Cicero's emphasis on the Bona Dea's required female *probitas* expands responsibility for the health of the state to the personal, not just the political, realm.[30]

The Bona Dea sanctuary was similarly important to the imperial family. Confirmation is found in Ovid's *Fasti:*

> . . . interea Diua canenda Bona est.
> est moles natiua, loco, res nomina facit,
>   appellant Saxum, pars bona montis ea est.
> huic Remus institerat frustra, quo tempore fratri
>   prima Palatinae signa dedistis aues.
> templa patres illic oculos exosa uiriles
>   leniter adclini constituere iugo.
> dedicat haec ueteris Clausorum nominis heres
>   uirgineo nullum corpore passa uirum.
> Liuia restituit, ne non imitata maritum
>   esset, et est omni parte secuta uirum.

. . . Meanwhile I should sing about the Bona Dea. There is a natural rock formation; this feature generates the name for the place: they call it the Stone (Saxum), and it makes up the better part of the mountain. On it Remus stood in vain, when you birds of the Palatine gave your signs to his brother Romulus first. The founding fathers built a temple on the gently sloping cliff, a temple that is taboo to men's eyes. The heir of the ancient family name of the Clausi dedicates this sanctuary, a girl who had never permitted the touch of any man on her virgin's body. Livia restored it, lest she fail to imitate her husband, and she followed his lead in every way. (Ovid *Fast.* 5.148–58)

Ovid places Livia's activity at this sanctuary within the context of the goals of Augustus' program of moral and urban renewal: her civic activity supported the same goals, and by the same means, as his. Indeed, Livia actively sponsored places and rituals that supported traditional female morality: marriage, fidelity, and childbirth.[31] In keeping with her other urban activities, Livia's attention to the Bona Dea's cult advertised her status as a *matrona* and a sponsor of *matronae*, the bulwark of female morality in Rome.[32]

Kleiner has recently argued that Livia's urban activity may have served more complicated political goals.[33] Not only did her building projects promote the importance of traditional female behavior in a successful Rome, but they also buttressed the importance of traditional social roles in that success. Her restoration of the Bona Dea sanctuary reinforced the moral code so important in the Princeps' design for a new Rome. It placed Livia in a patrician context; she was, after all, of the *gens Claudia* and brought that higher status to her husband, by birth less noble than she.[34] Her action, moreover, recalled the old-style religion that was featured so prominently in Augustus' rule. Importantly, it imprinted all these ideas (nobility, feminine decorum, religious tradition) into an urban site meant for women only—attesting the importance to women of all these factors as well as the part they play in them.[35] Finally, Livia's activity in the cult of the Bona Dea was an attempt to stabilize Roman values after their upheaval in the final years of the Republic—a response to the same crisis of morality that prompted Cicero to such strong invective against Clodius.[36] Livia's intervention in the Bona Dea's worship represents the imperial attempt to stabilize Rome's shifting paradigms of morality.

Augustus and Livia, in their activity at the Ara Maxima and the sanctuary of the Bona Dea, thus encouraged fixed and conservative gender roles as a strategy to guarantee Rome's well-being. Even if her restoration postdates our elegy, the impact of the monument is clear: the Bona Dea's shrine, like the Ara Maxima, reinforces traditional Roman gender roles and their complicity with public success. In fact these two monuments support the same message as Augustus' moral legislation of 18 BCE, the sweeping set of laws that regulated families by encouraging marriage and penalizing adultery, and the boldest statement yet of the importance of proper gender roles to the health of the state. The message: appropriate roles for women and men in a successful Roman society are prescribed and discrete. In the new Roman state, mapped onto the monuments sponsored by the Princeps and his wife, gender was prescriptive: men should be men, and women should be women.[37]

MONUMENTS, MORALITY, AND ELEGIAC HERCULES

Not so in Propertius' poetic city. The elegiac lover's refusal to conform to prescribed or rigid gender roles in his love poetry is well known; in Book 4 the elegist also refuses to succumb to such roles, encoded in the city around him. Combined or problematic gender roles pervade Book 4, often connected to urban places: Vertumnus's monument is both male and female (4.2); warrior Cynthia wages battle in feminine fashion on the Esquiline (4.8); and feminine Tarpeia exposes the cruelty of masculine ideology and makes her monument a testament not to her shame, but to her resistance to that oppressive ideology (4.4). Elegy 4.9 likewise participates in the disruption of traditional gender roles.

This elegy explains the origins of the Ara Maxima and the sanctuary of the Bona Dea. In doing so the poet takes great liberties with the myth of Hercules' arrival, with the cults of Hercules and the Bona Dea, and with the cityscape. He therefore sports with all aspects of his chosen poetic topic in Book 4: *sacra diesque canam et cognomina prisca locorum* ("I shall sing of the rites and festivals of Rome and of the hallowed names of her places," 4.1.69). Propertius' light treatment of places and myths of the Forum Boarium at once proves that he is the Roman Callimachus (4.1.64), author of refined and learned poetry. Propertius' landscape is a masterpiece of mannered sophistication, full of erudite details that stem from the Varronian, rather than Vergilian, tradition. Indeed, the connection of Hercules to the sanctuary of the Bona Dea is drawn directly from Varro (*apud* Macrobius *Sat.* 1.12.27–28), and the spirit of the poet is Varronian. For example, in 4.9.1–6 he offers etymologies for the Palatine (from *pecus*, evoked in *pecorosa*, 4.9.3; see Varro *Ling.* 5.53) and Velabrum (*uelificabat*, 4.9.6, and cf. Varro *Ling.* 5.44) as well as a possible *aetion* for the cult name of Hercules at the Ara Maxima (Hercules Invictus, evoked in *inuictos montis*, 4.9.3).[38] Later in the poem Hercules himself voices a bookish gem, when he negates local legend and names the Forum Boarium after his cows (4.9.19–20: *aruaque mugitu sancite Bouaria longo:/ nobile erit Romae pascua uestra Forum;* cows, hallow with your long lowing the Boarian fields; your pasture will be the noble forum of Rome; cf. Ovid *Fasti* 1.582). This playful and nontraditional landscape continues with Hercules' remarkable sensory feats: though he is a half a mile away or more, and though his cows are engaged in prolonged mooing, nevertheless the burly hero hears girls laughing behind the far-off closed doors of the Bona Dea sanctuary (4.9.19–23). Likewise the landscape is aquatically fickle: watery one moment (4.9.5–6), arid the next (4.9.22).[39] It is clear that Propertius' landscape is fanciful and contrived rather than austere and precise; what buildings existed at all, for example, when Hercules came to Rome? Certainly there was then no sanctuary of the Bona Dea on the Aventine; there would have been nothing on the Aventine, in fact. The very connection between the Ara Maxima and the Bona Dea sanctuary is also suspect; Varro's mention of it is our first in extant sources (*apud* Macrobius *Sat.* 1.12.27–28), and it may have been a late invention to link conveniently the two gender-specific cults.

More important than historical accuracy, however, is the commentary Propertius' poem and its places offer on the way the urban landscape contributes to Roman constructions of gender. Antiquarian inquiry of any sort was morally and politically charged in the late Republic and early Principate, an era when the past was used to valorize the present.[40] The tradition of the Ara Maxima was especially complex. Hercules in the Forum Boarium endorses not only imperialism but also traditional masculinity. Consequently, "when the antiquarians, historians and poets of the late Republic and early empire speculated on the myth and ritual of this particular cult site at the Ara Maxima, more was involved than the simple physical *location* of the cult. In this case, ideas of *place* lead straight to ideas of demarcation of *gender*, that is, to rival claims about the religious *place* of women. Stories of Rome *situated* the Roman system of cultural norms and practices."[41]

The same can be said for late Republican/early imperial interest in the
sanctuary of the Bona Dea. Through Hercules' actions at the Bona
Dea's shrine and the manner of his foundation of the Ara Maxima,
Propertius offers a serious social commentary that also touches on the
ways Roman buildings and places encode certain ideological positions.

As has long been recognized, Hercules' speech at the threshold of
the sanctuary is a *paraklausithyron* in the best tradition of the elegiac
lover, feminized and unconcerned with the state.[42] At the very least,
Hercules' appearance as an *exclusus amator* lightens the tone of the
poem and, with it, the poem's places:

> et iacit ante fores uerba minora deo:
> "vos precor, o luci sacro quae luditis antro,
>   pandite defessis hospita fana uiris."

> And before the doors he flings words not worthy of a god: "I beg you,
> who play in the sacred hollow of this grove, open your sanctuary as a
> shelter for weary men." (4.9.32–35)

This encounter at the doorstep undermines the solemnity of the hero's
advent into Rome. Hercules utters, after all, words that are inferior to
his divine destiny (*uerba minora deo*), and he prays, moreover, to girls
(*precor,* 4.9.33). More important for the present argument, his performance of the *paraklausithyron* transforms the hallowed sanctuary of the
Bona Dea, locus of aristocratic feminine virtue, into an elegiac house,
the realm of erotic sport (*luditis* and cf. *ridere,* 4.9.23) that is temporarily off-limits to the lover who waits at its doorstep. A typical erotic
threshold, it is decorated with garlands of a sort (*uittae,* 4.9.27) and
incense (*odorato igne,* 4.9.28). Likewise, Hercules' words and actions
transform the venerable priestess who guards the sanctuary doorway
into the elegiac *lena* who guards access to the *puellae* within[43]—a figure
who promotes behavior antithetical to the goals of the Augustan moral
program by fostering promiscuity among noble, unmarried women.

Indeed, Propertius conflates the May rites at the sanctuary of the
Bona Dea with those held in December at the home of the chief magistrate in order to eroticize the city's public landscape. By setting Hercules' *paraklausithyron* in a public place, Propertius participates in one
major ideological trend of the Principate: he blurs the distinction
between private and public. The city of Rome had always served as the
background for Propertius' amatory activities. In elegy 2.31, the newly

opened temple of Palatine Apollo provides the poet with an excuse for being late to meet his mistress. In 4.8 Cynthia forbids Propertius to flirt in the theater of Pompey or the Forum (4.8.75). In 1.16, the Capitoline hill (not primarily a residential area), more specifically the temple to Fides, is the setting for a *paraklausithyron*. As in poem 4.9, the *paraklausithyron* of 1.16 presents a remarkable overlay of erotic concerns onto public and venerable space.[44] The whole city is a playground for elegiac lovers.

The sanctuary of the Bona Dea, secluded and open to women only, lent itself especially to such amatory diversions, and other elegiac poets seized the opportunity to exploit the sanctuary's erotic possibilities. For Tibullus, the Aventine shrine is associated with adultery when he warns Delia's husband to beware a wife who goes to participate in the Bona Dea's rites (1.6.21–24). It is a pretext, Tibullus explains: she is merely using participation in the rite as an excuse to meet up with a lover:

> exibit quam saepe, time, seu uisere dicet
>   sacra Bonae maribus non adeunda Deae.
> at mihi si credas, illam sequar unus ad aras;
>   tunc mihi non oculis sit timuisse meis.

> As often as she goes out, beware, or if she says she is going to witness the rites of the Bona Dea that no man may attend. But if you trust me, let me go alone to follow her to the sanctuary; then I would not have to fear for my eyes. (1.6.21–24)

Tibullus, like Delia's husband, is jealous of her current lover. In offering to accompany Delia to the sanctuary, Tibullus hopes to rekindle their affair.[45] Ovid makes the connection between the Bona Dea's Aventine sanctuary and adultery even more explicit. In a lesson on deceiving a husband, he urges women to use the city's monuments. Theaters and circuses are crowded enough to allow for foul play, and the Bona Dea's temple offers a sure-fire escape from a jealous husband:

> quid faciat custos, cum sint tot in urbe theatra,
>   cum spectet iunctos illa libenter equos,
> cum sedeat Phariae sistris operata iuuencae
>   quoque sui comites ire uetantur, eat
> cum fuget a templis oculos Bona Diua uirorum.

What is a guardian to do, when there are so many theaters in this city, and when she goes readily to the races, when she sits in devotion with the sistrum of the Pharian heifer, when she goes where her escorts are forbidden to go, since the Bona Dea puts to flight the eyes of men from her temples. (*Ars am.* 3.633–37)

The elegiac tradition prompts us to see in Propertius' Bona Dea another allusion to elegiac—that is, adulterous—love. In Propertius' urban landscape, Livia's matronal decorum is incapacitated and Augustus, lurking behind Hercules, is put in the position of the excluded paramour.

Moreover, Hercules' foundation of the Ara Maxima is not, in Propertius' poem, the commemoration of victory over an enemy, as it had been in Vergil's and Livy's accounts and, indeed, in the Princeps' own "reading" of the monument. Rather, in the elegy the foundation of the Ara Maxima mimics the jealous act of a spurned lover.[46] Hercules and the priestess adopt elegiac roles, while Rome's monuments, so important in buttressing moral and social roles, become the setting for an elegiac lovers' dispute.

Given Hercules' historic association with Antony, Propertius' eroticization of the urban landscape is more than a playful elegiac trope. In elegy 4.9, the poet imbues Hercules with strong Antonian overtones that disrupt the "Augustan" meaning of the poem's monuments. In elegy 4.9 Hercules argues that he should be admitted to the all-female sanctuary because he has experienced life as a woman, in submission to the Lydian queen Omphale:

> sin aliquem uultusque meus saetaeque leonis
>   terrent et Libyco sole perusta coma,
> idem ego Sidonia feci seruilia palla
>   officia et Lydo pensa diurna colo,
> mollis et hirsutum cepit mihi fascia pectus,
>   et manibus duris apta puella fui.

If my face and the mane of this lion and my hair burned with the Libyan sun frighten anyone, I have also performed the servant's duties wearing a Sidonian dress and spun the daily wool with the Lydian distaff, and a soft strap has covered my hairy chest and I was a suitable girl for all my rough hands.[47] (4.9.45–50)

As mentioned above, Antony had claimed descent from Hercules, through the hero's little-known son Anton, and had used Hercules' iconography—the lion-skin, the club—in his own self-promoting images. This ancestral relationship backfired in the later years of civil wars, when the story of Hercules and Omphale was used as anti-Antonian propaganda against Rome's wayward general and his own foreign queen.[48] Hercules and Omphale, each in the other's clothes, appeared in Augustan art as an indirect way to criticize Antony and the luxury, corruption, and desire that threatened Rome and its moral foundations.[49]

Submissive Hercules brings Antony into this poem—all the more so because of the strong verbal resonance between Hercules' cross-dressing episode in 4.9 and the same episode in 3.11, the Cleopatra elegy:[50]

> Omphale in tantum formae processit honorem,
>   Lydia Gygaeo tincta puella lacu,
> ut, qui pacato statuisset in orbe columnas,
>   tam dura traheret mollia pensa manu.

> Omphale advanced to such a degree of honor for her beauty, a Lydian girl bathed in the lake of Gyges, that the man who had set up the Pillars of Hercules in the world he had tamed was working supple wool with his oh-so-hard hands. (3.11.17–20)

Elegy 3.11 draws an implicit parallel between Hercules and Antony.[51] Yet in poem 3.11 Hercules' servitude to Omphale and Cleopatra's mastery over Antony are not examples of moral decay or of political decline. The elegist does not condemn Hercules and Antony, but acquits them for falling prey to a woman. Indeed, the warning in the poem's opening (*exemplo disce timere meo*, 3.11.7) offers not shame or censure for the man who succumbs to a woman, but rather acceptance of her inevitable power. Thus, far from condemning Antony, Propertius' poetry shows some affinity for the defeated man whose public reputation of devotion to a woman at the expense of the state made him an attractive model for the elegiac lover. Propertius' use of Antony as an example for his own situation does not, as some have suggested, imply that Propertius was Antony's political partisan.[52] The elegist, after all, focuses not on Antony's political opposition to Octavian's regime, but rather on the tension between Antony's private affairs and Rome's public goals.[53]

In elegy 4.9, Antonian, personal, luxurious Hercules arrives at
Rome and founds the Ara Maxima, a monument Octavian linked to his
own defeat of Antony at Actium. Hercules' self-satisfied acceptance—
even boast—of his Antonian past sneers at the Princeps by bringing to
mind not only the Roman general vanquished in the battle of Actium,
but also the incompatibility of Antony's "elegiac" values with the new
Roman cityscape. Indeed Hercules' approach to the Bona Dea's sacred
spring—to drink it dry (*exhausto flumine*, 4.9.63)—hints of the Antonian; Caesar's lieutenant was notorious for his excessive drinking.[54]
Antonian Hercules thus challenges and casts doubts on Augustan Hercules, and Octavian's triumphal Ara Maxima becomes anything but
triumphal: it turns into a monument that memorializes not the victor
and his triumphant mores, but the victim and his suppressed mores. In
many respects, Propertius' Hercules is an embarrassment to both the
memory of Antony and to Augustus' fame, drawing attention to their
similarities and irreconcilable differences.

The incompatibility of cross-dressed Hercules with the new Augustan city is set into high relief by the state's recent attempt to regulate
male-female relationships and the first family's interest in urban sites
as a way to order gender. The repeated use of forms of the word *claudo*
in this poem (*inclusas*, 4.9.23; *clausa*, 4.9.25; *clausisset*, 4.9.43; *clausa*,
4.9.62) not only emphasizes Hercules' status as *exclusus amator*, but it
reminds the reader that this closed-off area is also a Claudian place
associated with Livia's *gens Claudia*. The Bona Dea's Aventine sanctuary had been dedicated by a Vestal Virgin named Claudia Quinta.[55] The
root *claud-* simultaneously evokes Livia's less upstanding Claudian
relation Clodius, who also had something to do with the Bona Dea.
Hercules, with his cross-dressing history, breaking into the Bona Dea
sanctuary, certainly recalls the scandal of 62 BCE and brings Clodius
anew into the respectable world of the Bona Dea's rites—thus exacer-
bating rather than palliating the moral crisis indicated by Clodius' sacrilege and addressed by Livia's restoration of the temple.[56] Of course, it
is impossible to know when Livia restored the Bona Dea's Aventine
temple; rather than suggest that she responds to Propertius or vice-
versa, I here posit only that the poet and the Princeps' wife contribute
conflicting thoughts to the ongoing ideological debate about gender
and monuments. Likewise, whereas the Princeps used the Ara Maxima to define and encourage the sort of masculine behavior that would
build the new state, Propertius sabotages the gendered message
encoded into this site by temporarily transforming Hercules into a
man-woman, unable to be defined by the cityscape and unclassifiable

in the Julian laws.[57] Elegy's systematic *aporia*, therefore, momentarily takes over the Roman landscape.[58]

Yet the elegiac effect on the city does not last. The priestess reaffirms Augustan principles and forbids Hercules' entry into the sanctuary because she denies his womanhood. Temporary feminization does not make Hercules a woman, and men are forbidden from the Bona Dea sanctuary: *interdicta uiris metuenda lege piatur / quae se summota uindicat ara casa* (this altar which protects itself in this remote shelter is forbidden to men and hallowed by a law not to be ignored, 4.9.55–56).[59] She cites Tiresias as an example of the dangers of intruding into a sacred space:

> magno Tiresias aspexit Pallada uates,
>   fortia dum posita Gorgone membra lauat.
> di tibi dent alios fontis: haec lympha puellis
>   auia secreti limitis unda fluit.

> At great cost to himself the prophet Tiresias caught a glimpse of Pallas Athena while she was bathing her strong limbs, her aegis set aside. May the gods grant you other fountains: this liquid flows for girls only, this spring without access of a threshold set apart. (4.9.57–60)

The priestess here alludes to the subject of Callimachus' fifth hymn, the so-called Bath of Pallas, in which Tiresias unwittingly stumbles upon the bath of the goddess and is blinded as his punishment. While the reference certainly serves to anchor this poem in the context of Alexandrian poetic techniques and to prove Propertius indeed to be the *Callimachus Romanus* (4.1.64), it also adds to the commentary on gender and space that the poem's primary *aetia* generate. A variation on the topos of "intrusion into the goddess's bath," Callimachus' hymn itself subverts expected gender roles. This topos, involving the unauthorized glimpse of a nude goddess, is much more suited to Artemis than to Athena.[60] Callimachus' innovation is in assigning a myth that highlights feminine chastity to the most masculine of goddesses.[61] Yet in citing this version of the myth, the priestess is suppressing—and so also evoking—the more popular tradition about Tiresias: namely, that he was himself cross-gendered.[62] In his intrusion, his indeterminate gender, and his Alexandrianism, Tiresias thus serves as an *exemplum* for Hercules at the doors of the forbidden sanctuary.

He is a topographical *exemplum* as well. At issue in both Propertius' poem and Callimachus' *Hymn to Athena* is access to forbidden spaces.

In both poems these spaces are remote, unurban. In Propertius' poem
the Bona Dea's sacred space is far off (*procul*, 4.9.23), enclosed (*inclusas*,
4.9.23; *clausa*, 4.9.25), off the beaten path (*deuia*, 4.9.27), secluded (*summota*, 4.9.56), and hidden (*secreti*, 4.9.60). Propertius' landscape is also
undeveloped:

> sed procul inclusas audit ridere puellas,
>   lucus ubi umbroso fecerat orbe nemus,
> femineae loca clausa deae fontisque piandos,
>   impune et nullis sacra retecta uiris.
> deuia puniceae uelabant limina uittae,
>   putris odorato luxerat igne casa,
> populus et longis ornabat frondibus aedem.

But far off he hears girls laughing from within, where a grove had encir-
cled a dell, the enclosed haunts of the women's goddess and fountains
that must be revered, and rites disclosed to no man without punishment.
Purple garlands were draped over her remote threshold, the smoky
house had gleamed with perfumed fire, and a poplar tree decorated the
shrine with its long branches. (4.9.23–29)

The setting of Athena's bath in the hymn is similarly untamed and
remote. The goddess bathes at the spring of Hippocrene on Helikon,
where the water flows beautifully (Ἑλικωνίδι καλὰ ῥεοίσα, *Hymn*
5.71–72). The hour is noon and quiet stills the remote landscape
(μεσαμβριναί δ' ἔσαν ὧραι, πολλὰ δ' ἀσυχία τῆνο κατεῖχεν ὄρος),
(*Hymn* 5.73–74). The natural locale is especially appropriate for the
goddesses; not only are such wild places conducive to divine epipha-
nies, but more importantly, these parallel places are situated so as to
protect the goddesses from the intrusion of profane visitors.

Hercules and Tiresias both approach these hidden and forbidden
springs thirsty, but there the similarity ends. Tiresias stumbles inno-
cently and unwittingly upon the forbidden sight:

> Τειρεσίας δ' ἔτι μῶνος ἁμᾶ κυσὶν ἄρτι γένεια
>   περκάζων ἱερὸν χῶρον ἀνεστρέφετο·
> διψάσας δ' ἄφατόν τι ποτὶ ῥόον ἦλυθε κράνας,
>   σχέτλιος· οὐκ ἐθέλων δ' εἶδε τὰ μὴ θεμιτά.

Tiresias, as yet alone with only his dogs, with a beard just darkening his cheeks, turned toward the sacred place. Feeling an unspeakable thirst, he came toward the trickle of the stream, wretch: unwillingly he saw what was unholy to see. (*Hymn* 5.75–78)

Hercules, on the other hand, seeks out the secluded sanctuary by choice: *huc ruit in siccam congesta puluere barbam* (he rushes to this place with dust matted into his dry beard, 4.9.31). What is more, Hercules enters the forbidden area deliberately, having been warned in advance of the place's restrictions:

> . . . ille umeris postis concussit opacos
>   nec tulit iratam ianua clausa sitim.
> at postquam exhausto iam flumine uicerat aestum,
>   ponit uix siccis tristia iura labris.

> . . . He shook the dark portal with his shoulders and the door, though closed, did not withstand his aroused thirst. But after he had conquered his burning heat and the river was dried up, he uttered these dread oaths with lips barely dry. (4.9.61–64)

His intrusion is laced with erotic nuance: *aestum* and perhaps *sitim* evoke sexual desire, desire that Hercules sates by draining the dregs of the river (*exhausto iam flumine uicerat aestum*, 4.9.63).[63] Having stretched his role of *exclusus amator* to its literal bursting point, Hercules uses force to break into the sanctuary—an action akin to rape and dependent on strict gender difference. He petulantly commemorates his return to amorous proactivity by establishing his own monument to rigid gender roles, the Ara Maxima for men only.

While Hercules' return to an active role may seem to reassert his more traditional, even excessive, masculinity,[64] the hero nevertheless remains ridiculous. The elegiac Hercules misinterprets himself and his role in the world and in the Roman city. In breaking into the sanctuary, Hercules seeks to demonstrate what he has argued earlier in the poem—that he is master of all places, from the heavens to the underworld:

> "audistisne aliquem, tergo qui sustulit orbem?
>   ille ego sum: Alciden terra recepta uocat.
> quis facta Herculeae non audit fortia clauae
>   et numquam ad uastas irrita tela feras,
> atque uni Stygias homini luxisse tenebras?

. . . .

"angulus hic mundi nunc me mea fata trahentem
    accipit: haec fesso uix mihi terra patet.
maxima quae gregibus deuota est Ara repertis,
    ara per has" inquit "maxima facta manus,
haec nullis umquam pateat ueneranda puellis,
    Herculis aeternum ne sit inulta sitis."

"Have you heard about the man who bore the world on his back? I am
that man: the world that I supported calls me Hercules. Who has not
heard the brave deeds Hercules did with his club, and about the arrows
never shot in vain at huge beasts? Who has not heard about the one man
for whom the shadows of Styx brightened?

. . . .

"This corner of the world receives me as I drag out my destiny. This land
scarcely welcomes me when I am weary. Let the Greatest Altar, which
has been vowed upon recovery of my herd, the altar made greatest," he
said "through these hands, never be open to girls for worship, lest the
thirst of Hercules remain ever unavenged." (4.9.37–41, 65–70)

In controlling all places (*orbem, terra, tenebras*), Hercules styles the earth
itself as beneficiary of his heroism (*terra recepta*, 4.9.38). His violent
entry into the Bona Dea sanctuary reveals that he sees himself as master of both feminine and masculine places as well (4.9.69–70). Hercules
also desires to control sacred as well as secular space. Though he is a
self-styled mortal and treated like a man by the priestess (*homini*, 4.9.41
and *uiris*, 4.9.55), he establishes an altar to himself (4.9.67–68), tacitly
asserting himself to be a god. He thus attempts to write his own apotheosis into the landscape.[65]
    We can hardly take this boastful Hercules seriously. The poem ends
ironically as the elegist's voice reemerges and casts doubt on Hercules'
topographical pretensions:

hunc, quoniam manibus purgatum sanxerat orbem,
    sic Sanctum Tatiae composuere Cures.
Sancte pater salue, cui iam fauet aspera Iuno:
    Sancte, uelis libro dexter inesse meo.[66]

This one, since he had sanctified the world that had been purified by his
hands, the Romans of Tatius' line style "Sanctus." Hail, father Sanctus,

whom harsh Juno now favors. Sanctus, may you wish to enter my book favorably. (4.9.73–74, 71–72)

The mention of purification, linked with an etymology for Hercules' Sabine name (4.9.73–74), flies in the face of his violation of the sanctuary of the Bona Dea. The verb *composuere* highlights the fact that this epithet is a subjective interpretation—one with which the elegist apparently disagrees. The poet stretches our trust further by saying that Juno herself now favors the god. To clinch the poem, Propertius prays for the god's quiet and propitious entry into it. May Hercules not enter Propertius' poem as he did the Bona Dea sanctuary.

Though Hercules' final actions—his forced entry into the Bona Dea sanctuary and his establishment of his own exclusively male shrine—attempt to reinforce a traditionally masculine control over the Roman landscape, this poem will forever link the Ara Maxima with indecorous, transvestite behavior coupled with the excesses of passion and the unmanly petulance of the god. In the end Propertius has exerted more control over the interpretation of the Ara Maxima than has Hercules. The perfumed scent of the god's feminine boudoir lingers in the Roman monument.

CONCLUSION

This poem, therefore, blends genre and gender with political innuendo and Roman monuments in a provocative response to the Princeps about the new Roman landscape. In the imperial city, the Ara Maxima and the sanctuary of the Bona Dea served to redefine Roman morality and, more importantly, Roman self-perception. By linking Roman tradition with gender roles, the Princeps redefined the successful Roman as one who acted like an old-style man. Elsner's formulation of how art acts upon viewers helps clarify the dynamics of this poem: a work of art both relies on the viewer's prior knowledge and experiences (reinforcing who he thinks he is), and adds something to his knowledge and experiences (redefining who he is by adding something new).[67] The monuments of elegy 4.9 reorient the Roman viewer to the new Rome and to his place in it. The Ara Maxima had always encouraged traditional male values; Augustus inserted himself into that picture as a paragon of those virtues and their protector in the civil wars against Antony, who conspicuously had not maintained that traditional male role. Augustus' actions there are complemented by Livia's restoration of the decorum of the *matrona* via her restoration of the Bona Dea shrine.

In paying attention to these urban sites, the Princeps and his wife tacitly acknowledge the power of place to define identity. In gaze theory, this phenomenon would be explained in a different way: that the viewer, rather than controlling what he sees and desires, is on the contrary transformed by the object of his gaze.[68] Augustan monuments thus render the Roman viewer passive, enacting upon him a message that informs, or rather transforms, him. The power of images in this poem is enough to transform Hercules from an elegiac lover into a traditional Roman man.

Nevertheless, Propertius' poem breaks the hold such monuments have over their viewer by reorienting the viewer's perspective. One might say that Propertius thus returns the Roman viewer to a more active role in looking at Roman places, by providing alternative ways of interpreting Roman monuments. Playing with Hercules' gender allows Propertius to redefine the evolving Augustan city and to interrogate the gender associations emphasized in certain places by the Princeps, by his wife, and by other literature of the day. As with all Propertius' topographical poems, this elegy's context within the book sets its themes in high relief. In this case, the poem's movements of gender and morality—from flexibility and permissiveness to crushing, violent rigidity—are paralleled by the surrounding poems: elegy 4.8, on a sexual threesome, and elegy 4.10, a poem focused on men and masculine achievement and rife with violence.

The elegist's poem on the origins of the Ara Maxima challenges traditional Roman mores as much as Propertius' earlier love poetry had. What is more, in writing a new Rome, Propertius challenges Augustus' authorship of the new urban landscape. The Ara Maxima stands as a monument not to the new regime but to the elegiac lifestyle. With his small voice, the poet answers back to the silent city.

CHAPTER 6

Spoils for the Poet

ELEGY 4.10 AND PROPERTIUS'
POETIC TRIUMPH

THOUGH CORNELIA marks the end of his oeuvre, Jupiter Feretrius brings to a close Propertius' journey through Rome's cityscape. It is a fitting finale for the elegist's topographical experiment. As I have argued above, in his other topographical elegies Propertius explores varying ways of "reading" Roman monuments, and the supple connection between monuments and the formation of Roman identity. Elegy 4.1 opens the dialogue with disagreement between the poet and his alter-ego Horos about the nature of Rome's cityscape, an opening that paves the way for the many voices and perspectives on Rome's monuments that follow. There is no one "Rome" that means the same thing to all subjects. Likewise, elegy 4.10 introduces perspectives on the temple of Jupiter Feretrius that cause us to question rather than affirm its place in Rome's urban and ideological landscape.

According to tradition, Romulus founded the shrine of Jupiter Feretrius to commemorate his victory over Acron, king of Caenina, whose armor he dedicated there.[1] Thereafter any Roman commander who defeated the enemy commander in single combat was awarded the right to dedicate the spoils as *spolia opima*—the special name given to spoils taken under these guidelines—to Jupiter Feretrius. This exceptional honor was only achieved twice again, by Cossus in the fourth century BCE, after his victory over the Etruscan king Tolumnius; and by Marcellus in the third century BCE, who vanquished the northern king Virdomarus. The temple contained these three sets of *spolia opima* and the implements of the Fetiales, priests responsible for the declaration of just war. Though very small, the temple towered as a monument to Rome's dominion.

In this chapter I explore how Propertius opens this monument up for discussion. He uses two primary strategies. One is to diminish the glory of the *spolia opima* by emphasizing the violence that precedes their dedication. Ignoring the celebratory dedication of the spoils in the temple of Jupiter Feretrius, Propertius dwells instead on the gruesome details of the deaths of Acron, Tolumnius, and Virdomarus. This ugly background tarnishes the temple's glory. In the elegist's reading, Rome's oldest temple commemorates not Rome's great victories but rather the violence that is at the heart of Rome's identity. This violence is made even more foreboding by the implicit connections the poet draws between it and the new order. Propertius laces his narrative with details that evoke Augustus and the imperial family. In doing so he is following the new emperor's cue: Octavian had restored the temple of Jupiter Feretrius in 32 BCE and controlled access to the right to *spolia opima* thereafter, thereby asserting his place as the culmination of Rome's founders and heroes. Propertius is content to leave him there as the pinnacle of martial achievement, but reinterprets that role by refocusing the tradition that led up to him. These brutal deaths can be laid at the Princeps' feet.

The poet's second strategy is to create a softer alternative to the violent tradition of *spolia opima* by exploiting the glory of the role of *Callimachus Romanus* he had assumed in elegy 4.1. Propertius' incipit for elegy 4.10 blends Callimachean imagery with that of the Roman triumph to cast Propertius as a Callimachean *triumphator*, achieving glory through rigorous poetic composition. Similarly, in the poem's finale Propertius offers rival etymologies for Jupiter Feretrius' name that again emphasize the power of words over places. Though he offers two possibilities for the name Feretrius (*ferre*, to bear *spolia* to the temple, and *ferire*, to strike down an enemy commander), the violent narrative that precedes this learned denouement induces us to prefer *ferire*. As monuments respond to and shape Roman identity, thus also words respond to and shape monuments. With the wordplay in these framing passages Propertius draws attention away from the historic achievement of *spolia opima* toward the achievement of his own poetry, and claims for himself access to that venerable space that houses Rome's highest honors.

FIGURE 11. Coin of Marcellinus showing the dedication of spoils at the temple of Jupiter Feretrius; the coin boasts not only Marcellinus' famous ancestry but also the family's perpetual honor as it is monumentalized in the city. Photo courtesy of the British Museum.

TEMPLE, SPOILS, AND PRINCEPS

Though the temple of Jupiter Feretrius was tiny and its contents rare, Octavian made it an important part of his early imperial ideology and intervened in its every aspect, rebuilding the temple itself, dusting off the Fetial implements and renewing the Fetial rites, and arbitrating later claims to dedicate *spolia opima*. His intervention provides a powerful example of how Octavian's topographical activity helped shape and define not only the new order but also his role in it. Restoring the temple and its rites lent the authority of Romulus to Rome's new founder at a time when his role was still in flux, and controlling access to the temple's honors helped him keep this authority.

No archaeological remains have been connected to this temple and its location on the Capitol is uncertain, but its design may be preserved on a coin of c.45 BCE, minted by a certain Marcellinus, which shows a tetrastyle building raised on a podium of a few steps, lacking a cult image (Figure 11).[2]

Cornelius Nepos, in his *Life of Atticus*, tells us that the noted scholar and Epicurean had urged Octavian to restore the dilapidated temple, whose roof had fallen into disrepair. The suggestion can be dated to the period immediately preceding the battle of Actium, and Nepos contextualizes it in a discussion of Atticus' political neutrality during these tense years of conflict. After describing Atticus' connections to

Octavian through their mutual regard for Agrippa, Nepos reveals a more personal connection between the two men:

nullus dies temere intercessit, quo non ad eum scriberet, cum modo aliquid de antiquitate ab eo requireret, modo aliquam quaestionem poeticam ei proponeret, interdum iocans eius uerbosiores eliceret epistulas. Ex quo accidit, cum aedis Iouis Feretrii in Capitolio, ab Romulo constituta, uetustate atque incuria detecta prolaberetur, ut Attici admonitu Caesar eam reficiendam curaret. Neque uero a M. Antonio minus absens litteris colebatur, adeo ut accurate ille ex ultimis terris, quid ageret, curae sibi haberet certiorem facere Atticum.

No day had passed on which Octavian did not write to Atticus, when he would ask him something about antiquity or would propose some question about poetry, and from time to time he would even chuckle at his rather wordy letters. From this sort of exchange it happened that, when the temple of Jupiter Feretrius on the Capitol, which had been founded by Romulus, was falling down with roof caved in because of its extreme old age and lack of upkeep, at Atticus' suggestion Caesar took to rebuilding it. Nor was Atticus' friendship cultivated any less by Antony in his letters, to the extent that Antony would take great care to make Atticus very aware of what he was doing even from the farthest parts of the world. (Cornelius Nepos *Att.* 20.2–24)

Nepos' praise for Atticus' neutrality does not obscure the fact that his friendship conveyed political advantage to those who would hold it.[3] Antony's pursuit of Atticus, for example, seems motivated by a desire to be no less a part of the great man's life than his rival. While Octavian seems motivated by a shared interest in antiquarian topics devoid of explicit political nuance, such interest in *arcana* on Octavian's part is surely not that of a hobbyist alone. As I mentioned above, recent studies have shown that it is a mistake to separate antiquarian from political interests during the fall of the Republic, when ideological positions find support and validation in precedent.[4] While Nepos glosses over Octavian's more pragmatic motives, he admits he wrote this chapter after Atticus' death in March of 32 BCE (*Att.* 20.1); the biographer's lopsided picture of Atticus' friendships might be the result of which dynast emerged victorious.

Caesar's heir gained certain political advantage from his attention to the temple of Jupiter Feretrius. Atticus' death dates the suggestion to the years before Actium, as does Nepos' mention of the insults exchanged between Antony and Octavian (*Att.* 20.5). Repairing this temple carried with it more than the general prestige connected with restoring Rome's fallen monuments (about which Augustus boasts at *Res Gestae* 19). The temple of Jupiter Feretrius was Rome's first shrine and Romulus' most prominent contribution to the urban landscape. By restoring the temple, Octavian became Rome's new Romulus, its latest and best founder. This likeness was not new; as early as 43 BCE Caesar's heir had flirted with the iconography of Romulus in order to gain political advantage when he was the newest man on the political playing field.[5] His restoration of the temple just before the battle at Actium helped define Octavian as a traditional Roman general at a time when Antony was out of the city and adopting new and foreign rather than traditional and Roman models of prestige. Octavian's reverence for Rome's traditions (as opposed to Antonian extravagance) can also be seen in the fact that in restoring the temple Octavian left intact its original shape and size, which was very small (Dionysius 2.34.4).[6]

In addition to restoring the temple itself, Octavian put to new use the Fetial instruments housed in the temple. The Fetiales were a priestly college established by Numa,[7] whose primary duty was to sanction foreign affairs on behalf of the Roman state (Cicero *Off.* 1.36). Among their specific duties, the Fetiales were supposed to send embassies, ratify treaties, and declare just war on enemies by throwing a special spear into enemy territory when all attempts at negotiation had failed.[8] The Fetial instruments—the *silex* stone used to render sacrificial animals unconscious, and the spear thrown in declaring war—were housed in the temple of Jupiter Feretrius.[9] Augustus includes his membership in this college in his own *Res Gestae* 7, having already exercised his rights as a priest: Octavian had declared war on Cleopatra in 32 BCE by throwing the Fetial spear in the Circus Flaminius in front of the temple of Bellona (Dio Cassius 50.4.4). This action characterized the war at Actium as a just war (and as a last recourse), and characterized the enemy as foreign.[10]

Octavian may have wished to put his personal stamp onto the temple's other contents as well. The honor would have likened him not only to Romulus but also to Julius Caesar, who had been awarded the right to dedicate *spolia opima* in 44 BCE.[11] Unfortunately, the victory at Actium was not such that *spolia opima* were an option for Caesar's heir. There may yet have been time for him to achieve this honor, but an unfortunate circumstance in 29 BCE forestalled that possibility. In that year Marcus Licinius Crassus, grandson of the triumvir, conquered Deldo, king of the Bastarnae, in single combat. Crassus' deed on the battlefield is recorded in great detail by Dio Cassius, who situates it in the context of Crassus' other successes in the east. Dio indicates that Crassus would have dedicated the *spolia opima*, had he been supreme commander when he stripped Deldo (51.24). It was determined that he was not eligible when Octavian intervened with evidence of a dubious precedent by which Crassus' claim could be denied: a linen corselet of Cossus inscribed with his consular rank.[12] The precedent of Cossus suggested that only a consul in office could dedicate *spolia opima*, a narrower definition than the tradition had previously held.

Crassus was excluded. Such a dedication would have been an embarrassment to the Actian victor, to be sure; he had not restored the temple of Jupiter Feretrius to lend its glory to another, or to facilitate oneupmanship of his own superlative triple triumph in 29 BCE. It might have caused deeper concern as well, as the honor of *spolia opima* would have lent prestige to a successful general already popular among his soldiers. The prefect Gallus had paid dearly for just such prestige.[13] Crassus was appeased with a triumphal ceremony, but not until the first constitutional settlement ensured that no such threat would arise again from a successful general in the field.[14] The threat did not arise, and Crassus fell from view.[15] The temple of Jupiter Feretrius remained the special province of the last man to enter it—the man who had restored it.

Having obviated the possibility of future dedications in the temple of Jupiter Feretrius,[16] but still desirous of the prestige of a rare military honor, Augustus found an alternative in the recovery of the Parthian standards lost at Carrhae in 53 BCE, especially resonant in that they had been lost by the grandfather of the Crassus whose claim to *spolia opima* was recently denied. As Romulus had done, Augustus set out to build a temple to house them dedicated to Mars Ultor on the Capitol, a small round temple that Dio says was decreed in emulation (ζήλωμα, 54.8.3) of Jupiter Feretrius. Images of this temple appear on coins and Dio says Augustus fulfilled his decree, but it seems it was never built and that the recovered standards were kept in the temple of Jupiter Feretrius until a permanent location could be found for them.[17]

That permanent location was the grand temple of Mars Ultor in the Forum of Augustus, a monument that clearly identified Augustus as the inheritor of all that was good in Roman tradition, including Romulus with his *spolia opima*. An image of Romulus *tropaiophoros* decorated one of the Forum's two axial niches; the other featured Aeneas with his father and the Penates. The paired decorations may be seen as visual symbols for Augustus's *uirtus* and *pietas*, respectively, and were repro-

FIGURE 12. Painting from Pompeii of Romulus and *spolia opima*. It is much more difficult to recognize the scene without the temple; the *elogium* would have identified it to the audience in Pompeii. After Rizzo, *La Pittura Ellenistica Romana* (Milan 1929), plate 194.

duced and displayed in places far from Rome. Though the statue of *Romulus tropaiophoros* does not survive, a painted copy of it does, from the Via dell'Abbondanza in Pompeii (Figure 12), as does the statue's inscriptional *elogium: Romulus Martis / filius urbem Romam / condidit et regnauit annos / duodequadraginta isque / primus dux duce hostium / Acrone rege Caeninensium / interfecto spolia opima / Ioui Feretrio consecrauit / receptusque in deorum / numerum Quirinus / appellatus est* (Romulus the son of Mars founded the city and ruled thirty-eight years. He was the first leader to consecrate *spolia opima* to Jupiter Feretrius, having killed

Acron king of the enemy from Caenina. Being received into the number of the gods, he was called Quirinus).[18]

It is interesting to note that the *elogium* provides not only the simple identification of the image but the history of the deed itself, as if the audience might not recognize Romulus *tropaiophoros* without the visual aid of the temple, and would need it explained and contextualized. The *elogium* also combines Romulus as urban founder, *tropaiophoros*, and son of Mars. Ovid's description of the temple of Mars Ultor at *Fasti* 5.545–98 emphasizes three elements: *pius* Aeneas, Romulus *tropaiophoros*, and the Parthian standards.[19] Their presence strengthened the association between Rome's legendary founders and their contributions to Rome and the new founder and his special contribution. The temple of Jupiter Feretrius was now a monument to the past, while that of Mars Ultor—new repository for special military honors— looked to Rome's future.[20]

This episode in the history of the temple of Jupiter Feretrius provides a striking example of how the Princeps adapted Roman monuments and their traditions to his own use—how many meanings became one, subsumed under the rubric "Augustan." Tradition about the *spolia opima* had thus far admitted a good deal of variation. Were all such spoils to be dedicated to Jupiter Feretrius, or were some fitting for Mars or Quirinus? How are the spoils connected with the epithet *Feretrius*, if at all? Was the honor of dedicating *spolia opima* available only to Roman generals, or to soldiers of any rank who had killed an enemy commander? As late as Varro, for example, this last point was still a matter of discussion; Varro had asserted that any soldier could dedicate *spolia opima* (*apud* Festus 204L).[21]

Into this tradition Octavian inserted his voice, casting the deciding vote for the one version of the story that supported his position. After his intervention, the temple of Jupiter Feretrius became a repository for honors now inaccessible in the new regime but for his approval.[22] The effect was perhaps underlined by the likelihood that the temple itself was inaccessible, before and after Octavian's intervention.[23] Octavian's authority regarding the temple and its arcane contents was indistinguishable from his authority in the military and political sphere. His was the voice that counted.

Octavian's coarse handling of the traditions of Jupiter Feretrius left a scar on its history, still visible in Livy's narrative about Cossus' achievement of the *spolia opima*. Having defeated Lars Tolumnius, Livy says, Cossus returned to Rome where he dedicated his spoils (4.20.1–4). In this description of the celebration, as elsewhere in his narrative, Livy is very clear that Cossus was of lesser rank when he won his spoils, subordinate to the dictator Mamercus Aemilius, the glory of whose triumph is stolen by the rarity of Cossus' honor. At this point Livy mentions the new evidence that the Princeps revealed to him, proving that Cossus was a consul in office fighting under his own auspices. Livy is explicit that Augustus' information contradicts his own research;[24] it is worth quoting his insertion in full (with words to be discussed below in bold typeface):

> Omnes ante me **auctores** secutus, A. Cornelium Cossum tribunum militum secunda spolia opima Iouis Feretri templo intulisse exposui; ceterum, praeterquam quod ea rite opima spolia habentur, quae dux duci detraxit nec ducem nouimus nisi cuius auspicio bellum geritur, titulus **ipse** spoliis inscriptus illos meque arguit consulem ea Cossum cepisse. Hoc ego cum Augustum Caesarem, templorum omnium conditorem aut restitutorem, ingressum aedem Feretri Iouis quam uetustate dilapsam refecit, se **ipsum** in thorace linteo scriptum legisse audissem, prope sacrilegium ratus sum Cosso spoliorum suorum Caesarem, ipsius templi **auctorem**, subtrahere testem. Qui si ea in re sit error quod tam ueteres annales quodque magistratuum libri, quos linteos in aede repositos Monetae Macer Licinius citat identidem **auctores**, septimo post demum anno cum T. Quinctio Poeno A. Cornelium Cossum consulem habeant, existimatio communis omnibus est. Nam etiam illud accedit, ne tam clara pugna in eum annum transferri posset, quod imbelle triennium ferme pestilentia inopiaque frugum circa A. Cornelium consulem fuit, adeo ut quidam annales uelut funesti nihil praeter nomina consulum suggerant. Tertius ab consulatu Cossi annus tribunum eum militum consulari potestate habet, eodem anno magistrum equitum; quo in imperio alteram insignem edidit pugnam equestrem. Ea libera coniectura est sed, ut ego arbitror, uana. Versare in omnes opiniones licet, cum **auctor** pugnae, recentibus spoliis in sacra sede positis, Iouem prope **ipsum**, cui uota erant, Romulumque intuens, haud spernendos falsi tituli testes, se A. Cornelium Cossum consulem scripserit.

Following all the authors before me, I have argued that A. Cornelius Cossus was *tribunus militum* when he brought the second dedication of *spolia opima* into the temple of Jupiter Feretrius. But moreover, because *spolia opima* are only considered to be those that a leader has stripped from a leader, and we do not recognize someone as leader except the one under whose auspices the war is waged, the very inscription on the spoils has made clear to those other authors and to me that Cossus cap-

tured the spoils as a consul. Since I had heard that Augustus Caesar himself, founder or restorer of all temples, having entered into the temple of
Jupiter Feretrius which he rebuilt since it was collapsing with age, read
this fact written on the linen corselet, I thought it would be tantamount to
sacrilege to deprive Cossus of such a witness of his spoils as Caesar, the
author of the very temple. But what error there might be in this matter,
that such ancient annals and that the records of the magistrates (which
linen books, stored in the temple of Juno Moneta, Licinius Macer cites as
his authorities again and again) hold that it was seven years later that A.
Cornelius Cossus was consul together with T. Quinctius Poenus, is a matter for common speculation for anyone. For it even happens that it is not
possible to shift such a famous battle into that year, because the three-year
period surrounding Cossus' consulship was lacking in war because of dis-
ease and want, to the extent that certain records, as if they were funeral
registers, supply nothing beyond the names of the consuls. The third year
from Cossus' consulship holds that he was tribune of the army with consular authority, and in that same year also *magister equitum;* under this
imperium he fought a second famous equestrian battle. That is all free conjecture. But, as I think, it is possible to turn to all sorts of opinions since,
when his fresh spoils had been deposited in the temple, in front of Jove
himself, to whom they were dedicated, and looking upon Romulus—
hardly witnesses to be disparaged with a false claim—the author of the
battle wrote that he, A. Cornelius Cossus, was consul. (Livy 4.20.5–11)

Historians of the past century read this passage with cynicism;
whether Livy could not reconcile his own research with Octavian's
information or whether he chose not to, the seams between Livy's
research and the Princeps' contribution are visible, creating the
impression that he succumbed either to pressure or decorum in revis-
ing his narrative.[25] Add me to the list of cynics, but what interests me
most in the context of this passage is not so much that Augustus inserted himself into tradition, but that Livy invites his readers to contemplate that insertion. The fact that Livy made the emendation apparent
to his readers suggests that it has value as an emendation more than as
an organic part of his text. In this instance, then, the process of writing
his history is as important as the history itself. A few years ago Miles,
exploring Livy's inability to reconcile his chosen sources with the
Princeps' information, concluded that the historian's *aporia* about
sources in the case of Cossus must also darken the reliability of his
every source and historical conclusion.[26] In other words, Livy resists the
closure demanded by the Princeps' discovery, though his resistance

simultaneously undermines his own history.

Indeed, Livy's passage seems to be a meditation on the word *auctor,* which appears four times in his digression. The word, a natural favorite in Livy's first book, evokes both authority and origination; his use of it to describe Augustus' relationship with the temple of Jupiter Feretrius is particularly worthy of note (*ipsius templi auctor,* 4.20.7). In the sentence immediately prior to that one, Livy calls the Princeps the founder or restorer of all temples (*omnium templorum conditor aut restitutor*). What does it mean, then, that he is the *auctor* of this one? To be sure, *auctor* is a common word for describing a builder or founder of a city.[27] In the passage above Livy compares this sort of authorship with other sorts, and each use of the word carries rhetorical weight in his account. The word is applied first to all those authors who wrote histories before him, and whose reports he followed until he had the Princeps' evidence. The unanimity of Livy's sources, as Miles suggests, lends compelling weight to their authority; one might say that this unanimity emphasizes rather the authority in these *auctores* than their origination of the tradition. Next the word refers to Augustus' relationship to the temple of Jupiter Feretrius, a usage that emphasizes origination rather than authority, or, to be more precise, authority through origination. Third, Livy uses the word to denote the linen scrolls that were Licinius Macer's authorities; these scrolls, records of the magistrates, combine the ideas of origination (since they are original contemporary records) with the authority of consensus; as with the *auctores* Livy followed in his unamended account, Macer's sources are plural. Finally, Cossus is called *auctor* of his deed on the battlefield—like Augustus, originator, yet unlike him originator of the deed itself rather than the proof of it: compare Cossus' *auctor pugnae* with Augustus's less than compelling *auctor templi.* Livy's digression thus draws attention to the process of change in Roman tradition, and to the competing voices of truth that operate within it.

Evolution and change in Roman tradition were not new phenomena. Evidence abounds for the additions, selections, and deletions made by various Romans to their legends, rituals, and customs. Nevertheless it is striking that the tradition of the *spolia opima* effectively froze with Octavian's intervention; his efforts not only went into reinterpreting the past, but closing off interpretations in the future. Just as the triumphal Fasti inscribed on Augustus' arch end with his own triple triumph—a visual, monumental reminder that no military glory would surpass his—so, too, the temple of Jupiter Feretrius, built anew by Octavian then surpassed by his Forum with its new sort of *spolia opima,* served as a reminder in the landscape of the change that accompanied the new leader. Regarding the *spolia opima*, one might say, Augustus had closed the conversation.

A REOPENING OF CLOSURE
Propertius and the Temple of Jupiter Feretrius

Some fifteen years had passed since the restoration of the temple and a dozen since Crassus' denied honors when Propertius turned his pen to the temple of Jupiter Feretrius. While any controversy had surely died down, the lapsed time also allowed for the new emperor's powers to coalesce and for Octavian to become Augustus. Harrison argues that it was important for the Augustan authors to get the details right; hence Livy amends his account, Vergil includes and honors three dedicants in his description of Rome's proto-heroes in the underworld, and Propertius follows suit. Harrison's reading of Propertius' poem rightly stresses its normative flair: "What strikes the reader is the fixity of the number three, which is treated as canonical and repeated at both the beginning and end of the poem: Propertius speaks as if no addition to the *spolia opima* had been contemplated since Marcellus in 222 BCE, and the whole thing is treated as an antiquarian matter. One suspects already that the Augustan line is being followed: the account is closed, and no addition is envisaged—not even from Augustus himself, the new Romulus, and certainly not from any other general."[28]

The fixity of the story is, I believe, exactly Propertius' point. The poet is content to work with a tradition delimited by the Princeps, and even takes it one step further; in subtle ways, he associates all three dedicants with Augustus himself. The new *auctor* of the temple thus becomes a player throughout the tradition of which he is the apex. Yet Propertius' description of the events within this tradition does not flatter any of its players, least of all its most recent. Rather, the poet's narrative dwells on the violence of the battles and expresses sympathy for the victims.

ROMULUS AND ACRON
A Wolf at the Gates

To Romulus, as founder of the tradition of *spolia opima*, Propertius gives his due: eighteen lines detailing his victory over Acron of

Caenina. This first and longest of the three tales sets the tone for what is to follow, and the poet begins explicitly by acknowledging Romulus as a model for the practice:

> imbuis exemplum primae tu, Romule, palmae
>   huius, et exuvio plenus ab hoste redis.

> You set the example with this first victory, Romulus, and you return heavy with spoils from the enemy. (4.10.5–6)

Propertius sets an ambiguous tone at once—*imbuis* means primarily "to dip, wet," and thus also, by extension, "to dye," and from there "to stain with blood."[29] In the lines that follow, the poet holds in the balance the positive and negative meanings of Romulus' achievement, creating an ambiguous origin for the tradition of *spolia opima* and Romulus' place in that tradition. As we shall see, not only are the spoils Romulus dedicates stained with the blood of the contest, but the language used to describe that contest evokes a passage of Vergil's *Aeneid*, published in 19 BCE, in a way that confounds the easy identification of Roman and enemy. What is more, Propertius adds another layer to his already ambiguous narrative by inserting details that bring Augustus himself into the poem as a new Romulus.

In the incipit of this poem Propertius promises to sing of the temple of Jupiter Feretrius and about arms dedicated within:

> nunc Iouis incipiam causas aperire Feretri,
>   armaque de ducibus trina recepta tribus.

> Now I shall begin to uncover the origins of Jupiter Feretrius, and the three sets of arms received from three leaders. (4.10.1–2)

As in elegy 4.6, in which Propertius promised to sing about the temple of Palatine Apollo but never really did, here also the poet is curiously silent about the actual armor Romulus dedicates. To be sure, Romulus' story begins with mention of the spoils that constitute the honor (*palmae*), but without any elaboration about them; they are simply spoils or, more precisely, spoil (*exuuio*); the use of the singular neuter rather than the usual feminine plural, as Richardson explains, "tends to give the word the value of an abstract idea" rather than a concrete dedication.[30] After a bit of background about Acron, Propertius offers two more tantalizing details about the spoils:

hic spolia ex umeris ausus sperare Quirini
   ipse dedit, sed non sanguine sicca suo.
hunc uidet ante cauas librantem spicula turris
   Romulus et uotis occupat ante ratis:
"Iuppiter, haec hodie tibi uictima corruet Acron."
   uouerat, et spolium corruit ille Ioui.

Having dared to hope for spoils stripped from the shoulders of Quirinus, he himself gave up his own instead, but not unmoistened with his
own blood. Romulus sees him brandishing his spear in front of the hollow towers, and cuts him off with prayers uttered: "Jupiter, this victim,
Acron, will fall for you." Romulus had vowed, and Acron fell as spoils
for Jove. (4.10.11–16)

First, Acron's spoils, still undefined, are nevertheless drenched in his
own blood. With this detail the poet evokes the violence of the contest
between Romulus and Acron without glorifying the actual spoils
achieved; the only real weapon the poet mentions is Acron's *spiculum*.
At 4.10.16 there is a hint at the specific wound that produced the blood:
occupat suggests the violence of a hewn throat.[31] Second, four lines later
we learn that Acron is himself the prize, offered as a victim to Jupiter.
Again, Richardson's comment hits the mark: "One expects *hic Acron
corruet uictima;* the inversion (sc. of *hic* to *haec*) makes his value as a victim seem greater than his value as a man."[32] The inversion also plays
on the pun with Acron's name: there falls the high one. It is not the
spoils themselves that matter to the Roman founder and his god—no
such symbolic honor will do. Rather, it is the dead body.

   In contrast to the abstract presentation of Acron's spoils, the poet is
oddly explicit about what armor Romulus himself wears, and his martial accouterment is primitive and fierce:

urbis uirtutisque parens sic uincere sueuit,
   qui tulit a parco frigida castra lare.
idem eques et frenis, idem fuit aptus aratris,
   et galea hirsuta compta lupina iuba.
picta neque inducto fulgebat parma pyropo:
   praebebant caesi baltea lenta boues.

The parent of our city and of virtue was used to conquering like this,
who tolerated the cold military camp since he came from a meager

home. As a horseman he was equally adept with reins and the plough, and his wolf-skin helmet was bedecked with a shaggy crest. His modest shield did not gleam painted with inlaid golden-bronze:[33] slaughtered cattle provided his pliant baldric. (4.10.17–22)

Romulus's crude leather armor recalls the skin-clad senators in Rome's proto-Curia, described in elegy 4.1 (*pellitos . . . Patres*, 4.1.12). The rustic details are meant to evoke an earlier, unsophisticated time and the hardy men who accompanied it. Romulus' wolf-skin helmet in particular suggests the tough quality of early Romans, proud as they were of their association with the wolf, whom the poet calls Rome's *altricem* and *optima nutricum* in the opening poem of the book (4.1.38 and 55 respectively). Romulus' personal relationship with the wolf makes his choice of the wolf-skin helmet all the more striking: it is not only Rome's totemic animal, but also Romulus' special badge of toughness. The fact that he wears the hide of his former nurse makes Romulus all the more savage. Finally, the adjective *hirsuta* cements the image; in Book 4, this word has always indicated something harsh and antithetical to elegiac values.[34]

The elegist's description of Acron and Romulus presents a complex intertextual engagement with Vergil's *Aeneid*—though not, as might be expected, with Vergil's account of the three dedicators of *spolia opima*. Rather, Acron at the gates of Rome evokes a passage from *Aeneid 9*, with specific verbal echoes marked in boldface type:

ergo etsi conferre manum pudor iraque monstrat,
obiciunt portas tamen et praecepta facessunt,
armatique cauis exspectant turribus hostem.

. . . .

. . . huc turbidus atque huc
lustrat equo muros aditumque per auia quaerit.
ac ueluti pleno **lupus** insidiatus ouili
cum fremit ad caulas, uentos perpessus et imbris,
nocte super media; tuti sub matribus agni
balatum exercent; ille asper et improbus ira
saeuit in absentis; collecta fatigat edendi
ex longo rabies et **siccae sanguine** fauces:
haud aliter Rutulo muros et castra tuenti
ignescunt irae, duris dolor ossibus ardet.

And so even if their shame and wrath lead them to join the battle, they [the Trojans] slam the gates shut and do what they have been told, and taking up arms they await the enemy in the hollow towers.

. . . .

. . . [Turnus] in turmoil ranges on his horse here and there along the walls, and he seeks an entrance through pathless ways. Just as a wolf on the prowl sitting watch at the full sheepfold, when he howls at the openings, beaten by winds and rains after midnight; the lambs, lying safe under their mothers, bleat incessantly; the wolf, harsh and made wicked with wrath, rages against the lambs he cannot get; his pent-up hunger wears him out for a long time and his dry jaw thirsts for blood: hardly otherwise do the furies enflame the Rutulian as he sees the walls and the camps, and pain glows in his hard bones. (Vergil *Aen.* 9.44–46, 57–66)

Propertius' phrase *hunc uidet ante cauas . . . turris* (4.10.13) echoes Vergil's *cauis exspectant turribus hostem* (*Aen.* 9.46) and likens Acron at the gates of Rome to Turnus at the Trojan camp. The likeness fits: both are Latin enemies of Roman founders, fighting at—and for the prize of—Rome. This parallel would implicitly liken Romulus to Aeneas, but Propertius' details make it impossible to remain comfortable about linking Rome's great founders in this respect. For one thing, in Vergil's text Aeneas is not actually watching from the towers, or even in the camp. He is away on a diplomatic mission, having left the Trojans with instructions not to provoke a battle nor to enjoin one on the open plain if they find themselves provoked.

Aeneas' clearly defensive proto-Romans invite the reader to consider Romulus' motives in attacking Acron. Propertius' poem is vague on this point, and it is unclear where the battle between Romans and Caeninans takes place, or why. The simplest explanation, and the one given by Livy, is that Acron and his Caeninans were the first to attack Rome after the rape of the Sabine women (Livy 1.10). Thus Acron seeking the gates (*portas . . . petentem,* 4.10.7) is attacking the gates of Rome in war; Romulus sees him from the walls and decides upon the spoils. Rothstein, however, noting that the fight takes place outside Caenina's walls, not Rome's, has suggested a different sequence of events: Acron presumably petitioned Rome and brandished his spear; Romulus decided upon and vowed the spoils; then Romulus killed Acron as the latter fled back to the gates of Caenina (*portas . . . petentem* in 4.10.7).[35] In Rothstein's reading, Romulus' attack was not entirely defensive. Yet in this case Rome has turreted walls (4.10.13, a patent anachronism) and

Caenina's entryways are described as *portas*—the word normally used for Roman gates. Surely Rothstein's interpretation is too much to rest upon the verb *redis* (4.10.6), but the specter of Rome on the offensive is nevertheless raised.

A further detail in Propertius' passage raises similar concerns vis-à-vis Vergil's narrative: Romulus' wolf-skin helmet. In Vergil's passage, Turnus pacing at the gates is compared to a wolf at a sheepfold, pacing and hungry, with jaw thirsty for blood (*siccae sanguine, Aen.* 9.64). Propertius' Romulus, decked out in wolf-skin, thus becomes Vergil's predator who has bathed Acron's armor in blood (*non sanguine sicca suo,* 4.10.12); Acron is not the wolf but the wolf's victim. Propertius preserves Vergil's diction but reverses his syntax. The complex allusion thus confounds any easy identification of Romulus as the defensive combatant in this battle. Acron's blood is the blood for which the Romulean wolf thirsts. Vergil's simile has become Propertian reality.

Given the resonance of Propertius' passage with the *Aeneid*, it is also tempting to see a contrast between Romulus' crude baldric and Pallas' elaborately imprinted one in the *Aeneid*. The elegist's founder wears a swordbelt made of rough leather; Vergil's youthful hero wears an engraved piece worthy of its own detailed ekphrasis, a piece that plays a decisive part in the ending of the great epic poem.[36] The presence of Pallas' *balteus* in the background of Romulus' poem is confirmed by the fact that Pallas himself, about to face Turnus in his last fight, anachronistically mentions the possibility of dedicating Turnus' armor as *spolia opima* (*Aen.* 10.449–50). This haunting echo evokes Pallas, I believe, to suggest Romulus' difference from him: where Pallas wore an engraved baldric worthy of his own youthful beauty and innocence, Romulus wears a belt of slaughtered hide fitting for his grittiness and tough experience in war. Unlike poor Pallas, Romulus defeats his Turnus and dedicates his spoils.

Romulus' ambiguity in this poem—his assimilation both to Aeneas and to Turnus, his similarity to and difference from heroes of a bygone era—is not confined to his historic achievement of the *spolia opima*. Rather, Propertius brings the Princeps into the story as well. As noted above, one of the reasons Caesar's heir was interested in restoring the temple of Jupiter Feretrius was the association with Romulus that he was cultivating in the years after Caesar's death. The timing of his intervention into the crumbling temple's history was calculated to lend Octavian the prestige of Rome's founder and, indirectly, to cast Antony as a foreigner uninterested in Rome's traditions. Propertius' brief description of Romulus' achievement reveals that he understood these motives. In no other version of this story, for example, is Acron named as a descendant of Hercules (*Acron Herculeus*, 4.10.9). As we saw in chapter 5, Antony had claimed descent from Hercules through his son Anton. As with the shifting associations with both Aeneas and Turnus, Acron's lineage brings the specter of civil war into this episode. Romulus versus Herculean Acron foreshadows Romulean Octavian versus Herculean Anton(y). The poet's use of past, present, and future verb tenses in the passage emphasizes this telescoping of time that allows Romulus and Augustus to be seen in parallel. At 4.10.14–16 Romulus sees Acron (*uidet*, looking sideways form the past), vows that he will fall (*corruet*, looking forward from the past), and Acron did indeed fall (*corruit*, looking back from the present). Past, present, and future come together, and with them Romulus and Augustus.

SECOND THOUGHTS
Cossus' Victory and Sympathy for the Fallen

The elegist's account of the next episode in the history of the temple of Jupiter Feretrius is equally stark and equally difficult to read as celebratory. The second man to dedicate *spolia opima* in the temple was A. Cornelius Cossus, whose rank had become such an important precedent for the new emperor before his first constitutional settlement. Propertius is not explicit on the famous debate about whether Cossus was consul or *tribunus militum* when he defeated Tolumnius,[37] but he does construct his narrative in a way that unsettles the honor of the dedication.

Where Romulus had defended Rome against an enemy force at its gates (at least at first; see above), Cossus' victory over Tolumnius takes place at Veii in the context of Roman expansion:[38]

Cossus at insequitur Veientis caede Tolumni,
    uincere cum Veios posse laboris erat;
necdum ultra Tiberim belli sonus, ultima praeda
    Nomentum et captae iugera terna Corae.

But Cossus follows with the slaughter of Veian Tolumnius, when it took some work to be able to conquer Veii; not yet was the sound of war

heard beyond the Tiber, the farthest prize so far being Nomentum and
the three acres Cora offered when it was captured. (4.10.23–26)

Though Barber 1960 (1953) transposes lines 25–26 and thus reads the
couplet as the end of the Romulus episode rather than as part of the
Cossus story (because, presumably, Rome *had* fought beyond the Tiber
before its expedition to Veii), I find the original order offered in the
manuscripts does no injustice to the facts and smoothes the transition
between stories; Cossus' victory is part of one long process of Roman
expansion, and these lines enact the same sort of temporal elision that
occurred in Romulus's story with the variety of verb tenses the poet
used. In its original position (as reproduced above), the couplet
explores the continuum, contrasting Rome's "domestic" fight against
Caenina with its war "abroad" against Tolumnius' forces.[39] One scholar terms the Roman action "brigandage," and Propertius' mention of
Cora's scant acres suggests land redistribution, and with it, a motive of
expansion.[40] The effect of a Roman offensive is heightened by the way
Propertius represents the battle itself:

> forte super portae dux Veiens astitit arcem
>   colloquiumque sua fretus ab urbe dedit:
> dumque aries murum cornu pulsabat aeno,
>   uinea qua ductum longa tegebat opus,
> Cossus ait "Forti melius concurrere campo."
>   nec mora fit, plano sistit uterque gradum.
> di Latias iuuere manus, desecta Tolumni
>   ceruix Romanos sanguine lauit equos.

By chance the Veian leader stood atop the stronghold of the gate and
confidently addressed the crowd from his city. And while the ram was
striking the wall with its bronze horn, where the long vine-work was
protecting the machine of war, Cossus said, "Better for the brave to meet
in the open field." Without delay each one sets his feet on the plain. The
gods helped the Latin troops, Tolumnius' severed neck bathed Roman
horses with its blood. (4.10.31–38)

Tolumnius, the elegist says, was giving some sort of speech from atop
his gates when Cossus forced the fight. This detail is curious; no other
author includes it. What sort of speech was the Veientine leader giving?
Was he taunting the enemy below? Was he exhorting his own troops to

valor? Was he trying to negotiate with the besiegers? Roman tradition paints Tolumnius with more negative colors; he had killed Roman envoys to Fidenae, and Rome's attack was to avenge this atrocity (Livy 4.17.1–6). Propertius, on the other hand, leaves room for doubt about Tolumnius' culpability, as Tolumnius does nothing in the poem other than defend his own walls. The word *Latias* is also curious in this passage, and further supports the idea of Roman expansion. To be sure, at the most basic level it draws a contrast with implied *Etruscas manus*, but one wonders, are the Caeninians defeated by Romulus now included among the *Latias . . . manus?*

As with his treatment of Romulus, Propertius mentions little or nothing about the spoils Cossus captured and focuses instead on the enemy commander's death. This death frames his discussion of Cossus' deed, as 4.10.23 opens the narrative with Tolumnius' slaughter (*caede*), and 4.10.38 ends it with the details of this slaughter. Again, the elegist attends to the gore, creating a vivid tableau of the Etruscan's severed head spurting red blood onto nearby horses. Livy suggests that Cossus killed Tolumnius with many spear-thrusts, and then took his head back to Rome on a stake (4.19.5). Propertius takes the story one step further: for Tolumnius' blood to spurt, the heart must still have been beating at the moment of decapitation. Cossus did not defile the dead body, as in Livy's version; rather, the decapitation was the death. The vivid *sanguine* that bathes nearby horses in Cossus' narrative, appearing in the same *sedes* it had at 4.10.12 to describe Acron's gory spoils, links these two dedications of *spolia opima* in the blood that stains them.

As with Romulus' tale, there is no triumphant return to Rome for Cossus in Propertius' poem, and the death that frames this second portion of the narrative itself undermines celebration of the *spolia opima* as an achievement. But the most striking element of the elegist's version is the interjection of a powerful and beautiful lament for lost Veii. This lament falls at the center of the poem and lends to the whole a feeling of melancholy and sympathy for Rome's victims:

> heu Vei ueteres! et uos tum regna fuistis,
>   et uestro posita est aurea sella foro:
> nunc intra muros pastoris bucina lenti
>   cantat, et in uestris ossibus arua metunt.

> Alas, ancient Veii! At that time you were still a kingdom, and the golden throne still sat in your forum. Now within the walls sounds the horn of

an unhurried shepherd, and they harvest fields upon your bones.
(4.10.27–30)

With *heu* at 4.10.27 we witness the poet's pain, and the repeated -*ue*-
sounds that follow extend his vocalic cry. The second-person pronouns
and adjectives compound the effect, emphasizing the personal connection between the poet and the fallen city and drawing us as readers
into this lament. The repetition of the second person underscores Veii's
decline from prosperity to ruin—you(r) kingdom, your throne, your
bones.

Propertius' portrait of lost Veii is rich with resonance. The *topos* of a
great city fallen into ruin recalls and reverses the *topos* of the humble
settlement grown to magnificence that Propertius had applied so effectively to Rome at 4.1.1–14, and simultaneously blends two popular
images of Etruria found in Roman literature: that of Etruria as a grand
and vast land stretching to the sea, and as the simple and rustic land
that runs along the Tiber.[41] The elegist's Veii is a great kingdom that has
become a rustic village. To this nostalgic and melancholy Etruria Propertius adds a powerful and conventional image of the effect of war on
the landscape—the plowing of bones.[42] Vergil had earlier used this
image to lament the grim realities of civil war at the close of the first
book of the *Georgics:*

> scilicet et tempus ueniet, cum finibus illis
> agricola incuruo terram molitus aratro
> exesa inueniet scabra robigine pila,
> aut grauibus rastris galeas pulsabit inanis,
> grandiaque effossis mirabitur ossa sepulcris.

> There will come a time when the farmer, working the soil with his
> curved plow, will find in those lands rough javelins corroded by rust, or
> he'll hit empty helmets with his heavy hoe, and he will wonder at the
> huge bones that appear when graves are dug up. (*G.* 1.493–97)

The passage from the *Georgics* juxtaposes Italian fecundity and Italian
death. For Propertius, though, the image of bones in fields is not
national but personal. He had used the image twice earlier in his poetry, in the startling *sphragis* to the first book (1.22) and in its partner-
poem that precedes it, the sepulchral epigram of a man named Gallus
who dies during the civil wars in Umbria in 41–40 BCE (1.21). In these

two poems, Propertius stops talking about Cynthia and reveals his personal history. He is an Etruscan who witnessed the civil wars fought on his native soil and was dispossessed of his home.[43] Both 1.21 and 1.22 mention the bones of the dead on Etruscan soil:

> et quacumque super dispersa inuenerit ossa,
>   montibus Etruscis, haec sciat esse mea.

> (sic mihi praecipue, puluis Etrusca, dolor,
> tu proiecta mei perpessa es membra propinqui,
>   tu nullo miseri contegis ossa solo),
> proxima supposito contingens Umbria campo
>   me genuit terris fertilis uberibus.

And wherever she finds bones scattered over Etruscan hills, let her know that they are mine. (1.21.9–10)

(thus it is especially painful for me, Etruscan dust, that you permitted the limbs of my wretched kinsman to be scattered, that with no soil do you protect his bones), nearby Umbria, touching on the field settled below, bore me, Umbria fertile in its rich earth. (1.22.6–10)

Propertius' closure to Book 1 forces a rereading of the rest of the book and reinterprets the lover-poet who dominates the earlier poems. He repeats his disdain at 2.1.29; in a famous and lengthy *recusatio*, Propertius mentions in the context of other imperial feats he won't celebrate in song the *euersos focus antiquae gentis Etruscae* (the overturned hearths of the ancient Etruscan people). As Nethercut has shown, the passage is structured so as to taint all the emperor's exploits with the stain of civil war.[44] The elegist's sore memories of a civil war that ravaged his homeland and his kin help explain his audible disdain for typical pursuits of Roman men and his preference to dally in a love affair.[45] Lest there be any doubt about the connection between Propertius' poetic choices and his painful Umbrian background, the seer Horos in elegy 4.1 confirms the painful nexus of the elegiac poet, the bones of the dead, and Etruria's fertile fields. Having offered his own credentials as a seer and chronicled his successes, Horos points his prophetic finger at Propertius and details the elegist's past:

> Umbria te notis antiqua Penatibus edit—
>   mentior? an patriae tangitur ora tuae?—

qua nebulosa cauo rorat Meuania campo,
  et lacus aestiuis intepet Umber aquis,
scandentisque Asis consurgit uertice murus,
  murus ab ingenio notior ille tuo.
ossaque legisti non illa aetate legenda
  patris et in tenuis cogeris ipse lares:
nam tua cum multi uersarent rura iuuenci,
  abstulit excultas pertica tristis opes.

Ancient Umbria gave birth to you from well-known Penates—am I
lying? Or have I hit upon the borders of your fatherland?—where the
murky Mevanian river moistens the hollowed-out field, and the Umbrian lake grows warm with the summer-baked waters, and the wall of
lofty Assisi rises to its height, a wall all the more renowned because of
your talent. And you collected the bones of your father, which should
not have been collected at such a young age, and you are forced into a
lowly estate. For although many bulls used to turn over the soil in your
fields, a grim surveyor's rod took away the riches you had cultivated.
(4.1.121–30)

Horos' identification of the poet comes just before his impassioned
plea for Propertius to write love elegy rather than national aetiology
(*Apollo . . . uetat insano uerba tonare Foro*, "Apollo forbids you to thunder in the raging Forum," 4.1.133–34). In other words, Propertius'
Umbrian background makes him unsuited for poetry that celebrates
Roman places. Elegy 4.10 fulfills Horos' prophecy; the temple of
Jupiter Feretrius resonates too closely with Umbrian defeat. Perhaps
because of how personal it sounds, the lament in 4.10 is considered one
of Propertius' most powerful set-pieces,[46] and it is impossible not to
share his grief for what was lost. Like the closing poems of the first
book, the lament for Veii in elegy 4.10 casts a shadow on the whole
poem. By its concentrated focus on the victim and the losses involved
in one episode of Roman glory, the poet turns our perspective to other
victims in Rome's steady march to imperial mastery over Italy.

Because of the evocations of the poet's own losses in Etruria, his
scornful attitude is directed not only at Rome's general tendency
toward militarism, but toward the specific manifestation of that attitude in 41–40 BCE, when Octavian destroyed Perusia. Details peculiar
to Propertius' account of Cossus and Tolumnius seem calculated to
raise the specter of recent civil war in this poem about the attachment
to martial valor. The destruction of Perusia lingers in ancient sources as

a particularly grim episode in the civil wars that followed Caesar's death.[47] Perusia, upset at Rome's encroachment on its territory for land on which to settle Roman veterans, enlisted the aid of Lucius Antonius against Octavian.[48] As a result Octavian besieged Perusia for many months, until the Perusians were forced to surrender. In a massacre known as the *arae Perusinae*, Octavian had the senators from the town beheaded as a sacrifice to Julius Caesar. What truth the legend of the *arae Perusinae* preserves is unknown, but it is certain that stories of the executions had been magnified into a tale of massacre early on.[49] As mentioned above, where tradition holds that the Romans attacked to avenge the ambassadors killed by Tolumnius, Propertius connects the Roman invasion to a desire for land:

> necdum ultra Tiberim belli sonus, ultima praeda
>   Nomentum et captae iugera terna Corae.

> Not yet was the sound of war heard beyond the Tiber, the farthest prize
> so far being Nomentum and the three acres Cora offered when it was
> captured. (4.10.25–26)

Likewise, whereas in Livy's account the battle between Cossus and Tolumnius was fought on the plains outside Fidenae, Propertius' conflict is a siege of Veii like the one at Perusia. The elegist even describes Tolumnius barricaded within the gates of Veii as the Romans attacked with siege engines:

> forte super portae dux Veiens astitit arcem
>   colloquiumque sua fretus ab urbe dedit:
> dumque aries murum cornu pulsabat aeno,
>   uinea qua ductum longa tegebat opus.

> By chance the Veian leader stood atop the stronghold of the gate and,
> confident, addressed the crowd. And while the ram was striking the
> wall with its bronze horn, where the long vine-work was protecting the
> machine of war. (4.10.31–34)

Such towered gates are anachronistic to Cossus' time, but not to 40 BCE; a second-century gate such as the one described at 4.10.31 still exists at Perugia, and is called the *porta Augusta*.[50] Finally, in Livy's account Tolumnius was killed in battle and then beheaded. Propertius'

Tolumnius, like those sacrificed at the altar to Caesar, was decapitated while still living.

... desecta Tolumni
ceruix Romanos sanguine lauit equos.

... Tolumnius' severed neck bathed Roman horses with its blood.
(4.10.37–38)

In Propertius' poem, Veian Tolumnius raises the specter of the *arae Perusinae*. The elegist thus sheds generic tears of lament for a great city destroyed, and real tears for the losses of his own day.

M. CLAUDIUS MARCELLUS AND DYNASTIC CLOUT

The elegist's account of M. Claudius Marcellus' entry into the history of the temple of Jupiter Feretrius is almost perfunctory; he seems to include details only to emphasize how paltry are the spoils themselves and, of course, the vivid death of the enemy, the Gallic king Virdomarus:

Claudius at Rheno traiectos arcuit hostis,
　Belgica cum uasti parma relata ducis
Virdomari. genus hic Rheno iactabat ab ipso,
　mobilis e rectis fundere gaesa rotis.
illi ut uirgatis iaculans it ab agmine bracis
　torquis ab incisa decidit unca gula.

Claudius held off the enemy that had invaded from the Rhineland, when the Belgian shield of the huge leader Virdomarus was brought back to Rome. He used to boast that his clan came from Rhine itself, quick to pour out javelins from his guided chariot. As he came, hurling his javelin, from his troops with his striped trousers the twisted torque fell from his slit throat. (4.10.39–44)

Here for the first time Propertius details the spoils to be dedicated in the temple of Jupiter Feretrius; the word *relata* at 4.10.40 indicates they were brought back to Rome. They are the stylized, almost exaggerated accouterment of a barbaric northerner.[51] One wonders what sort of triumphal spectacle would be provided by some striped pants and a necklace. Even Virdomarus' shield is small; the poet draws attention to the contrast between huge Virdomarus and his modest *parma* (4.10.40). Yet even as this huge menace, descendant of the Rhine, boasts and vaunts from his chariot, Marcellus dispatches him quickly and without sentiment (recall that Romulus and Cossus had each spoken a vow or challenge before killing their enemies). Like Acron and Tolumnius, Virdomarus dies by a blow to the neck. The guttural stops, voiced and unvoiced, in line 4.10.44 mimic the gurgling sounds of a slashed throat: *torquis ab incisa decidit unca gula.*

Propertius calls Marcellus by his *gentilicium*—Claudius. There is no metrical reason for him to do so, and the choice is startling; he could have called him Marcellus. Vergil had: all three dedicators of *spolia opima* are included in the parade of heroes in *Aeneid* 6. Of the three Marcellus' achievement is given most detail—five lines (6.855–59), compared to Romulus' two (6.779–80) and Cossus' one (6.841). The prominence of Marcellus in Anchises' account adds pathos to the appearance of the younger Marcellus, Augustus' nephew, whose potential for *spolia opima* will be cut short by his untimely death. Grimal believes that Propertius' choice to write a poem about *spolia opima* is the elegist's tribute to the lost Marcellus, and that the elegy must have been written earlier than 16 BCE.[52] But why not mention the possibility in elegy 3.18? And why, then, call the historical victor in 4.10 Claudius?

In my view Propertius uses the name Claudius to connect the *spolia opima* once again to the recent exploits of the imperial household, telescoping past and present as he had done with his accounts of Romulus and Cossus. Claudius was Livia's *gentilicium* and that of Augustus' two stepsons, Tiberius and Drusus. In 16 BCE—as it happens, the date traditionally assigned to the publication of Propertius' fourth book—Lollius suffered a terrible defeat at the hands of the Germans, a disaster that came to be called the *clades Lolliana.* Augustus sent Tiberius and Drusus north to deal with the enemy. Omens on the eve of their departure were bad, and the Princeps restored the faith of the gods by repairing the temple of Quirinus on the Quirinal hill. Augustus mentions this restoration in the same breath as that of Jupiter Feretrius at *Res Gestae* 19, and his attention to Quirinus seems a subtle tribute to the city's first founder. The brothers had soon pacified the transalpine regions; within three years Drusus was commander of the armies along the Rhine (with Tiberius back in Rome as consul). Drusus would continue to fight on the German frontier—as far as the Elbe—until his death in 9 BCE. Suetonius mentions that Drusus planned to dedicate *spolia opima* from his German victories (*Claud.* 1), but was prevented by his death; after Drusus' funeral Augustus paid tribute to this lost possibility by dedicating his own fascular laurels to Jupiter Feretrius.[53]

Propertius' use of the name Claudius evokes Augustus' heirs and their exploits to the north. The elegist's jumbled geography contributes to the allusion. In 222 BCE Marcellus defeated Virdomarus at Clastidium. There Romans defeated a mixed army of northerners— Gauls, primarily Insubrians, with some German allies. Tradition holds Virdomarus as the Insubrian king—i.e., a king from Cisalpine Gaul. Propertius' man, in contrast, though he wears Celtic trinkets, comes from beyond the Rhine, indeed boasts of his ancestry from the Rhine, and carries a Belgian shield. This conflated geography is more than poetic carelessness. Virdomarus' background thus described assimilates his threat to the one being met by the imperial sons. Although Suetonius situates Drusus' attempt at dedicating *spolia opima* later in the German campaign, it is tempting to wonder whether there were suggestions of it in the early years of the action, just after Lollius' defeat—especially if the restoration of the temple of Quirinus in 16 BCE was meant to pave the way for a dedication of *spolia opima* within the imperial family. It is also possible that Propertius' poem was written somewhat later than 16 BCE; that is the *terminus post quem* given to the book's publication by the mention of Scipio's consulship in 16 BCE.

The possibility that Tiberius and Drusus' campaign in the north was yet unfinished when Propertius wrote his poem might explain the perfunctory tone of this episode within it. Propertius leaves the details up to the imperial sons. Nevertheless, after the bloody deaths of Acron and Cossus, and the lament for Veii, the achievement of *spolia opima* does not seem as glorious as perhaps the imperial family might hope. The elegist's perspective on this martial honor is not flattering, and before it is won the Claudian victory in the north is tarnished by the blood from Virdomarus' severed throat.

These are the stories of the dedicators of *spolia opima*—what about the temple in which they were to be dedicated? In telling of the three historical achievements of this rare honor Propertius has been silent about the urban location that commemorates it. He does not even attend much to the spoils captured in battle, preferring to describe Romulus' crude equipment rather than Acron's, ignoring Cossus' dedication, and accentuating Virdomarus' exotic clothes and undersized military weaponry. Instead, he has drawn attention to the moment of death that facilitated each dedication to Jupiter Feretrius. In fact, the temple and its contents are all but nonexistent in the poem, and all that remains palpable—red and wet—is the blood that spatters them. Bloodstained by association is the Princeps as well, whose lurking presence haunts all three episodes of this rare Roman achievement. The Propertian reader, accustomed to sweet love poetry, may remember this human blood whenever he visits the temple of Jupiter Feretrius, or sees other signs of his new emperor in the city around him.

CALLIMACHUS ROMANUS CLIMBS THE CAPITOL

Propertius frames his unsettling narrative of the history of the *spolia opima* with passages that draw attention to the poet hard at work. A similar frame operates in elegy 4.6. There, the poet as *uates* introduces the celebration of Apollo and his temple on the Palatine, then returns after the narrative of Apollo's deeds at Actium to lead a sympotic night of revelry. As we saw in chapter 4 above, this poetic frame acts as a foil for the battle narrative it contains and reinterprets it in ways that favor the poet; Propertius as *uates* has not only a more pleasant task than Apollo or his protégé in battle, Octavian, but also a greater effect on the way his readers interpret the monumental topic of the poem (the temple of Palatine Apollo) than its imperial builder. Poetry creates monuments. Likewise in elegy 4.10, the poet's self-conscious introduction and conclusion frame and interpret the central narrative. Propertius begins his poem with a brief statement of his resolve to compose it and the great rewards his poem will bestow on him. He ends with a series of etymological suggestions that draw the reader's attention to the power of (his) words to construct our interpretation of visual arts. This metapoetic frame draws attention to poetic achievement as a fitting—and preferable—alternative to the pursuit and winning of *spolia opima,* and enacts Propertius' own "restoration" of the tiny temple on the Capitol.

Propertius opens his temple as the triumphant *Callimachus Romanus* he had promised to be at elegy 4.1.64:

> nunc Iouis incipiam causas aperire Feretri
>   armaque de ducibus trina recepta tribus.
> magnum iter ascendo, sed dat mihi gloria uires:
>   non iuuat e facili lecta corona iugo.

Now I shall begin to uncover the origins of Jupiter Feretrius, and the three sets of arms received from three leaders. I climb a great path, but glory gives me strength: a crown gathered from an easy height gives no pleasure. (4.10.1–4)

This incipit recalls two great Alexandrian poems. The word *causas,* or origins, is the Latin translation for *aetia,* the title of Callimachus' masterpiece.[54] The rest of the incipit derives from Aratus, who, like Propertius, begins his great didactic poem *Phaenomena* with Zeus: ἐκ Διὸς ἀρχώμεσθα (Let us begin from Zeus, *Phaen.* 1). Aratus was admired by his contemporary Callimachus as an artist who had treated a grand theme at length with consummate *leptotes,* or "subtlety" (*Epigr.* 27). With his evocation of these two poets, Propertius reinforces his allegiance to the aesthetic sensibilities for which Callimachus' name was a beacon; the Roman elegist is not only like Callimachus, but he is like a poet Callimachus admired. His double allusion creates a poetic triad of mutual admiration.[55]

The second couplet develops the poet's Callimachean stance and describes his written achievement in terms that resonate with the slender Muse. In writing this little poem he climbs a great path—*magnum iter,* 4.10.2. "Great" must here mean "steep" as in "ambitious," as commentators have suggested—casting his brief poem on Jupiter Feretrius as the rare and demanding sort that pleases Apollo in Callimachus' hymn to the god (2.105).[56] But if *magnum* also means "great" as in "wide," Propertius' composition constitutes a Callimachean misdemeanor. The great path he climbs contradicts the Alexandrian master's injunction not to travel the wide and common road (μὴ καθ᾽ ὁμὰ δίφρον ἐλᾶν μηδ᾽ οἶμον ἀνὰ πλατύν . . . , *Aet.* fr.1.26–27). I believe the couplet is richer with the tension between "wide" and "steep" preserved. Propertius did not promise at 4.1.64 to be Callimachus; he promised to be *Callimachus Romanus.* As scholars have recognized, the elegist's application of Alexandrian poetic rigor to the grand themes of Roman rites, days, and the names of places expands and redefines Callimacheanism.[57] The ambitious poem on the temple of Jupiter Feretrius is the capstone of this promise.

Propertius thus naturalizes the *Aitia*'s self-conscious incipit. The narrow Callimachean path becomes a great Roman road, of the sort that made Rome famous through the world: well crafted, even beautiful, and offering bold access to distant wonders. Good old-fashioned Roman glory lends strength to the struggling poet. As Callimachus' path is naturalized into a Roman road, so, too, is the poetic persona naturalized into a Roman traveler. Climbing his difficult poetic hill, with the promise of glory at the top, the poet enacts a sort of Roman triumph. In this poem about armor and warfare and dedications to Jupiter on the Capitol, the poet's difficult climb up the steep hill reminds of the procession up the *cliuus Capitolinus* by victorious commanders awarded the great honor of a triumph. The temple of Jupiter Feretrius lay atop the Capitol just before the end of the triumphal procession. As Rome's first temple, it was the destination of the triumphal ceremony until the bigger temple to Jupiter was built nearby over two hundred years later.[58] Those making the journey with *spolia opima* were rare indeed—three men only achieved this honor, as Propertius reminds us twice at 4.10.2. Climbing his difficult path, Propertius makes himself equal to them.[59]

The last line of the proem follows suit in Romanizing Callimachus. The elusive crown that the poet finds pleasing surely evokes the rare droplets of Deo (Demeter) that Callimachus' Apollo prefers over the muddied Euphrates (*Hymn* 2.105–12). But it is important to note that Propertius seeks a *corona* (crown) rather than the *serta* (garland), even though he had earlier eschewed the former as harsh while preferring the latter as more refined (e.g., 3.1.19–20, and cf. 4.1.61–62). His prize is nothing less than the symbol of Roman martial and civic glory—to be sure, the honor given to the triumphant general. This *corona* is Propertius' poetic *spolia opima,* and his poem appropriates imperial honors.

The triumph had proven to be a rich theme for Cynthia's poet in Books 1–3—as a foil for his own private pursuits, as in 2.1, or as a metaphor of his *militia amoris,* as at 2.4. The triumph appears several times in Book 4, a phenomenon Galinsky attributes to Propertius' "new concession to the Augustan spirit."[60] I believe the triumph recurs in the fourth book for different reasons. As a powerful Roman metaphor for achievement in the public realm and as a celebration that involves rites, days, and the names of places, the triumph is a potent symbol of the way Roman identity is encoded in the cityscape. Propertius' Callimachean triumph buccaneers for his poetry the honors normally given to Roman generals—in fact, none of the three dedicators of *spolia opima* gets as far up the Capitol in the poem as does the poet himself. Propertius' rich incipit at once elevates the status and prestige of elegiac poetry to one of Rome's central honors; shatters the monopoly on Roman virtue and glory previously held by martial achievement; overwrites onto the triumphal route and the Capitol a new kind of victory ritual; and dedicates to Jupiter Feretrius a new kind of spoil—a poem, rarer and more precious than Virdomarus' striped pants.

The power of words over places returns at the end of the poem, in which Propertius poses alternative etymologies for Jupiter Feretrius's epithet:[61]

> nunc spolia in templo tria condita: causa Feretri,
>   omine quod certo dux ferit ense ducem;
> seu quia uicta suis umeris haec arma ferebant,
>   hinc Feretri dicta est ara superba Iovis.

Now three sets of spoils are established in the temple: for this reason he's called Feretrius, because leader strikes (*ferire*) leader by sword under sure omen; or because they used to carry (*ferre*) these conquered weapons on their shoulders, hence the proud altar of Jupiter Feretrius has its name. (4.10.45–49)

His refusal to choose between these options opens, rather than closes, possibilities and leaves the connection between the past, the present, and the city unresolved.[62] Note that the poet uses "or" rather than "and"; his etymologies are offered as alternatives that Romans can choose, depending on how they view the monument. As noted above, Propertius' poem says almost nothing about the transportation of spoils back to Rome, their carriage up the Capitol, or their dedication to Jupiter; the closest he comes to validating the etymology from *fero* is at 4.10.40, when he mentions that Virdomarus' little *parma* was brought back (*relata*), presumably to Rome (and cf. *tulit* at 4.10.18). While Propertius refuses to take sides on *ferre*, he does have much to say about wounding with swords, as each of the three conquered foreign commanders provides armor splashed with his own blood. The fact that these three violent acts are divinely approved with sure omen (*omine . . . certo*, 4.10.46) implicates the gods in Rome's glorification of carnage, following up on the suggestion earlier in the poem that the gods guided Latin forces (*di Latias iuuere manus*, 4.10.37).[63]

Callimachus Romanus would replace it with the glorification of poetry. The wordsmith posits fanciful phonetic echoes of the epithet by combining *f-*, *r-*, and *t-*sounds: for example, in *frenis . . . aratris* (4.10.19), in *fretus* (4.10.33), and in *fortis* twice (4.10.32 and 36).[64] These more fanciful echoes defamiliarize the temple and the identity it manifests in its name, opening new vistas for interpretation and naming. So also does the unspoken *fere tria*, "roughly three," an etymology whose specter is evoked by the very text that vanishes before our eyes

with ever shrinking narratives. The text thus uses its own disappear-
ance as a strategy to provoke its audience into wondering where any
fourth dedication has been lost or ruled out, thanks to the Princeps—
and the poet.

CONCLUSION

Critics have noted the complete absence of the feminine in this poem.[65]
There are no women in preference for whom the poet can mask his distaste for the Roman masculine, martial values that are embedded in the
monuments around him (and that had been reasserted by Hercules in
elegy 4.9). Rather, Propertius makes it clear to the reader what has happened, indeed what must happen, to adorn the temple of Jupiter
Feretrius—death. By focusing on the victims whose spoils decorate the
city, the elegist exposes uncomfortable fissures in the connection
between Roman monuments and Roman identity.

Propertius is careful in this poem to associate Romulus' ambiguous
victory with the birth of the city. At 4.10.17 Romulus is the parent of the
city and of virtue—*urbis uirtutisque parens.* In a very concrete sense this
is true: Rome's first shrine arose from Romulus' battle, and so the city
is a result of his martial virtue. Yet I believe Propertius' comment is
more general and pervasive than that. Romulus' battle, his victory, and
his dedication are paradigmatic of the ways and means by which
Rome's cityscape evolved. Manubial temples were common in the city,
as were temples to gods appropriated from enemies either with the
gods' consent (e.g., via *euocatio*) or without it. By Propertius' day Rome
was filled with monumental reminders of its expanding hegemony.
Romulus set—or stained—the first example for this connection
between the Roman city, Roman virtue, and warfare. The poet explores
this connection by playing with words that echo the *ui(r)* in *uirtutis:* it
appears in *uincere* alongside *uirtutis* in the same line (4.10.17), in *uictor*
at 4.10.8, in *uictima* in 4.10.15, and picks up again in *Virdomari* in
4.10.41 and *uirgatis* in 4.10.43. *Vis,* too, lurks behind these words.

Propertius' formulation *urbis uirtutisque parens* foreshadows the
honorific title given to Augustus in 2 BCE: *pater patriae.* Though it is
extremely fanciful to suggest that the Senate and people were influenced in this decision by Propertius' poem, written a dozen years earlier, it is interesting to note that Augustus' honorific title involved the
Roman cityscape no less than did the title Propertius bestowed on

Romulus.⁶⁶ At *Res Gestae* 35 Augustus himself reveals that the title *pater patriae* was to be inscribed on his own Palatine home, on the Curia (which he had rebuilt), and on his Forum Augustum—three different places in the city that testified to his role as its (re)founder and (re)builder. Propertius' poem anticipates what Augustus would do with the title *pater patriae* in Rome, only to unsettle it.⁶⁷ Wherever Romulean virtue is encoded in Roman buildings and places, Propertius' poem encourages us to see bloodstains and victims. For the elegist, there is one overwhelming response to the city thus built, a response uttered by the book's last speaker directly upon the heels of elegy 4.10's disturbing urban vision: at 4.11.1, Cornelia says "stop" (*desine*).

The Rise and Fall of Cities

WHAT IS LAST is first; the last topographical poem in Propertius' tour of Rome describes Rome's first public monument. The elegist's description of the temple of Jupiter Feretrius proves that *arcana* are not arcane. On the contrary: from the beginning, Rome's buildings responded to and shaped the Romans' sense of themselves, and stood for Romans of all eras as reminders of who they had been and who they had become. Many of these monuments continue to shape the self-identity not only of Romans, or even of Italians, but of all those who inhabit Rome's legacy. From Napoleon's Arc de Triomphe in Paris; to the U.S. Capitol building in Washington, D.C.; to the Government-General building in Seoul, recently demolished as a symbol of Japanese colonial rule; to the Memorial Coliseum in Los Angeles where teams compete at American football, Roman architecture continues to endorse strong ideological positions on such matters as manly virtue, statecraft, and imperialism.

Cynthia's poet demonstrates with uncomfortable clarity the extent to which Roman identity is encoded in its buildings and places. Throughout Book 4 Propertius scrutinizes the monumentalization of various ideological positions in Rome, poking and prodding Rome's monuments to see what further meanings they might admit. The result is a poetic book rife with different voices and different perspectives on the eternal city, perspectives that often call into question any sleepy or complacent adherence to Rome's traditional values.

Propertius' achievement in building a written city rivals Augustus' achievement in building a marble one. In elegy 4.1 the elegist promises to do just that:

moenia namque pio coner disponere uersu . . .

. . . .

scandentis quisquis cernit de uallibus arces,
ingenio muros aestimet ille meo!

For I would try to lay out the city walls in my holy verse . . . whoever sees these citadels rising above the valleys, let him judge their walls by my genius! (4.1.57, 65–66)

We, his readers, are to judge Roman buildings by Propertius' genius, not Augustus'. The incipit for elegy 4.10, written at the end of his "architectural" project, marks his success. Propertius triumphs, climbing his own scripted Capitol (*magnum iter ascendo*, 4.10.3) in the Rome that is his own, not the Princeps', creation. Where the Augustan building program urges a sense of individual duty to the state (the Basilica Aemilia), a sense of wonder at Rome's place in the world and the emperor's place in Rome (the temple of Palatine Apollo), a sense of the proper relationship between traditional gender roles and success (the Ara Maxima and the sanctuary of the Bona Dea), and a sense of the manifest destiny guaranteed by Roman martial aggression (the temple of Jupiter Feretrius), Propertius encourages instead caution about a state that assumes too much control over private affairs, awareness of the civil strife that enabled Augustus' Principate, skepticism about the virtues encoded into traditional roles for men and women, contrition at the human cost of Roman expansion—and, above all, a Vertumnus-style open-mindedness in what monuments mean and how that meaning is conveyed.[1]

Perhaps this aspect of the book explains the curious choice of monuments pesented in Book 4; they are all part of Rome's public rather than private face, all more central than peripheral, but they are not necessarily Rome's "greatest hits" nor its freshest wonders. Propertius all but ignores, for example, the theater of Marcellus and the new emperor's mausoleum, the temple of Jupiter Tonans and even the Forum Augustum already under way and unlike anything Romans had ever seen before. With the exception of the temple of Palatine

Apollo, the elegist rather chose to elaborate on places already imbued with a long history into which the Princeps inserted himself. The pre-existing history of most of Propertius' sites emphasizes the changes of his own time as part of a process of identity formation rather than its result. Rome was not yet imperial in 16 BCE. The poet's task was to show it becoming so. Though his is not the most flashy Rome, the elegist's city—his poems on Roman rites, days, and the names of places, issued from his tiny breast (*exiguo . . . e pectore* 4.1.59)—nevertheless persists in ringing in our ears. Propertius' entry into the urban landscape argues forcefully that Roman identity is not something created from the top that trickles down, but rather something that is negotiated, discussed, and disputed at all levels. A Princeps is only as successful in crafting a new Rome as Romans are willing to accept it without pause.

The poet succeeds in another way as well. Time has proven true Propertius' boast from elegy 3.3.19–26—that monuments and pyramids, mausolea and temples will fall, but Propertius' *ingenium* will endure.[2] Pound's version at *Homage to Sextus Propertius* 1 captures the idea with a bold Ozymandias-like flair:

> Happy who are mentioned in my pamphlets,
>   the songs shall be a fine tomb-stone over their breasts.
>   But against this?
> Neither expensive pyramids surpassing the stars in their route,
> Nor bones modeled on that of Jove in East Elis,
> Nor the monuments or effigies of Mausolus,
>   are a complete elucidation of death.
> Flame burns, rain sinks into the cracks
> And they all go to rack ruin beneath the thud of years.
> Stands a genius a deathless adornment,
>   a name not to be worn out with the years.

Propertius' poems remain intact—unraveling at some textual seams, to be sure, but nevertheless still there to be read and appreciated. In contrast, none of the buildings or monuments he describes in Book 4 remains. Augustus' city and the messages embedded in it endure only as long as the marble from which they are built. The transience of the physical world is a theme that runs throughout Book 4. It has pride of place at the beginning of the book's introductory poem. To start his tour of Rome, Propertius introduces the contrast between Rome's current splendor and its rustic beginnings:

hoc quodcumque uides, hospes, qua maxima Roma est,
  ante Phrygem Aenean collis et herba fuit;
atque ubi Nauali stant sacra Palatia Phoebo,
  Euandri profugae procubuere boues.
fictilibus creuere deis haec aurea templa,
  nec fuit opprobrio facta sine arte casa;
Tarpeiusque pater nuda de rupe tonabat,
  et Tiberis nostris aduena bubus erat.
qua gradibus domus ista Remi se sustulit, olim
  unus erat fratrum maxima regna focus.
Curia, praetexto quae nunc nitet alta senatu,
  pellitos habuit, rustica corda, Patres.
bucina cogebat priscos ad uerba Quiritis:
  centum illi in prato saepe senatus erat.
nec sinuosa cauo pendebant uela theatro,
  pulpita sollemnis non oluere crocos.

All that you see here, visitor, where great Rome stands now, was but hill and grass in the days before Trojan Aeneas. And where stands the Palatine sanctuary for Phoebus Protector of the Sea, the exiled cattle of Evander used to take their rest. These golden temples arose out of statues made of clay, nor was it any shame to live in a house built without pretense. The Tarpeian Father thundered from his bare rock, and Tiber was a neighbor to our cattle. Do you see where the house of Remus rises up yonder on its high steps? Once a single hearth was the extent of the brothers' kingdom. The Curia, which now gleams aloft with the Senate in its ceremonial toga, once held skin-clad Elders, humble hearts, those. A shepherd's horn used to assemble Romans of yore: then "the Senate" was often any hundred men in a field. Nor did supple curtains hang in the hollow theater back then, and the platforms did not smell of ritual saffron. (4.1.1–16)

As mentioned in chapter 1, the newer buildings cited in these opening lines all have a strong Augustan flair: the temple of Palatine Apollo; a thundering Jupiter—i.e., Jupiter Tonans on the Capitol; the house of Remus, probably the temple of Quirinus restored in 16 BCE; the Curia, restored by Augustus after a fire in 29 BCE; and the theater of Marcellus, built in honor of the Princeps' nephew and dedicated in 13 BCE, a decade after his death. This golden Augustan city stands in stark contrast to pastoral proto-Rome. Like Vergil, who employed the same juxtaposition of past and present from the perspective of the

past, Propertius invites contemplation on Rome's change over time.
But unlike Vergil, whose temporal trajectory points only toward the
rise of Rome, Propertius points toward its eventual decline as well.[3]
Elegy 4.10 brings full circle the movement from rustic to rich and back
to rustic, juxtaposing the former splendor of the great Etruscan city
Veii, defeated by Rome, with its current, conquered humility:

> heu Vei ueteres! et uos tum regna fuistis,
>   et uestro posita est aurea sella foro:
> nunc intra muros pastoris bucina lenti
>   cantat, et in uestris ossibus arua metunt.

> Alas, ancient Veii! At that time you were still a kingdom, and the golden
> throne still sat in your forum. Now within the walls sounds the horn of
> an unhurried shepherd, and they harvest fields upon your bones.
> (4.10.27–30)

Many readers have noted the correspondence between risen Rome in
4.1 and fallen Veii in 4.10, but few have teased out its implications for
Propertius' view on monuments and identity.[4] Cities rise and cities fall.
Their transience in the elegist's work is not so much a commentary on
the persistence of nature as on the fragility of man's achievements; his
focus on the past is not so much a nostalgic preference for simpler
times as an examination of how Rome's very beginnings contain the
seeds of both its rise and its eventual fall. Ruined Veii, viewed with pity
and despair, emphasizes the vulnerability of monuments and cities,
and with them the vulnerability of the men who build them and the
identity they foster. Against the failings of the political and physical
worlds, only music—the *bucina pastoris*—will survive.

NOTES

Introduction

1. I use Barber's 1960 (1953) Oxford text with my own translations, unless otherwise noted.

2. "The Organization of Opinion" is chapter 30 of Syme's 1939 book, reissued in 1960. The fact that he devotes only one chapter to literary and visual propaganda in no way diminishes his achievement; we are still trying today to answer the questions Syme asked.

3. See also Kennedy 1992, who demonstrates that the concept "Augustan" was under negotiation then as much as it still is today.

4. Barchiesi 2002: 4, and see also Spencer 2001: 265 for a similar statement. Barchiesi is here discussing Ovid's *Fasti*, a text that has a head start over Propertian scholarship in this direction; in addition to Barchiesi 2002, see Newlands 1995, Barchiesi 1997a, and Hinds 1992a and 1992b. A similar dialogue is emerging in our understanding of the relationship between Ovid's written landscapes and the painted landscapes of Pompeii; see Hinds 2002 for an exploration of this exchange. Barchiesi 2003 goes a long way in articulating the broader opportunities and dilemmas posed by examining " . . . how texts and images cooperated in a Roman discourse about the paradoxes of the new state of things" (11); his discussion ranges over a variety of poetic texts from the Augustan age.

5. So too White 1993: 182–90. In discussing the proliferation of written Romes in the early Augustan years, White argues " . . . that the catalyst in this case was Augustus himself, and that he influenced the poets not by any direct approach to them, but by a campaign of public works which was steadily transforming the appearance of the city" (187).

6. Favro 1996: 228–30.

7. Boucher and Benediktson each devote a chapter to Propertius' visual mode ("La sensibilité de Properce: Tempérament visuel" in Boucher 1965: 41–64, and "Propertius' Poetics of Imagism" in Benediktson 1989: 103–16 and 150–51). Papanghelis 1987: 3–5 elevates this visual sensibility above all others, considering it the approach to life and poetry that governs and subordinates other ways of framing experience.

171

8. Boucher 1965: 41–42 and Papanghelis 1987: 207 both draw attention to the pervasive presence of art in the period in which Propertius flourished.

9. See the discussions of focalization as a critical term in Genette 1980: 186–89 and Bal 1985: 100–102.

10. Hardie 1993 discusses the ways Horace uses the visual arts as a parallel to poetry, in that there is " . . . a shared vocabulary of symbols and images which may be realized either in poetry or in sculpture and painting" (124).

11. Harrison 2001: 71–72, and see also Leach 1988: 3–24, Becker 1995: 4, and Fowler 1991.

12. Fowler 1991 and 1996.

13. Fowler 1996: 73. Laird 1993 also discusses the difference between ekphrasis of real objects and ekphrasis of imagined objects.

14. Kennedy 1993 is the starting point for any pursuit of this instability in Latin letters; Greene 1998, Janan 2001, P. A. Miller 2003, James 2003, and DeBrohun 2003 are book-length meditations on the problems of discourse in elegy; Janan and DeBrohun focus on Propertius Book 4.

15. Greene 1998, and see also Wyke 1987b and 1989, Sharrock 1991, and Gold 1993.

16. James 2003: 35–36; D'Elia 1981: 75–76.

17. P. A. Miller 2003: 23. Miller's book argues for the interdependence of Latin love elegy and the upheavals of the changing political and social order in this period (see also Dufallo 2003 for a specific instance of this interdependence in elegy's transformation of a Republican oratorical trope). Janan 2001: 7, arguing against Veyne's approach to elegy's contradictions as a game (Veyne 1988), makes a similar appeal to elegy's socio-historical context as the framework within which to understand the genre. D'Elia 1981: 74–75 sees two necessary conditions for the appearance of Latin love elegy: the particular forms of elite values and status that emerged in the Augustan age, and the youth of the poets themselves.

18. Cornelius Balbus was the last man outside the imperial family to celebrate a triumph, for a victory over the Garamantes in 19 BCE (Velleius Paterculus 2.51.3). See Syme 1960 (1939): 402–5 and Severy 2003: 80–81 for the general accumulation of military commands within the imperial family.

19. For example, Suetonius emphasizes in the last sentence of his biography (*Aug.* 101.4) that Augustus left public finances in the hands of his slaves and freedmen; see Severy's discussion of the role of the emperor's freedmen and slaves in administering the state (Severy 2003: 144–52). See also Syme 1960 (1939): 353–55.

20. Elsner 1995: 4.

21. Alföldy 1991, and cf. Elsner 1996.

22. See Favro 1996: 4–11 and 227 for a discussion of cognitive mapping within Rome, and Schmeling 2000 for the mental mapping of Rome in the wider world.

23. For topographical analyses of individual poems in Book 4, see, e.g., O'Neill 2000 on elegy 4.2 and Spencer 2001 on elegy 4.9.

24. Rothwell 1996; Fantham 1997.

25. Vasaly 1993: 41. Similar treatments exist for other Roman authors; see, for example, Dyson and Prior 1995 on Roman verse satire; Jaeger 1995 on topography in the *Carmina* of Horace; and Scott 1997 on images of Rome in Vergil's *Aeneid*.

26. Edwards 1996: 2.

27. D'Ambra 1998: 13 discusses " . . . the construction of social identity by external forces that dominate individual choices and freedoms." Kennedy 1993: 36 offers

" . . . the ideology of the individual . . . is *a* theory, *an* ideology, of personality which is not uncontested, and is always open to the argument that personality is not an essence which pre-exists experience, but is actively being constructed and re-constructed within the discourses in which people operate." So, for example, "Tibullus" is neither the lover nor the soldier nor the poet, but the incongruity among these three enacted roles (17). See also Elsner 1995: 125.

28. Both P. A. Miller's and Janan's titles encapsulate the negotiation between self and society.

29. Such studies are particularly rich for the early Roman Republic and for the Second Sophistic. See Cornell and Lomas 1997 for the Republic, and the collection of essays in Goldhill 2001 (mostly literary) and Laurence and Berry 1998 (mostly archaeological) for the Second Sophistic.

30. Johnson 2001: 7.

31. I cite Pound's *Homage to Sextus Propertius* from his later reissue of that poem in *Diptych Rome-London* 1994 (1958). The selection here is from p. 8.

32. The epigrams of Callimachus are the closest Greek model for Latin love elegy; lyric poets also employed the elegiac meter, but without the thematic or stylistic cohesion that could constitute a genre. Propertius' fourth book, in contrast, draws on Callimachus's *Aitia*, itself an experimental use of the elegiac couplet.

33. See, respectively, Hallett 1973; Wyke 1987b and 1989; Greene 1995; and Sharrock 2000 for these positions.

34. This dynamic is discussed by Clausen 1964 and Cameron 1995: 454–84; DeBrohun 2003: 3–9 treats Callimacheanism in Propertius' poetry. The numerous studies pertaining to the Callimachean program of Propertius' fourth book will be cited in the context of the discussions below.

35. Cynthia's social class and marital status resist easy categorization; even when she functions as a courtesan (as she perhaps does in elegies 1.3 and 2.7; see James 2003: 36–41), the poet treats his affair with her as illicit and stuck in irresolvable tensions. D'Elia 1981: 75–77 argues that in this respect the poet is on fresh ground for elegiac verse. As he points out, the disparity of Cynthia's status and her lover's finds no precise analogue in Callimachean love poetry; rather, this socioeconomic pairing finds its model in Roman comedy. Veyne 1988: 67–84 discusses the sort of woman the elegiac mistress could be, if real, then (85–100) posits that her specific status doesn't really matter and need not remain consistent; for elegy's generic game, she need only be unattainable. See Gold 1993 and P. A. Miller 2003: 7 and 61–73 for discussions of her discursive variability and the ways this variability challenges any stable categorization of the poet's own role.

36. Alfonsi 1979 (1945); Grimal 1953; Boucher 1965; d'Elia 1981; and DeBrohun 2003.

37. Tränkle 1983; Stahl 1985; Sullivan 1976; Gurval 1995; and Janan 2001.

38. DeBrohun 2003 offers a sustained meditation on how "Callimachus" changes as a discursive force in Book 4's new project.

39. The speaking door in elegy 1.16 and Gallus in elegy 1.21 perform a similar, though more limited, role in Book 1.

40. Boyle 2003.

41. Cairns 1992: 67.

42. Alfonsi 1979 (1945): 73–74. The other reason is that, after the *Aeneid*, such an undertaking would have been inopportune.

Chapter One

1. Though some critics (notably Murgia 1989) read the Propertius-Horos pair as two discrete poems, scholarly consensus overwhelmingly supports one complex poem rather than two discrete poems. I agree with the consensus; too many correspondences of theme and language link the two parts for them to be separable. See most recently P. A. Miller 2003: 186 for a compelling advocacy of unity.

2. Octavian dedicated the temple of Palatine Apollo in 28 BCE, and made his home on the Palatine in a house without pretense; thundering Jupiter alludes to the temple of Jupiter Tonans, dedicated in 22 BCE after the Princeps' escape from a lightning strike; in 16 BCE Augustus and his stepsons Tiberius and Drusus restored the temple of Quirinus, here called the Domus Remi; and Propertius mentions the Curia, whose restoration Octavian completed in 29 BCE (it had been begun by Caesar in 44 BCE). Propertius' reference to the Domus Remi is somewhat hard to pin down; because of the high steps it cannot refer to the Casa Romuli, which was at any rate never expanded into something grand and so would not fit the "then and now" scheme of his opening lines. Two problems with identifying it as the Temple of Quirinus are easily explained: *Remi* is substitution for the metrically impossible *Romuli,* and the speaker seems to address his *hospes* from a vantage point on the Palatine (*ista* implies some distance).

3. Stahl 1985: 255.

4. Weeber's 1978 treatment of these lines argues that they stave off the demand for epic by incorporating something of Vergil's great poem.

5. In contrast, Tibullus' paean to the humble old village on the Tiber leads up to his fervent prayer for a new Golden Age that will restore the lifestyle of the rustic—and romanticized—past (Tibullus 2.5, and see Rothwell 1996: 829–32), while Ovid decidedly prefers Rome's modern comforts to her ancient simplicity (*Ars am.* 3.115–28).

6. Newman 1997: 265.

7. See Janan 2001: 134 and MacLeod 1983: 142 for this sense of estrangement. As we shall see below, in addition to its comment on Roman temporal identity, the image of the *Romanus alumnus* also speaks to Roman cultural identity.

8. DeBrohun 2003: 51–67. The answer Propertius provides, she argues, is that it grew through *arma,* a notion that casts a shadow both on the growth of the city and the parallel expansion of Propertius' own poetry.

9. See Bing 1988: 7 and note 34.

10. See also G. Zanker 1987: 120–21, who summarizes the phenomenon thus: "aetiology was capable of being used as a vehicle for providing a much-needed sense of cultural continuity for the Greek intelligentsia resident in the newly founded city of Alexandria in the first half of the third century BC . . . this . . . will have helped alleviate the problem of cultural identity experienced by early Alexandrian Greeks."

11. Janan 2001: 134.

12. Callimachus *Aet.* 1.20: βροντᾶν οὐκ ἐμόν, ἀλλὰ Διός; see below for the generic implications of this passage.

13. Boucher 1965: 124 draws attention to this allusion as one of Propertius' strategies for rejecting a political life. Though he does not discuss it *per se,* the Epicurean resonance of the Vergilian passage adds fascinating depth and irony to the astrologer Horos' advice.

14. At 4.1.55, the wolf is similarly called the best foster mother (*optima nutricum*).

15. Johnson 2001: 10.

16. *TLL* s.v. *alumnus* 1796.52: *alumnus ad terras, regiones, urbes, sim.* See Propertius 2.33.15 (*fuscis Aegyptus alumnis*, Egypt with its dark nurslings), 4.1.37 (*nil patrium nisi nomen Romanus habet alumnus*, the Roman foster child has nothing of his ancestors except the name), 4.2.9 (*ille [sc. Tiberis] suis tantum concessit alumnis*, the Tiber granted so much land to his foster children), and 4.3.67 (*domitis Parthae telluris alumnis*, when the foster children of Parthia have been defeated).

17. See, e.g., Richardson 1977 *ad* 4.1.59; J. F. Miller 1982: 384; and DeBrohun 2003: 11.

18. *OLD* s.v. *disponere* 1a., and see also *TLL* s.v. *disponere* 1422.44, referring specifically to architectural layout.

19. MacLeod 1983: 143–44 also points out the poet-as-founder and sees the omen-taking at 4.1.68 as part of the ritual of foundation performed by the *ktistes*. DeBrohun 2003: 42 offers another, complementary interpretation of the parallel between city-building and poetry-writing. The growth of Rome from small simple town to grand expansive city, she argues, mirrors the poet's proposed expansion of his work from small and (relatively) simple elegy to grander and more complex aetiology. She deftly adduces, among other things, the poem's opening line, in which *hoc quodcumque vides* evokes both the cityscape and the poetry scroll as it is unrolled (36).

20. Newman 1997: 269.

21. For *opus* as a poetic word, see *OLD* s.v. *opus* 3a (genre) and 9c (a work of literature). For *surgo* as an architectural word, see *OLD* s.v. *surgo* 7a.

22. The famous story of Romulus' birds is told at Livy 1.6–7.

23. See P. A. Miller 2003: 187: "The poems in Book 4 ultimately represent a crisis in naming." By this he is referring to Propertius' habit of exploiting the full spectrum of meanings possible in elegy's syntax and diction, but the crisis in naming extends to the ways monuments' names call into question other ways of understanding their meaning.

24. Though not poetic catchphrases *per se*, these images all suggest a departure from neoteric delicacy. See MacLeod 1983: 144–45. Most suggestive is the chariot, which comes from Vergil *Georgics* 2.542.

25. *Contra* DeBrohun 2003: 185 ("a part of his song") and P. A. Miller 2003: 186 ("a small portion from his song").

26. Richardson 1977 *ad* 4.1.134 draws attention to Propertius' probable education for a career in politics.

27. "Matrix" is the word used throughout Conte 1986 for the horizon of expectations on the part of the reader that arise from a text's genre, against which the features of the text may be measured.

28. Richardson 1977 *ad* 4.1.45 reads Brutus the founder, especially given the *secures*, which evoke the consulate; Camps 1965 *ad* 4.1.45 sees the tyrannicide also. The catalogue of men appears *passim* in 4.1.2–50.

29. See DeBrohun 2003: 75 n.75. The five women of the first half appear scattered through the catalogue of men, more specifically, from 4.1.21–51.

30. DeBrohun 2003: 185.

31. Wyke 1987a explores how elegy 4.1's split-gender program manifests itself

in the multiple female perspectives—Arethusa's, Tarpeia's, Cynthia's, and Cornelia's—that follow in the rest of the book.

32. Recent examinations of the dual program of the introductory poem include Hutchinson 1984, who sees a juxtaposition of old and new that plays throughout the book; Warden 1980, who reads in the introduction and the other poems in Book 4 an alternation of aetiological and amatory poetry; Wyke 1987a, for whom gender is the shifting focus in 4.1 and throughout the book; and Stahl 1985: 255–79, for whom "war" (= Augustan) and "love" (= anti-Augustan) are the operative poles of interpretation. For J. F. Miller 1982: 381–82 with n.46, MacLeod 1983, and DeBrohun 2003: 33–85, the two halves of the poem indicate one complex rather than two discrete perspectives.

33. Perhaps Horos believes the omens failed because men have abused the gods for gain (*nunc pretium fecere deos,* 4.1.81); it is tempting, if fanciful, to see this accusation's applicability to Roman temples, built to the benefit of Rome or its citizens.

34. The mention of Conon brings Callimachus directly into the poem yet again, and with him Catullus. Conon had advised the royal court that a new constellation appeared in the sky; it came to be known as the Lock of Berenice and was celebrated in Callimachus's famous poem of that name, and in Catullus's reworking of Callimachus's poem (poem 66). Archytas, a mathematician, also theorized about the infinity of the universe; Horace *Carm.* 1.28 celebrates him. Horos' name also links him with the sun god and master of Hellenistic poetry *par excellence*—Apollo—through his namesake Horos, Egyptian sun god; see DeBrohun 2003: 19–20.

35. See MacLeod 1983: 149: "The implication is that in dealing with Rome's past Propertius would have to be a prophet of gloom as well as of gladness, to reveal how Cassandra was raped as well as what she foretold, to report impious words and deeds as well as pious ones. . . ."

36. Murgia 1989, believing that this sentiment makes no sense in Horos' mouth, transposes this couplet to 4.1's first half so that Cassandra utters it after 4.1.52. This transposition is not necessary: Horos speaks cryptically throughout, he responds explicitly and subtly to Propertius' aims and claims in 4.1's first half (*contra* Murgia 1989: 261: "Horos' monologue in 71–150 can reflect no knowledge of the poem which is 1.1–70"); and Ovid's evocation of the passage need not situate it in 4.1's first half (again, *contra* Murgia 1989: 261–62).

Chapter Two

1. Indeed, elegy 2.1.5–16 employs very similar language to demonstrate the poet's flexibility. DeBrohun 1994 reads Vertumnus' multiform persona as a signal of elegy's new indecorous, amalgamated identity in Book 4. Dee 1974 sees the *poikilia* manifested by the god as a testament to Propertius' self-proclaimed status as the Roman Callimachus in 4.1.69. For Shea 1988, 4.2 is a continuation of the program set out in 4.1 that elaborates on the multiple forms of the elegies that are to follow; Janan 2001: 15 and Newman 1997: 275–77 also treat the poem as programmatic. Finally, O'Neill 2000 provocatively reads Vertumnus' urban location in Rome's "red-light district" as a function of the poem's—and the book's—amatory undertones.

2. See Radke 1979 (1965): 318–20; Marquis 1974: 497; and Pinotti 1983: 90–91 for the various possibilities in interpreting Varro's text.

3. The mirror is reproduced in Marquis 1974: 498, with bibliography.

4. The consonant cluster -*lt*- easily shifted to -*rt*-. For the connection to *uertere* see, for example, Propertius 4.2.47, Ovid *Fast.* 6.409–410, and Porphyrio *ad* Hor. *Epist.* 1.20.1.

5. Devoto 1940: 246–247 discusses the proto-Latin form, and see Cristofani 1985 s.v. Voltumnus.

6. Colonna 1987 examines Etruscan precedents for the vocal patterns of Vertumnus' name, but Prosdocimi and Morandi, both responding to his arguments in the same volume (68–69), see Indo-European roots for the name. Prosdocimi suggests -*wetos*- (year) at play in the name and connects Vertumnus to the changing of the year, while Morandi sees the various meanings of the cluster -*urt*- (to turn, change, mix), indicating Vertumnus as a god of movement (*vascolare* is the word Morandi uses) and distribution (*mestolo*).

7. Porphyrio mentions the *sacellum* (*ad* Hor. *Epist.* 1.20.1).

8. Vortumnus in the times of Diocletian and Maximian, *CIL* 6.804.

9. Colonna 1987: 61 and figure 1; Coarelli 1992 (1983): 229–30; and see also Putnam 1967 for a precise description of the whereabouts of the monument. Cristofani, responding to Colonna 1987 in the same volume (68), argues that this dating is improbable because there was nothing in that urban sector before the Cloaca; he prefers a third-century BCE date for the *signum Vortumni*. Nevertheless, the bend of the canal around the monument is quite convincing. The *signum's* location within the *pomerium* (Colonna 1981: 163) also indicates the monument's antiquity in Rome.

10. Propertius 4.2.12–18 and 23–46.

11. Varro *Ling.* 5.46; Propertius 4.2.51. Varro's Etruscans fought under Caele Vibenna; Propertius' under Lycomedius (= Lucumo).

12. Vicus Tuscus named for Etruscan settlers at the time of Sabine wars: Varro *Ling.* 5.46 and Propertius 4.2.49–52, and Servius *ad Aen.* 5.560. After Porsenna's soldiers: Livy 2.14.9, Dionysius of Halicarnassus 5.36.4, and Festus 486–87L. After Tarquinius Priscus' supporters: Tacitus *Ann.* 4.65.

13. Richardson 1992 s.v. Vicus Tuscus

14. Cornell 1995: 156–59 demonstrates a strong Etruscan presence in (but not conquest of) Rome even before the Tarquins, and the existence of a cultural *koine* that allows for the horizontal mobility of Etruscans from Etruria to positions and ranks of similar prestige in Rome. His conclusions lend weight to Varro's and Propertius' early placement of Vertumnus in the city.

15. The goods traded on the Vicus Tuscus are too many to name here; see Aronsen in Steinby 1993–2000 s.v. Vicus Tuscus for details.

16. Richardson 1992 and Astolfi in Steinby 1993–2000, both s.v. Horrea Agrippiana.

17. As Radke says (1979 [1965]: 318), "bedeutsam ist auch die nichtrömische Bevölkerung dieses Stadtteiles."

18. See O'Neill 2000 for the seedy side of Vertumnus.

19. Ziolkowski 1992: 183–85 collects the sources: see, for example, *Inscr. It.* 13.2.494–95.

20. Fulvius Flaccus' triumph in 264 BCE is recorded in the triumphal Fasti (*Inscr. It.* 13.2 547). Festus 228L tells of the painting of Fulvius Flaccus in the temple.

21. For Beard, North, and Price 1998: 132–34, Vertumnus' arrival is a clear case of *euocatio*, and reveals an interesting shift in perspective on the practice: Vertumnus' would be the last known *euocatio* to result in a temple in Rome itself. After 264 BCE, conquered gods might be given a temple within Roman territory, if not Rome itself, marking a shift in the definition of "Roman"; whereas for Volsinii "Roman" meant "in Rome," afterward "Roman" meant "under Roman purview." Orlin 1997: 15, however, cautions against overstating the occurrence of *euocatio*, and later suggests (61–63) that foreign gods almost always came to Rome via the official channels of the Senate in consultation with the Sibylline books. Orlin doesn't consider Vertumnus' case explicitly, but his discussion of Camillus' dedication to Juno Regina through *euocatio* (the only case of the practice of *euocatio* explicitly stated in the sources) reveals many similarities between the two cases: both generals defeated Etruscan strongholds, both relied on key Etruscan gods already present in Rome, and both dedicated Aventine temples to these gods. Indeed, Flaccus' act may even suggest imitation of Camillus.

22. See Haynes 2000: 328–29 and Harris 1971: 115–18 for a discussion of Rome's political motives in 264 BCE. For the statues and their propaganda, see Pinotti 1983: 79; Gruen 1992 is an invaluable resource for the broader dynamics of cultural change in the third century. Haynes 2000: 330 records that two bases bearing Flaccus' name and traces of bronze statues have been found in the Forum Boarium.

23. Orlin 2002 discusses the Aventine, which lies between the Pomerium and the city walls, as a liminal space that marks the transition of foreign cults into Roman ideology.

24. Torelli 1995: 44–51.

25. See Andreussi in Steinby 1993–2000 s.v. Aventinus Mons.

26. Plebeian secession to the Aventine is noted by Livy at 2.32 and 3.50. For the *lex Icilia* see Dionysius of Halicarnassus 10.31–32 and Livy 3.31.1.

27. Livy 1.45. Dionysius of Halicarnassus 10.32 reveals that the plebs kept their treasury in the *aedes Dianae*, making it doubly marginalized as a plebeian and foreign place. For Diana's *dies natalis*, see Degrassi 1963: 494–96.

28. See Venditelli in Steinby 1993–2000 s.v. Dianae (*aedes*).

29. Livy 5.21–31, and see also Ziolkowski 1992: 194.

30. Clothing given to the Manneken Pis, often bestowed upon it by visiting dignitaries, is kept by the state. We do not know what became of clothing and offerings left at Vertumnus' statue.

31. Elegy 4.2 does not figure in the broad treatments of Stahl 1985, Rothwell 1996, Fantham 1997, or Janan 2001.

32. Umbria had long ago been absorbed into Etruscan territory, and Propertius himself seems to consider Umbria and Tuscany interchangeable; see, e.g., 1.22.6 (*Etrusca*) and 1.22.9 (*Umbria*).

33. Wyke 1987a: 156. Elegy 3.2.9 names both gods as Propertius' inspiration, and he writes hymns to each as well: 3.17 celebrates Bacchus, while 4.6 sings of Apollo.

34. Shea 1988 catalogues the poem's self-conscious literary puns, as Vertumnus speaks of his forms (characters, 4.2.1) and body (of work, 4.2.1), his signs (seals, 4.2.2), index (summary, 4.2.19), and figures (of rhetoric, 4.2.21).

35. Dee 1974. Other hallmarks of Callimacheanism appear in the poem, such as the epigrammatic trope of addressing a passerby and, of course, etymologies.

36. Shea 1988: 71.

37. Wyke 1987a: 156–57 and DeBrohun 1994: 53–56. Both scholars use the word "bipolar," though to different ends. For Wyke Vertumnus contributes to "a bipolar poetics, a programme comprising surprising and sometimes playful transformations of narrative voice and a range of elegiac tones" (157). For DeBrohun, Vertumnus seems to model the "bipolar poetics of Book IV" (54) in that his "wardrobe changes serve as an enabling strategy that allows the wearer to change from one identity to another, even its polar opposite" (55). In DeBrohun's reading, this bipolarity heralds not a new blended decorum for elegy but rather a meeting place between two usually incompatible poetic ideals (62, expanded in DeBrohun 2003: 172–75).

38. O'Neill 2000.

39. See Miller and Platter 1999, especially 453.

40. Marquis 1974 and Pinotti 1983 both stress the god's diverse ethnic heritage, as I do, and discuss some of the same passages in the poem as hallmarks of this diversity. Marquis' primary interest is in the diversity of Roman religious practices, not in Vertumnus' monument. Pinotti reads the poem as a paean to Rome's assimilation of other people that treads a delicate line between conformity with Augustan ideals and anti-conformity. It will be apparent from my notes the debt I owe to these two articles.

41. Propertius' language in this poem lends support to the theory, discussed above, that Vertumnus' official arrival resulted from an *euocatio:* Vertumnus' language at 4.2.4 recalls the ritualistic formula for *euocatio* as found in Macrobius *Sat.* 3.9.7–8. The resonance is discussed in Pinotti 1983: 79.

42. For Suits 1969: 486, the nuance is somewhat different: Vertumnus is proud to have an older Roman connection than his Aventine counterpart, and proud not to have deserted his original fatherland. Marquis 1974: 493–94 likewise reads this episode somewhat differently; Vertumnus had been in Rome so long that he had become naturalized by 264 BCE and did not mind becoming officially Roman at that time. To Pinotti 1983, Vertumnus' preference for a statue rather than an ivory temple straddles the delicate line of conformity; by rejecting the ivory triumphal temple Vertumnus avoids celebrating the achievements of the *gens Fuluia*, so recently connected to Antony; yet he simultaneously shows distaste for the splendid new Augustan monuments, such as the temple of Palatine Apollo. Boucher 1965: 147–48 explains the poet's choice of Vicus Tuscus Vertumnus over Aventine Vertumnus in terms of its resonance with daily rather than public life; the statue's antiquity lends it an accessible *"charme particulier"* (148).

43. Propertius probably leaned heavily on the Varronian tradition, but it is important to recall that Propertius' poem is a construction whose truth need not trade in factual accuracy; see Feeney 1998: 176. Interestingly, Varro adds a different Sabine element to the story, saying he was introduced to Rome by Titus Tatius, who built his first altar there: *et arae Sabinum linguam olent, quae Tati Regis uoto sunt Romae dedicatae; nam, ut annales dicunt, uouit Opi, Florae, Vedioui Saturnoque . . . idem Larundae, Termino, Quirino, Vortumno* (and the altars indicate the language of the Sabines, altars that were dedicated at Rome in fulfillment of a vow of Titus Tatius when he was king; as the annals say, he dedicated to Ops, Flora, Veiovis and

Saturn, Larunda, Terminus, Quirinus, Vertumnus; *Ling.* 5.74).

44. For Marquis 1974: 494 n. 14, these lines evoke 4.1.31, where Propertius counts as the three original elements of Rome the Sabines, the Romans, and the Etruscans.

45. Here I accept Postgate's emendation *credis id* along with Camps 1965 and Fedeli 1984, rather than Barber's 1960 (1953) *credidit* (accepted also by Richardson 1977), which, though attested in the best manuscripts, necessitates a lacuna. *Credis* preserves the epigrammatic feeling of the poem, with Vertumnus continuing to address passersby, and I find *seu* an unproblematic conjunction since it connects two etymologies in 4.2.9–10 and 11–12.

46. Dee 1974: 46–48.

47. Shea 1988.

48. Augustus *Res Gestae* 25.

49. Hardie 1998: 34. For Thomas 1982: 36–51, this passage emphasizes the costs of Roman expansion to Italy or, as he puts it in his commentary on the *laudes* (1988 *ad* 2.136–76), the result of "civilized man imposing his will on a natural, innocent or unwarlike world." Similarly Ross 1987: 215–19 sees the Italian Golden Age as a fiction. On the other side, Miles 1980: 119–29 and Gale 2000: 214–19 see the exaggerated praise of Italy as encomiastic or, at least, as a fantasy that encourages a sense of wonder. Still others refuse to choose between Vergil's celebration of Italy and the imperialism so closely connected with it (Perkell 1989: 100–7; Boyle 1986: 83–84).

50. See above for a discussion of Vertumnus' name; Devoto 1940 is especially helpful.

51. Cicero *Leg.* 1.5: *Ego mehercule et illi et omnibus municipibus duas esse censeo patrias, unam naturae, alteram ciuitatis* (I believe, by god, that he—and all citizens— have two fatherlands: one is the fatherland of their birth, the other is the land of their citizenship). Set in the countryside near Arpinum, this dialogue between Cicero, Atticus, and Quintus dramatizes the combination of Roman and municipal identity.

52. Johnson 2001: 7. The converse to the ambivalent émigré is the non-Roman who wants to be fully Roman—a phenomenon that is patently Roman in its perspective, given our sources. "Sidonian Dido" as examined by Hexter 1992 explores how easy it is for the Roman or Romanized reader to read Vergil's Dido as one such eager proto-Roman, while reading her as such ignores Vergil's hints and teasers about her Tyrian roots.

53. Publius Cornelius Scipio Aemilianus Africanus is a perfect example of the blending of natal and adopted identity.

54. Johnson 2001: 9–10.

55. For *signa* as a poetic plural for *signum Vortumni* see Marquis 1974: 492 (along with acerbic note 6) and Rothstein 1898 *ad* 4.2.2. For *signa* as *indicia*, see Suits 1969: 381 and Camps 1965 *ad* 4.2.2.

56. Wallace-Hadrill 1997 and cf. Rawson 1985: 102–3 and 233–49.

57. See Varro *Ling.* 6.78: *fictor cum dicit "fingo," figuram imponit* (when a designer says "I shape" he imposes a shape).

58. See Suits 1969 for the Priapea as a background text for this poem.

59. De Brohun 1994.

60. Hardie 1992: 75.

Chapter Three

1. Varro *Ling.* 5.41; Livy 1.10; Dionysius of Halicarnassus 2.38ff. (who cites Fabius Pictor [fr. 8P] and Cincius [fr. 5P]); Ovid *Fast.* 1.260–61 and *Met.* 14.776–77; Valerius Maximus 9.6.1; and Plutarch *Rom.* 17 (citing Antigonus, *FGrH* 816 F2) all support the traditional version. The traditional version also appears in a relief sculpture from the Basilica Aemilia, and on two coins: a Republican denarius from the Social War (*RRC* 244.2a–c with plate 45.7), and another denarius from the Augustan age (*BMCRE* 1.29–31 with plate 1.16).

2. See Richardson 1992 s.v. Tarpeia Rupes for a list of ancient sources that mention this feature of the rock.

3. A systematic discussion of the growth and use of Tarpeia's legend is much needed. Two such studies have appeared but are outdated and narrowly focused (Dumézil 1947 and Gansiniec 1949). A better model is Wiseman 1995.

4. Calpurnius Piso *apud* Dionysius of Halicarnassus 2.40, the first source to mention her veneration, puzzles over it. In order to explain the discrepancy between Tarpeia's treason and her veneration at Rome, Piso exonerates Tarpeia by making her a double agent. Also, Festus 496L mentions a statue to Tarpeia in the vicinity of the Temple to Jupiter Stator, but no vestiges of this remain and its date is unknown; Festus' statue also indicates a version of the myth that does not condemn Tarpeia.

5. Varro *Ling.* 5.41.

6. Plutarch *Rom.* 17 offers this option without attributing it to anyone in particular.

7. Simylus' elegy is quoted in Plutarch *Rom.* 17.5.

8. The "betrayal-for-love" motif, analogous as it is to many Greek myths, seems older than the "betrayal-for-greed" motif found in the traditional Roman version, and perhaps indicates Greek origins for Tarpeia's myth. See Hubbard 1975: 119–21 and Bremmer and Horsfall 1987: 68–70. As Bremmer and Horsfall suggest, Simylus' amorous Tarpeia and the contextualization of her treason during the Gallic sack may indicate that his elegy preserves an earlier version of her myth than that found in other sources. This version was then supplanted by the story of Manlius and the geese, and the myth of Tarpeia was retrojected to the Sabine wars. As Bremmer and Horsfall note, however, this reconstruction must remain conjecture and does not, in any case, require Simylus' elegy to predate Propertius'.

9. *RRC* 244/2a–c with plate 45.7.

10. For a renewed Sabine synoikism, see Morel 1962: 36. For a call to Sabine nationalism, see Gansiniec 1949: 25. In both cases Titurius' cognomen *Sabinus* seems to indicate Sabine sympathy. For a pro-Roman interpretation of the coin, see Evans 1992: 124–25.

11. See Cicero *Att.* 4.16.8 for the elder Aemilius' restoration; Plutarch *Caesar* 29 mentions Caesar's involvement; and Cassius Dio 49.42 covers the dedication by the younger Aemilius.

12. A full description of all parts of the frieze is given in Carettoni 1961. Most scholars date the frieze to the Julio/Aemilian restoration of 55–34 BCE; others see the frieze as a new creation of the Augustan age. For the earlier dating, see Carettoni 1961: 65; Arya 1996; and Albertson 1990. For the Augustan date, see

Kampen 1991b. P. Zanker 1988: 82 comments on the new Julian flair of the building without dating the frieze, and see also Evans 1992: 129–34.

13. Grimal 1951: 212–14 and 1953: 26–27. He sees this connection operative in Propertius' poem and reads the poem as laudatory of Augustus, but the Sabine-Numa connection is more applicable to the Julian use of the legend. As Albertson 1990 notes, the frieze as a whole seems to celebrate not only Romulus as an ideal king, but also Rome's evolving calendar—both themes that were pertinent to Caesar's rule

14. *BMCRE* 1.29–31 with plate 1.16. Turpilianus' coin is clearly modeled on the earlier denarius by L. Titurius Sabinus.

15. See Morel 1962: 38 for Turpilianus' Sabine roots. The pun may be at work in Propertius' elegy, 4.4.1, *Tarpeium nemus et Tarpeiae turpe sepulchrum* ([I shall tell of] Tarpeia's grove and Tarpeia's shameful grave). More on this pun later.

16. Wallace-Hadrill 1986.

17. Grimal 1953: 26–27.

18. See Kampen 1991b: 455–58, who includes the frieze as an Augustan innovation.

19. See Favro 1996: 130 and 156 for an overview of the phenomenon of dynastic imprinting in the Augustan city.

20. The Ara Pacis is the other conspicuous example of monumental women in Rome; this coincidence lends some support to Kampen's dating of the fragments to the Augustan rather than Julian period (Kampen 1991b: 450). See also Kleiner 1978, who argues that the women on the Ara Pacis are represented in their traditional, familial roles. They would thus also reinforce the marriage legislation.

21. Raditsa 1980.

22. Warden 1978: 180. See Carettoni 1961: 28 for a convincing discussion that this figure is Tatius.

23. For the gendered ambiguity of the erotic gaze see especially Kampen 1996b: 20–21.

24. Carettoni 1961: 32–36 describes the marriage scene, without commenting on its resonance as an anti-model for Tarpeia.

25. The message about the danger of unregulated female conduct was all the more emphatic in the context of the Basilica's other decorations. The Basilica had already been adorned with metal shields by Lepidus, its restorer in 78 BCE (for which see Favro 1996: 189). Given the prevailing explanation for Tarpeia's death (namely, that she was crushed by the shields of Tatius' troops) and the ideological association of the *Clipeus Virtutis* or Shield of Virtue, with Augustus after 27 BCE (*Res Gestae* 4.2), Tarpeia's resonance was complex: the Princeps, with his shield of Roman morality, would crush any such threat to Rome's greatness.

26. P. A. Miller 2003: 193.

27. Warden 1980: 108–9 links the reader's sympathy for Tarpeia and understanding of her dilemma with the shift of focalization the poem offers. Readers understand, in the frame of the poem, that Tarpeia's love constitutes sacrilege, but through her monologue they come to "experience the vitality of Tarpeia's love" (109).

28. Here I disagree with Tissol 1997: 149, who sees Propertius' Tarpeia as a naïve girl who deceives herself by ignoring Scylla's punishment, though she acknowledges her illicit love.

29. *Amor* and *Roma* are common terms in Propertian scholarship, generally applied to elegiac values or themes (*Amor*) and patriotic values or themes, including aetiology (*Roma*). See, for example, Wyke 1987a and DeBrohun 2003: 22–24 for the ways these two forms of discourse meet within poems.

30. Perrone 1991 defends persuasively the emendation of the manuscripts' *esse* to *ora* in 4.4.34, citing comparanda, paleographic plausibility, and the good sense required by the text (*esse* would render the couplet repetitive of the one before).

31. I prefer Camps' emendation of *nuptae* to *nupta* at 4.4.59 and his revised punctuation; the meaning remains the same, while the grammar is decidedly less awkward (Camps 1965 *ad* 4.4.59–60).

32. As DeBrohun 2003: 194 points out, Tarpeia's elision of her wedding clothes with her Vestal costume illuminates her own precarious situation and the uneasy mingling of *Amor* and *Roma* in Book 4 generally. In her reading, *molliet* adds an elegiac touch to martial Tatius.

33. Miles 1995: 211–19 discusses how the Roman myth of the Sabine women and the marriage legislation of Augustus promote marriage as an institution with greater societal than personal impact. See also Treggiari 1991: 90–94 for a more concrete expression of this desire.

34. Beltrami 1989.

35. Propertius 2.7 is the most explicit statement of this disdain.

36. Livy 1.4.

37. Ovid *Fast.* 3.11–24 and Dionysius of Halicarnassus 1.77.1.

38. Richardson 1977; Goold 1990.

39. Richardson 1977 *ad* 4.4.69–70.

40. So too is Tarpeia's broken water jar, according to Janan 2001: 74. Like the water that slips out of the broken jar, Tarpeia's sexuality escapes the confines of her priesthood. For Stahl 1985: 283, the tension is best expressed in Propertius' description of Tarpeia as a *mala puella* 4.4.17. The elegiac *puella* (as opposed to a *uirgo*) has sexual potential that she devotes to her lover. Were Tarpeia to break faith with the goddess she serves, she would be a bad (i.e., disobedient) mistress. Reading *mala puella* another way, unable to fulfill this sexual potential, Tarpeia is a bad (i.e., unaccomplished) mistress.

41. Beard 1980 and 1995.

42. Miller and Platter 1999: 453.

43. Stahl 1985: 285, and see also Scivoletto 1979 on Propertius' amatory landscape in Books 1–3.

44. Richardson 1977 *ad* 4.4.3–14.

45. Livy 1.55.5 gives as an etymology for the Capitol an actual head found there. Edwards 1996: 69–95, in her chapter "The City of Empire," discusses the religious and military messages the hill delivered to Romans, their subjects, their clients, and their enemies. See also Jaeger 1993 for the continued symbolic importance of the Capitol in Livy's day.

46. Though the Gauls had come close to occupying it, the Capitol had never been occupied by enemies (Livy 5.33ff.). Horace even describes eternity in terms of this hill in his famous *Carm.* 3.30, *usque ego postera / crescam laude recens, dum Capitolium // scandet cum tacita uirgine pontifex* (I shall grow fresh with future praise, as long as the Pontifex with the silent Vestal Virgin climbs the Capitol).

47. For this phenomenon, see Stambaugh 1988: 243–86. Cosa boasts an *arx*-style

Capitol; Timgad, a flat version.

48. Stehle 1989 discusses the "triumphal" arrival of two goddesses, Venus Erycina and Cybele, into Rome. The symbolic procession of these goddesses into the city to the location of their new Roman sanctuaries—in Venus' case, on the Capitol—resembled the triumphal ceremony in form and purpose. Tarpeia's journey down the Capitol reverses that procedure.

49. There may be multiple puns in this first line. Boyd 1984 sees *se-pulchrum* as its own play on *turpe*, with the privative *se-* commenting on Tarpeia's shameful situation. *Tarpeiae turpe sepulchrum* may also joke at the moneyer Turpilianus' name. Wallace-Hadrill 1986: 77 sees the pun operating in the other direction: Tarpeia's appearance on his coin puns Turpilianus' own name. However this pun operates, such multivalent play on names recalls, again, Vertumnus in elegy 4.2.

50. Tatius' camp encloses either the Lacus Iuturnus or the Tullian Spring. Camps 1965 *ad* 4.4.14 seems to opt for the former, while Richardson 1977 *ad* 4.1.3–14 clearly opts for the latter. Richardson's reasons are more compelling; it would be easy to encircle the Tullian Spring within a camp at the site of the future Curia.

51. Camps 1965 and Goold 1990 both print *scelus*.

52. Stahl 1985: 282–83. He finds the same contrast between "(Julian) arms and (pastoral) lover" in 2.34, a poem that values Vergil's *Eclogues* higher than his *Aeneid* (283).

53. See chapter 1 above for a discussion of the old-and-new Rome in elegy 4.1. Specific military and political monuments are situated in the proto-Roman pastoral landscape: the temple of Palatine Apollo (4.1.3), the Curia (4.1.11–12), and the house of Romulus (4.1.9–10). As noted in chapter 2 above, the characters that appear in 4.1's first half are, by and large, male figures from Roman history or women serving masculine interests. Even Tarpeia occurs in masculine form as *Tarpeiusque pater* (4.1.7), a name for Jupiter.

54. Stahl 1985: 254–55. See my introductory chapter above for a discussion of the term "focalization" as it applies to Propertius' poetry.

55. Suetonius *Aug.* 29.2.

56. Grimal 1951: 206. To Grimal, Tatius practicing on his horse must evoke the equestrian statue of Caesar (Tatius' descendant) in his Forum (1951: 208).

57. *OLD* s.v. *proludere* 1a.

58. For *ludere* as an erotic and poetic word, see, for example, Catullus 50.2. If Grimal 1951: 208 is correct that Propertius' readers would understand sporting Tatius as a prototype for Caesar's equestrian statue, then Tarpeia's interpretation of Tatius' activity is all the more misguided.

59. As O'Neill 1995 has shown, Tarpeia's urn acts as a metaphor for the more onerous, patriotic poetry Propertius eschewed in Books 1–3. When Tarpeia drops the urn, she rejects (consciously or not) her role as subject in such weighty nationalistic discourse and becomes the lover she wants to be.

60. In elegy 1.3, the lover adorns the sleeping Cynthia so as to create an erotic tableau that matches his feelings. He, like Tarpeia, is transfixed by his gaze upon the tableau. See Valladares 2001.

61. See above, note 31, for the textual emendation.

62. Fantham 1997: 135.

63. For Boucher 1965: 148, Tarpeia's punishment keeps the myth's moral intact, despite the elegiac focus on her amorous intentions.

64. From the Capitol: 4.4.29–30: *ab arce . . . uicino . . . Ioui.* To the Forum: *hinc,* 4.4.15.

65. The reader recalls that Ariadne, too, would be abandoned by the lover she helped. This is nowhere explicit in Tarpeia's mention of Ariadne, but as Whitaker 1983: 164 notes in summarizing the use of myth in Propertius (he does not discuss Tarpeia), " . . . we expect to find, and frequently do in fact find, other subtle and allusive links between the two."

66. *murus erant montes* (4.4.13) suggests the flatness of the valley where Tatius is encamped, and *patriamque iacentem* 4.4.87 hints at the flatness of the Capitol where the Romans are encamped.

67. Stahl 1985: 285 says this of Tarpeia's urban incongruity: "Tarpeia's thoughts are not at home in her country, but in an apolitical, individual, lyrical and pastoral world of her wishes." Janan 2001: 78 discusses the contribution the Maenad /Amazon simile (4.4.71–72) makes to the poem's surreal landscape. Why, Janan wonders, is a woman from Strymon running along the banks of the Thermodon? "Always, before thought can overtake it in this poem, the feminine is already elsewhere" (78). Warden 1978 also sees a spatial dimension to this simile, for the Maenad "bursts forth from her house out into the streets, the movement expressing as it were the making public of private emotions" (181). In her urban incongruity Tarpeia is like the women of the second half of poem 4.1 (see chapter 1 above), who find themselves in a poem whose climax and primary message is "Avoid the Forum" (4.1.134).

68. Gold 1993.

69. Stahl 1985: 285–98 offers the lengthiest treatment of the likeness between Propertius and Tarpeia, but see also Wyke 1987a.

70. She cites Ariadne and Scylla, blending variants of Scylla's myths to suit her amatory purposes. Her frequently shifting thoughts and her abrupt transitions are the effects of her heightened emotion and the tensions of her situation.

71. Her path is narrow and difficult, and she pursues trickling, not gushing, water; cf. Callimachus *Hymn* 2.108–12. For a fuller discussion of these nuances, see King 1990.

72. Other models include Ariadne's extended complaint in Catullus 64 and some of Dido's speeches in the *Aeneid* (such as *Aen.* 4.590–629). Indeed, Tarpeia's mention of Ariadne may be an allusion to Catullus' poem. Boyd 1984: 86 with note 6; Tissol 1997: 143–53; and Wyke 1987a: 163 all discuss the literary pedigree of the Tarpeia elegy.

Chapter Four

1. Grimal 1951 and 1953: 19; Cairns 1981 and 1984; Fedeli 1988: 92; Stahl 1985: 248–55; Johnson 1973; Janan 2001: 102–4; P. A. Miller 2003: 203–9; Connor 1978; Gurval 1995: 249–78; Nethercut 1983: 1840–41.

2. Williams 1968: 51–57, esp. 53; Sweet 1972; Arkins 1989; J. F. Miller 1982: 392–96.

3. See Barchiesi 2003: 2 for a discussion of this unique opportunity presented in our sources; he offers by way of example the different pictures Propertius and Ovid present for the Danaid portico, even though they mention the same decorative features (Danaids, Danaus, columns, etc.).

4. The vow at Naulochus is common tradition, found in Velleius 2.81.3 and Cassius Dio 49.15.5. Several Fasti attest its dedication date (*CIL* 1.316, 325 and 329 = the Fasti Praenestini, Amiterni, and Antiates, respectively).

5. For citations about all aspects of the temple, see Gros in Steinby 1993–2000 s.v. Apollo Palatinus.

6. Gurval 1995: 87–136.

7. P. Zanker 1983, and see also Favro 1996: 227.

8. See Galinsky's discussion of this dimension of the complex (Galinsky 1996: 219–20).

9. For the Danaid-portico, see Propertius 2.31.4; Ovid *Am.* 2.2.3–4, *Tr.* 3.1.60–62; Ovid *Ars am.* 1.73–74. In the latter two texts Ovid also mentions Danaus with unsheathed sword. Their husbands, the sons of Aegyptus, are attested by the scholiast for Perseus 2.55–56, cited in Bo's 1969 edition *ad loc.* The altar group is mentioned in Propertius 2.31.7–8; Pliny *HN* 34.17 alludes indirectly to the altar group, mentioning a heifer of Myron that was celebrated in familiar poetry.

10. Suetonius *Aug.* 29.3 and Cassius Dio 53.1.3 tell us about the library; Porphyryo *ad* Horace *Epist.* 2.1.214–18 attests to the statues of authors displayed there.

11. For the ramp to Augustus' house, see Carettoni 1988: 264 with figures 154–55. The park is attested by Solinus 1.18 (*silua quae est in area Apollinis*) and may or may not be part of the original complex.

12. P. Zanker 1983: 23–24. Vermeule 1977: 50 also sees this architecture as a transition piece between the Hellenistic complexes and later imperial complexes, such as Athens' Hadrianic Olympieion.

13. Late sources even mention a statue of Augustus with the attributes of Apollo in the context of the library. Camps 1967 *ad* 2.31.5–6 cites the scholiast for Horace *Epist.* 1.3.17: *sibi posuerat effigiem habitu ac statura Apollinis* (he had erected here a likeness of himself in the dress and posture of Apollo). See also Servius on *Ecl.* 4.10 (Vergil: *tuus iam regnat Apollo;* Servius: *et tangit Augustum, cui simulacrum factum est cum Apollinis cunctis imaginibus* [Vergil: your Apollo already reigns; Servius: And here he means Augustus, whose portrait was made with all the features of Apollo]).

14. Octavian's other early building projects assert the same theme. Octavian's mausoleum, built by 28 BCE, for example, attests his desire for burial in Rome (tradition) and evokes Hellenistic *mausolea* (innovation), such as the famous eponymous tomb of Mausolus at Halicarnassus. See P. Zanker 1983: 24–25 for the Roman context of the temple.

15. Candilio in Anderson, Giuliano, and Nista 1989: 85 discusses the stylistic resonance of the Danaid type and its analogue, the bronze Herculaneum dancers.

16. Apollo with his lyre may recall Euphranor's fourth-century BCE sculpture from the Metroon in Athens.

17. Gros in Steinby 1993–2000 s.v. Apollo Palatinus. Standing behind Apollo on the Sorrento base is the Sibyl, handing over her books into his keeping. The Sibylline books were kept in the temple sometime after 12 BCE (Suetonius *Aug.* 31.4).

18. Barchiesi 2003: 5–6 draws attention to the additional polysemy inherent in the use of—and more importantly, the description of the use of—Greek artworks in Rome.

19. Walker 2000: 71. P. Zanker 1988: 247–252 also discusses the inscription of ethics into Greek arts and draws upon the thoughts of Dionysius of Halicarnassus

and Horace *Ars poetica* to illuminate the confluence of literary, ethical, and visual values in the Augustan age. I would add Vitruvius' *De architectura* to his list.

20. His use of obelisks, especially the use of one as the gnomon of his famous and complicated solarium, inserts the Princeps into Roman space and time and likens his own role to that of the Hellenistic ruler-king. See, for example, P. Zanker 1988: 184.

21. See above, note 9.

22. Kellum 1993 (1986): 80–81 discusses this resonance; the Danaids and their fiancés are Greeks living in Egypt, like Cleopatra, and some ancient sources give Cleopatra as the name of one of the Danaids. According to Vermeule 1977: 49, Lanciani, collecting evidence for these decorations, confirmed the presence of columns of *giallo antico* and of the group of the Danaids; around three centuries earlier, some twenty Danaid torsos had been found on the spot but were mistaken for Amazons, who would ironically have fit just as well with the decorative scheme of the complex.

23. The waterbearers in *nero antico* currently in the Antiquario Palatino may be these Danaids, or may be replicas of a slightly later Julio-Claudian date. See P. Zanker 1983: 27 and Candilio in Anderson, Giuliano, and Nista 1989: 85–90.

24. This is the interpretation of LeFèvre 1989: 24 and later of Spence 1991: 14. Fowler 1991: 30 points out one serious problem with this interpretation—namely, that it is difficult to separate the Danaids from their guilt, even in (especially in) Augustan literature.

25. P. Zanker 1983: 30 posits this interpretation, and cf. Kellum 1993 (1986): 81: "In broader terms, however, these statues in the temple portico served not only as Cleopatra surrogates, but as an ultimate symbol of fratricide and civil war."

26. Kellum 1993 (1986): 80 points out that the guilty maidens consider supplicating Apollo at Aeschylus *Supp.* 214–15.

27. *BMCRE* 1.95 with plate 3.15. Slightly later coins from the imperial mint at Lugdunum seem to depict the same Apollo, though he lacks the platform with rostra; see *BMCRE* 1.459–62 with plate 11.7–9, and 478–86 with plate 12.1, 3–8. The reverse of both coins boasts Apollo *citharoedus* with plectrum and lyre and the legend ACT below.

28. P. Zanker 1983: 31. Alternately, as Kellum 1993 (1986): 82 believes, the coin could depict the cult image within the temple, which Propertius also describes in process of song. To Gros in Steinby 1993–2000 s.v. Apollo Palatinus, the coin more likely represents the victory monument at Nicopolis.

29. Gurval 1995: 279–91 argues against the identification of Apollo on Antistius Vetus' coin as the courtyard's god based on the incongruities between it and Propertius' description.

30. See, for example, Kellum 1993 (1986): 77–79.

31. While she admits their Actian evocation, Strazulla 1990 is cautious about reading the temple's terracottas as unequivocally Actian. For additional resonance of the gorgoneion, for example, see Strazzula 1990: 30.

32. Fowler 1991: 30–31.

33. Gurval 1995: 127–31.

34. Boucher 1965: 49 rightly notes that the semi-religious, ideal tone of Horace's poem befits his lyric genre, while Propertius' elegy effaces the fact that the place is, indeed, a temple.

35. Though Cynthia's name is not mentioned, she may be assumed to be the addressee. The fact that she is addressed in the last line of elegy 2.30 reinforces the impression.

36. See Fowler 1991 for a discussion on the ways ekphrasis intersects with narratology, and see the discussion of focalization in the introductory chapter above.

37. Richardson 1977: *ad* 2.31, introductory note.

38. Cf. Vergil *G.* 3.16, which accomplishes the same thing: *in medio mihi Caesar erit templumque tenebit* (in the middle will be my Caesar and he will inhabit the temple) holds Caesar in the middle of the line as he will be in the temple.

39. Fowler 1991: 29.

40. See, above, note 13.

41. Ovid calls them an *agmen* at *Am.* 2.2.4; the two elegists' passages together suggest they perhaps overwhelmed the courtyard.

42. Richardson 1977 *ad* 2.31.4.

43. Richardson 1977 *ad* 2.31.7, citing Pliny *HN* 34.57 and Petronius 88.

44. Though Vergil's temple is surely a metaphor for the epic poem he has in mind (Thomas 1988 *ad* 3.34), several details of the description evoke the Augustan building program. Barchiesi 1997b: 273 and Spence 1991: 14 both read the proem to *Georgics* 3 as a text in part about Apollo's new temple, then under construction.

45. Barchiesi 1997b: 272–73.

46. As Gurval 1995: 130–31 points out, only here does Propertius evoke victory and defeat, and only to lament the vanquished.

47. Indeed, Apollo has replaced Cynthia as a source of inspiration. See 2.1.3–4: *non haec Calliope, non haec mihi cantat Apollo. / ingenium nobis ipsa puella facit* (Calliope doesn't sing these things to me, nor does Apollo. My girlfriend creates all my inspiration).

48. Camps and Richardson 1977, for example, both in their introductory notes to 2.32, transpose something to smooth the transition (Camps delays 2.32.1–2 until after 2.32.9–10 and divides the poem; Richardson advances 2.32.7–8 to the beginning of the poem but retains the poem's unity).

49. Barchiesi 2003: 2 advises that "when we use Propertius to reconstruct the figurative program we should also pay attention to allusion and intertextuality." He goes on to discuss the complex reworking of Niobe drawn from Callimachus' *Hymn to Apollo* and Propertius elegy 2.31.

50. The poet's earlier scorn for Actian themes is most explicit in elegy 2.1; P. A. Miller 2003: 203–4 sees this detail as an indication of the contrast between the approach of the subjective elegist in 2.1 and that of the displaced subject in 4.6.

51. See the critical treatments mentioned in note 1, above, with the exception of those of Cairns, Grimal, and Fedeli. Miller 2003: 204–5 explores the limitations of applying the terms "patriotic" or "unpatriotic" to this poem.

52. This is the sustained argument of Gurval's 1995 book *Actium and Augustus:* that Actium was not necessarily the turning point, nor was it immediately understood as such, but that in the decades following the battle it took on new meaning as a crux between the old order and the new.

53. Arkins 1989: 248 draws attention to the ways this line defamiliarizes language, thus also defamiliarizing the battle of Actium which had become, as Arkins asserts, yesterday's news (246–47).

54. This monument, described by Strabo 7.7.6, burned soon after it was erected;

Strabo's report relies on hearsay.

55. Johnson 1973: 158–59 describes the artifice in this passage.

56. Mader 1990 *passim.*

57. For DeBrohun 2003: 222–23, loose-tressed Apollo calls to mind the Apollo who fosters elegiac poetry, in contrast to fierce-faced Apollo of epic poetry. Boucher 1965: 52–53, noting the existence of warrior Apollos in Greek art, proposes the possibility that a real artwork lay behind elegy 4.6's fierce Apollo.

58. Mader 1990: 325 mistakenly suggests that both Apollos, *doctus* and *heroicus,* were present in the complex (*doctus* outside, *heroicus* inside).

59. Barber 1960 (1953) does not capitalize this word, but, as described above, I believe it must in this context evoke the official title of Rome's first man.

60. See P. A. Miller 2003: 205–7 for an interesting discussion about the problems that arise from Propertius' backward-flowing consequentiality in this poem.

61. This is a common interpretation of the name change of 27 BCE. See, for example, Syme 1960 (1939): 313.

62. See 4.1.9.

63. Ahl 1985.

64. In light of the poem's two puns on the name "Remus," the repeat reader might see disturbing humor also in the poem's programmatic statement, *Musa, Palatini referemus Apollinis aedem* (4.6.11).

65. The word *moritura* also links Cleopatra with Dido; it is almost Dido's epithet in *Aen.* 4, appearing four times in the same form: 4.308, 4.415, 4.519, and 4.664.

66. Richardson 1977 *ad* 4.6.67 notes the confusion, but no one has made much of Propertius' periphrasis.

67. See, e.g., Pillinger 1969: 190–92; Sweet 1972: 170–71; J. F. Miller 1982: 393–95; P. A. Miller 2003: 203–4; and DeBrohun 2003: 214–15.

68. These are catalogued by J. F. Miller 1982. Miller is more cautious than I about the relationship between the poems: "We cannot insist on these 'echoes' too strongly, but it is still reasonable to say, in light of the other parallels between the two works, that Propertius probably used *hy.* 2 as a precedent for his poetic proclamation in a ritual context" (395).

69. See Haslam 1993 on *Hymn* 2.

70. Cairns 1981 and 1984.

71. J. F. Miller 2003.

72. See, for example, elegy 2.10.10, where Propertius had called the *cithara* his own instrument.

73. See also DeBrohun 2003: 220–25 and 233, who sees in the exchange of costume a comment on the new habit of elegy in Book 4; in her reading, even with his bow set down the god is still *Apollo victor,* a symbol of elegy's uncomfortable adjustment to grander themes.

74. Most MSS read *perque,* but the emendation seems necessary and felicitous. See Richardson 1977 *ad* 4.6.74.

75. Calame 1993: 51 notes these instances, calling them the "musical isotopy." Calame's words on these correspondences are suitable to Propertius' poem, *mutatis mutandis:* "So the celebrated programmatic scene where, kicking Phthonos back, Apollo opposes the river-song to the poetic drops of water from a pure source is equally an echo of the killing of the monster plaguing the site of the future sanctuary at Delphi."

76. Fedeli 1984 *ad loc.* emends to *tu deus,* against the manuscript tradition, and is supported by Lentano 2002, who argues that the line reveals a cultural anxiety over paternity and identity. Propertius' playfulness and tongue-in-cheek attitude toward the powers that be lend support, in my mind, to the manuscript tradition. P. A. Miller 2003: 207–8 discusses the ideological reasons for emendation.

77. This word rings loudly against the erotic *fides* expressed by Cynthia at 4.7.53; for the contrast, see Janan 2001: 101.

Chapter Five

1. Grimal 1953; Holleman 1977; Coli 1978.

2. McParland 1970; Pinotti 1977; Warden 1982; Cairns 1992; DeBrohun 1994; Anderson 1964 and 1992.

3. Janan 1998 and 2001; Lindheim 1998; Cyrino 1998; Fox 1998 and 1999; and Spencer 2001.

4. This date is attested in the Fasti Amiterni (= *CIL* 1².244):

HERCVLI · INVICTO · AD · CIRCVM · MAXIM

Rites to Hercules Invictus at his sanctuary next to the Circus Maximus.

5. For the triple triumph see the Fasti Antiati (= CIL 12.248):

AVGVST[VS] · TRIVMP[HAVIT]

Augustus celebrated a triumph,

and the Tabula Barberiniana (= *CIL* 1².77):

IMP · CAESAR · DE · DALMA[TI]S · EID · SEX
TRIVMPH · PALMAM · DEDIT
IMP · CAESAR · [EX · AEGY]PTO · XIIX · K · SEPT
TRIVMP[H]AVIT

Imperator Caesar celebrated a triumph over the Dalmatians on the Ides of Sextilis (August). He offered the palm branch. On the 18th day before the Kalends of September Imperator Caesar celebrated a triumph over Egypt.

6. Triumphators even clothed one of the Forum Boarium's many statues of Hercules in triumphal garb for the procession, and victors sometimes dedicated new statues or altars to the god. See Coarelli 1988: 165 for a discussion of the role of Hercules in the triumphal celebration, and Fox 1998 for a discussion of Hercules as a model imperialist.

7. Donatus *Vit. Verg.* 91 = Suetonius. *Vit. Verg.* 27. See Grimal 1988 for a discussion of Octavian's possible motives in timing his triumph thus.

8. See P. Zanker 1988: 44–45 and Gurval 1995: 92–93 for a collection and discussion of the sources for this association. The connection between Antony and Hercules appears in ancient literary sources (Appian *B. Civ.* 3.16–19 and Plutarch *Ant., passim)*, on coinage (*RRC* 494/2a with plate 58.23, with Antony on the obverse and Anton on the reverse), and in sculpture (preserved in a carved ring from Pompeii and perhaps at play in the lost *De Antoniis statuis* of Messala Corvinus, partisan of Octavian in the thirties; see P. Zanker 1988: 58). Though Gurval argues that the connection was within the bounds of Roman tradition and need not imply any political aims, I agree with Zanker that the cultivation of the association, particularly its Alexandrian precedent, was politically motivated.

9. See chapter 4, above, for the Actian nuances of the temple complex.

10. Thus Galinsky 1996: 222–24. I am grateful to John Pollini for pointing out to me that previous representations of this episode show the demigod running away with the tripod, such as is seen on the red figure vase from Vulci by the Berlin painter, or on the relief from the Siphnian treasury at Delphi. See Flacelière and Devambez 1966: 93–95 with figs. XI (1) and XI (2). Hercules' revised pose and calm stance in these reliefs suggest reconciliation rather than opposition.

11. It is even possible that the Princeps restored the Ara Maxima in the early 20s BCE among the 80-odd other unnamed shrines he mentions restoring in *Res Gestae* 20.4. For a contrasting view, see Huttner 1997, who denies any official or deliberate connection between the Princeps and Hercules.

12. Schultz 2000. For other restrictions at the Ara Maxima, see McDonough 1999.

13. At [Aurelius Victor] *Origo gentis Romanae* 8.5, the exclusion of women from worship at the Ara Maxima is coextensive with its control by the patrician Potitii and Pinarii. According to this source, Appius Claudius Caecus used bribery to change both restrictions. This account suggests that at some time the stricture against women was lifted. See Schultz 2000: 296 with note 23, and see also Mueller 2002 for a discussion of the mythic dimensions of the cultic changes in 312 BCE as the product of Augustan-age concerns over the extinction of *gentes.*

14. See most recently Fredrick 2002 about the connection between masculinity and nationalism in Augustan images. For another version, see Kellum 1997.

15. Janan 1998 demonstrates this connection in Vergil's *aetion* of the Ara Maxima, and see also Fox 1998 for the linkage of Hercules with masculinity and imperialism in other Augustan sources.

16. Hercules in the *Aeneid* has attracted a vast bibliography. In addition to Janan's 1998 study, see Winter 1910: 227–37; Galinsky 1972: 153–66; and Galinsky's 1984 entry in Della Carte 1984–1991, s.v. Hercules. Hardie 1986 explores the cosmic dimensions of the hero's appearance as a reenactment of Hesiod's Gigantomachy (110–18) and as a reinstatement of the hero's deeds and enemies vis-à-vis Lucretius' dismissal of their import (213–19). Grimal 1988 discusses the political nuances of Vergil's narrative sequence.

17. Galinsky 1972: 241 mentions this relationship in the reverse order: "it is hardly accidental that Octavian scheduled his great triple triumph on the day of the official annual festival of Hercules at the Ara Maxima . . . it is exactly on this day that Vergil has his Aeneas arrive at the site of Rome and, on that occasion, he develops most extensively the analogies between his own hero and the greatest hero of the Greeks."

18. Miles 1995: 220–24, and cf. Konstan 1986, who explores the tension between individuality and plurality from a different angle.

19. *Ampliorem* also signals the possible origins of Augustus' name from *augeo*.

20. Brouwer 1989 is a convenient collection of all the sources regarding this goddess and her worship.

21. Ovid *Fast.* 5.147–58 and Macrobius *Sat.* 1.12.21.

22. Flory 1984: 318 n. 29 suggests that the women had to be *uniuirae*, but this is unlikely. Livia, for example, would thus be excluded.

23. Social status may also have motivated Clodius' intrusion; he may have wished to assert his rights as a patrician (which he still was), or to curry favor among plebeians. See Brouwer 1989: 263; Tatum 1999: 85–86; and Fox 1998: 15 for speculation as to Clodius' motives. Tatum's discussion leaves in no doubt how serious Clodius' offense was.

24. Cicero speaks publicly against Clodius for his sacrilege throughout *De Domo sua, De haruspicum responso, In Pisonem,* and *Pro Milone.* For Caesar's divorce as connected to the scandal, see, e.g., Cicero *Att.* 1.13.3; Brouwer 1989: 365 n.318 posits Pompeia's childlessness as the real reason for the divorce.

25. A cursory scan of Brouwer 1989: 15–143 reveals men and women, freedmen and slaves, local politicians and private persons dedicating to the goddess. Brouwer discusses this variety at pages 254–67.

26. At Rome her primary sanctuary was restricted to women, as was the official nocturnal celebration, but elsewhere it was not. Roman literary sources therefore reflect the Bona Dea's official Roman rites rather than her broader, unregulated worship. See Brouwer 1989: 257–58 for this explanation.

27. For Cicero, according to Brouwer, the Bona Dea is guarantor of all that is holy and right about Roman tradition—all that Clodius violated—while the dedicants of inscriptions were concerned not with the goddess as a political symbol, but with her ability to help and protect individuals. See Brouwer 1989: 260 for Cicero's influence and 396 for nonpolitical responses to the goddess. Leach 2001 adds to Brouwer's conclusions the Roman cultural primacy of the masculine; Cicero used Clodius' cross-dressing as a way to effeminize his opponent, and thus devalue his political authority.

28. For Bömer 1957 *ad* 5.147, the discrepancy between the archaeological sources and literary sources results from a transition in the goddess's worship in the first century BCE from a strict, aristocratic, and gender-specific following to one that was gender inclusive and socially diverse. It is possible that the impetus for such an expansion of the goddess's appeal was perhaps the influx of foreign religious beliefs and practices in the first century BCE.

29. Cicero's strongest vitriol against Clodius comes in his *De haruspicum responso.* See, for example, *Har. resp.* 44: *P. Clodius a crocata, a mitra, a muliebribus soleis purpureisque fasceolis, a strophio, a psalterio, a flagitio, a stupro est factus repente popularis* (Clodius has cast off his yellow robe, his headband, his delicate sandals and his violet stockings, his breastband, his harp, his debaucheries, his adultery, and he has suddenly become a man of the people). Similar strong language is used in the fragments from *In Clodium et Curionem,* particularly fragments 5 and 23 with Crawford's 1994 commentary *ad loc.*

30. The shift from political to personal responsibility is marked at the end of the Republic, accompanied by a shift in the semantic range of words and ideas such as

concordia, libertas, and *amicitia.* For *Concordia/concordia* see Flory 1984: 315; for *libertas* and *amicitia* see DuQuesney 1984 and Kennedy 1992; and for the general trend of semantic and moral transition, see Wallace-Hadrill 1997.

31. The force and focus of Livia's urban activity is well discussed by Kleiner 1996 and Flory 1984. Livia restored the shrines of Pudicitia Patricia and Pudicitia Plebeia (28 BCE), Fortuna Muliebris (7 BCE), and Concordia (15–7 BCE); the last is linked by its date of dedication to Mater Matuta, Fortuna Virgo, and the Matralia festival for married women and *uniuirae.*

32. To be sure, one inscription even attests that the women of Forum Clodi took Livia's sponsorship of family values so seriously that they celebrated her birthday at the sanctuary of the Bona Dea. See Brouwer 1989: 104–5 (= *CIL* 11.3303) and Flory 1984: 320. See also Purcell 1986.

33. Kleiner 1996, but see Flory 1984 for a different view.

34. See Syme 1960 (1939): 229 for Livia's social status and Octavian's marriage to her as a felicitous means of social climbing.

35. The shrines to Pudicitia Patricia and Pudicitia Plebeia speak clearly to this aim. So, too, the porticus to Concordia. Livia dedicated this porticus in 7 BCE on the site of the extravagant villa of Vedius Pollio, willed to Augustus in 15 BCE. The return of this land to public use was a marked political statement against the excesses of the late Republican aristocracy. Her dedication thus complemented Augustus' *Lex Iulia de modo aedificiorum urbis,* a law with practical and sumptuary overtones passed around 7 BCE (it restricted the size of buildings in Rome). The portico was dedicated on the heels of Tiberius' victorious return from Germany; it is possible that he co-sponsored the dedication (Dio 55.8.1). Livia's sponsorship of this site, therefore, reinforced traditional social roles, traditional gender roles, and Augustan dynastic succession. Kleiner 1996: 32 and Flory 1984: 329 discuss such other possible motives for her dedication.

36. Whatever Clodius' motive had been in 62 BCE (for which see above, note 23), Livia's attention to the cult repopulated it with the better sort of Claudian devotee.

37. See Kleiner 1978 for this dynamic on the Ara Pacis panels. Kleiner argues that the Ara Pacis casts women in traditional female roles, i.e., wives and mothers. Kampen discusses the same message as seen in Severan art and other Augustan art (Kampen 1988 and 1991a).

38. Pinotti 1977 discusses these details. Add to Pinotti's list an allusion to the etymology of the Aventine from *aduentus* (Varro *Ling.* 5.43) at 4.9.3 (*uenit ad . . . montes*). *Inuictos* in 4.9.3 is attested in late manuscripts; the line is corrupt.

39. Anderson 1992: 101–2 draws attention to the humor, even absurdity, of the topography in this poem, as a hallmark of the poem's playful rather than cultic tone. For Spencer 2001: 264–65, such details emphasize the reader's perceptual reality only to destabilize it.

40. Rawson 1985: 236: "it is always at least worth inquiring whether a Roman antiquarian has political views." See also Wallace-Hadrill 1997. For a less charged interpretation of Propertius' antiquarianism, see Feeney 1998: 117 ("the category of 'ritual' does not constitute a focus of enquiry for him as it does for us: he has his eye on gender and genre, and is making these cults and myths work within that frame"). Still further away from politically motivated antiquarianism is Cairns 1992: 66 ("Propertius 4.9 is an elegy, not a piece of scholarship"); for Cairns the poem's literary, unresearched, even fictional content nevertheless serves real devotional contexts.

41. Beard, North, and Price 1998 vol. 1: 174 (original emphasis) and cf. the first chapter of Staples 1998.

42. Anderson 1964.

43. The celebrants are called *puellae* by the poet at 4.9.23, by the priestess at 4.9.59, and by the hero at 4.9.69. Everyone involved agrees on who they are. Anderson 1964 discusses the effect of the *paraklausithyron* on the characters of the poem but not on its places; DeBrohun 2003: 134–43 expands Anderson's treatment and examines the ways the religious *limen* and the lover's *limen* overlap to redefine hero Hercules as an elegiac lover, albeit a nontraditional one who refuses to follow elegiac convention by breaking through the closed door. For DeBrohun, Hercules' action is symbolic of the ways Propertian elegy in Book 4 similarly occupies a new poetic space.

44. Corbeill (2005), and note the *corollae* and *faces* that adorn the temple door at 1.16.7–8.

45. Shades of adultery color the other mention of the Bona Dea's rites in the Tibullan corpus. Though nominally acquitting himself of sacrilege on the eve of his death, at 3.5.7–8, the dying Lygdamus contrasts himself to friends who sport at Baiae (notorious as a place for liaisons) and then protests that he has not revealed the Bona Dea's secrets—i.e., he has been discreet about affairs.

46. Anderson 1964: 9.

47. I read the adjective with concessive force in the ambiguous line 50. The contrast with *mollis* in line 49 points to such a reading.

48. Plutarch *Antony* may exaggerate Antony's Herculean affinity (see Gurval 1995: 92 n. 14), but the abundance of detail bids for some truth. *Ant.* 4 tells us that Antony enhanced his natural physical resemblance to the hero by dressing in a low-belted tunic with a heavy cloak, and by swaggering; at *Ant.* 36 Antony uses Hercules' polygamous example to defend his own promiscuity; and at *Ant.* 60 the destruction of a temple of Hercules by lightning was considered a prodigy against Antony.

49. Kampen 1996a and P. Zanker 1988: 58–59. Since Roman ideology posited a connection between Roman success and Roman morality (i.e., behavior appropriate to one's gender and social status), sexual deviance and political instability formed a mutually reinforcing set of ideas. See generally Edwards 1993 for the best expression of this connection. Kampen 1996a demonstrates that after the Augustan age, as the East began to lose its negative resonance, Omphale and Hercules underwent a gradual shift toward respectability, appearing in funerary sculpture and on coins.

50. Both passages mention the specific feminine duties Hercules performed while in service to Omphale. The coincidence of the words *mollia, dura,* and *pensa* in each passage, combined in one sentence, with the hands being *durus* in both cases, cements the allusion. As DeBrohun 2003: 159 n.10 points out, *idem ego* signals "a sort of Alexandrian footnote" to the earlier poem.

51. Though Antony's name is left unspoken in 3.11, I disagree with Gurval 1995: 195 that his example does not figure prominently in Propertius' poem. To be sure, Propertius' focus in 3.11 is the power of women and not the defeat of men. Nevertheless, Antony's subjugation is hinted at in 3.11.29: *quid, modo quae nostris opprobria uexerit armis* (what about the woman who recently brought such shame upon our weapons?), and he is unmistakably evoked at 3.11.31–32: *coniugii obsceni*

pretium Romana poposcit / moenia (she demanded the city of Rome as the fee for her unclean marriage).

52. Griffin 1977 suggests this, but Gurval's 1995 argument to the contrary convinces me. See also Tränkle 1983, who sees Propertius' position toward the new regime as consciously aloof but not, nevertheless, Antonian or Republican.

53. This is the thesis of Stahl 1985: 234–47.

54. Plutarch *Ant.* 2.4 and cf. Cicero *Phil.* 2.44–45. Krostenko 2001: 293–96 discusses the political importance of Antony's display.

55. See above, note 21, for sources. It is tempting also to see an allusion to Appius Claudius Caecus, the censor linked with the history of the cult of Hercules at the Ara Maxima: he transferred jurisdiction over this cult from the patrician Potitii and Pinarii to the state. He also built Rome's first aqueduct, called the Aqua Appia. Perhaps *non clausisset aquas* in 4.9.43 hints at this public work.

56. See Spencer 2001: 273–75 for more embarrassments to Livia from the tradition of the Bona Dea.

57. Though his emphasis is not on the poem's monuments, Fox 1998: 15–16 reaches the same conclusion in his study of Hercules' transvestism. Touching upon Livia's restoration of the sanctuary, he writes: "Such an aggressive display of gender disorder is out of accord with the emphasis on harmonious state and family relationships to which Livia's proximity to the poem appeals. . . . Hercules here is acting as a symbol of resistance to any kind of ritually enforced socio-sexual order."

58. Miller and Platter 1999: 453–54 note how elegy draws attention to tensions and anxieties in Roman beliefs and behaviors as one of its primary generic strategies: "Augustan elegy, therefore, is an oppositional discourse, not so much because it represents a determined univocal opposition to a given set of values—Augustan or otherwise—but rather in the sense that it is constructed out of values whose inherent contradictions make conflict between elegy and Roman ideology a necessary condition of the genre's existence." For elegy's most pervasive *aporetic* notion, i.e., gender roles (which are not simply inverted but rather are hybridized or otherwise made ambiguous), see Greene 1995, and Wyke 1987b and 1989.

59. For Lindheim 1998, Hercules' and the priestess's differing views of how to define gender constitutes another layer of this elegy's *aporia*. It asks whether gender is constructed (i.e., defined by behavior and appearance—this is Hercules' method), or essential (defined by anatomy, the priestess's method). A similar *aporia* is posed by Janan 1998 and 2001, in whose reading Hercules' indeterminate gender confounds binary gender categories (and other binary categories) themselves.

60. Haslam 1993: 124 with note 28 suggests that the topos may have originally been assigned to Artemis. See also O'Hara 1996: 175 with note 4, who notes Artemis' humiliation as late as Eustathius.

61. Depew 1993: 66–69 traces the masculine outline of Callimachus' Pallas.

62. In the context of Hercules' transgendered experience, the name Tiresias also recalls an older version of his myth, from pseudo-Hesiod's *Melampodia*. Ovid preserves the tale at *Met.* 3.316–38. Tiresias, experienced as both a man and as a woman, was punished for his extra knowledge. To be specific, Hera blinded Tiresias for asserting the supremacy of women in attaining sexual pleasure. In the Hesiodic version, the gendered implications of Tiresias' punishment are even stronger: not only has the seer blurred the boundary between male and female—a threat to discrete gender roles—but he has also valued the female over the male

experience, upsetting the hierarchy normally resident in the binary system. See Janan 2001: 143–45 for discussion of the ways Tiresias' presence in elegy 4.9 unsettles traditional gender identifications. Similar gender upsets befall Tiresias in a lost poem of unknown date, assigned by O'Hara 1996 to the Catullan era. Though O'Hara, too, connects Tiresias' sex changes to elegy's tendency to meddle with traditional gender roles, he admits how dangerous it is to express certainty (179 and 215).

63. *Sitis* appears with a sexual connotation at Ovid *Rem. am.* 247; for *aestus* see, e.g., Propertius 2.33.43. See Anderson 1964: 12 with notes 26–27 for this and further erotic nuances in Hercules' actions, and cf. Warden 1982: 239 n.30.

64. For Cyrino 1998, this emergence is the purpose of the transvestism. Hercules' transvestism is an experiment that, functioning like a carnivalesque diversion, confirms the re-emergent masculinity of the hero. Such diversions, popular in Roman rituals and discourse, release the tensions that build up in Rome's highly stratified daily life. Cyrino discusses both Achilles' and Hercules' cross-dressing myths in detail and concludes that only the manliest of men could dress in female clothes and remain masculine: the transvestism of each hero " . . . serves primarily a conservative function: to reaffirm his high-octane sexuality" (217).

65. Ovid's Hercules does the same. At *Fast.* 1.581, Hercules himself founds the Ara Maxima, thus styling himself a divinity. As this *aetion* immediately precedes Augustus' appearance in the *Fasti*, Barchiesi 1997a: 97 finds Hercules' proactivity pointedly ironic.

66. I follow Barber's 1960 (1953) rearrangement of the last four lines of the poem; transposing the couplets prevents the jerkiness of address to reader then poet then reader and ends the poem with a prayer to the god (Camps 1965 *ad* 4.9.73ff., *contra* Richardson 1977 *ad* 4.9.73–74, who retains the MSS order and believes that 4.9.73–74 is an aside to explain Hercules' epithet). I reject the emendations *Sancum* for *Sanctum* in 4.9.74 and *Sance* for *Sancte* in 4.9.71 as unnecessary; the repetition of forms of *sanct-* is at home in an aetiological elegy.

67. Elsner 1995: 4–5.

68. P. A. Miller 2001 and see also Kampen 1996b: 20–21.

Chapter Six

1. Flower 2000 discusses the formation of this tradition in clear detail. She argues that the tradition of *spolia opima* arose with Marcellus' desire for extraordinary honors, and that Romulus' and Cossus' dedications were invented to provide a precedent.

2. *RRC* 439/1 with plate 52.18. The moneyer is probably P. Cornelius Lentulus Marcellinus, quaestor of 48 BCE. Marcellinus was surely trying to capitalize on the clout of the Marcellus name; see below.

3. See generally the comments in Horsfall 1989.

4. Wallace-Hadrill 1997 and cf. Rawson 1985: 102–3, 233–49. Atticus had pursued antiquarian topics long before his acquaintance with Octavian. During Cicero's lifetime he had composed his *Liber Annalis* tracing great families and events from the city's foundation—certainly a useful tool during the first century BCE's power struggles. See Cicero *Brut.* 14 and *Att.* 6.1, and Nepos *Att.* 18. P.

Zanker 1988: 103 posits that Atticus' suggestion was itself politically motivated (i.e., not neutral). It need not have been for Octavian to use it to his advantage, but overt partisanship on Atticus' part would explain Antony's interest in cultivating Atticus' friendship.

5. Specifically, ran the legend, he saw an omen of twelve birds as justification of his participation in a civil war. Suetonius *Aug* 95.2 and Dio Cassius 46.46.2–3 duly record the event; cf. Wiseman 1995: 144. For Romulus' role in the propaganda of Caesar's heir, see Gagé 1930: esp. 140–45.

6. Livy 1.33.9 reports that Ancus Marcius had enlarged the temple to commemorate new military victories.

7. Dionysius of Halicarnassus 2.72. Livy attributes the creation of the college to Ancus Marcius (1.32) and describes their rites in detail under his kingship, but the rites appear earlier when Tullus Hostilius uses them (1.24).

8. Livy 1.24 and 32 offers the fullest discussion of their rites and duties, but see Wiedemann 1986 for a discussion of the problems with the sources and the evolution of the rites.

9. Paulus ex Festus 92 = p. 81 Lindsay: *Feretrius Iuppiter . . . ex cuius templo sumebant sceptrum per quod iurarent et lapidem silicem quo foedus ferirent* (Jupiter Feretrius . . . from whose temple they took the scepter by which they swore and the silex stone by which they struck their treaty).

10. As Wiedemann 1986 suggests, Octavian might have introduced the act of throwing the spear into symbolically foreign territory in Rome (instead of into actual enemy territory) as part of the ritual Fetial activity. He adds (482), "of course, once that had been done, it became an age-old tradition forthwith." Wiedemann suggests that justification for the spear throwing might have been found in Varro's *Calenus;* as for the location in Rome (482–83), the (new) location for this sort of ritual within Rome demonstrates more its propaganda value than its sacramental significance; it was as important for Romans to see the ritual as it was for the gods to see it.

11. Dio Cassius 44.4.3. Some take Dio's reference as anachronistic, and the honor as given to Octavian instead (Platner and Ashby 1929 s.v. Iuppiter Feretrius, *aedes* and Syme 1959: 44 n. 85); but the coin of Marcellinus from 44 BCE (*RRC* 439/1 with plate 52.18) suggests the topic was in the air, and the arguments of Harrison 1989: 408–9 are compelling.

12. Rich 1996 argues that Crassus never requested the honor of dedicating *spolia opima.* I am inclined to disagree, but in any case he may have been forestalled.

13. Gallus and Crassus were connected in other ways as well. Syme 1960 (1939): 310 brings to attention *CIL* 6.21308, which shows a Licinia, daughter of Paullus and wife of Gallus, buried in the tomb of the Crassi.

14. Recent opinion has separated the Crassus affair from the settlement, arguing that the settlement must have been well under way when Crassus became (in)eligible for his claim (see Flower 2000: 50). Crassus may not have caused the settlement, but it is difficult to separate the potential embarrassment his situation created from the terms that precluded the possibility of its being repeated; see Syme 1960 (1939): 309ff. for the still compelling arguments.

15. Levick 1975: 158–59 suspects his presence behind the trial of Primus in 23 BCE.

16. Members of the imperial family may have been exempt from the stricture:

Rich 1999 plausibly suggests that Drusus hoped to dedicate *spolia opima* and that this would have been acceptable to the Princeps.

17. *BMCRE* 1.315 with plate 5.20, 1.366–75 with plates 7.18–20 and 8.1–5, and 1.704 with plate 17.2 all show a round temple with the legend Mars Ulto(r), with the legend *signis receptis* on the reverse. P. Zanker 1988: 186–87 and Càssola 1970: 25–26 (following Platner and Ashby 1927 among others) believe the Capitoline temple of Mars Ultor was actually built, but Simpson 1977 makes strong arguments against the existence of this temple. Reusser in Steinby 1993–2000 s.v. Mars Ultor (Capitolium) discusses the controversy that arises from the coins, but declines to vote. As for the temporary storage of the standards in the temple of Jupiter Feretrius, Horace *Carm.* 4.15.6 speaks of the standards as a benefit to our Jove (*nostro Ioui*); of course, there were three temples to Jupiter on the Capitol at the time, but the special nature of these spoils to me admits the possibility that *nostro Iovi* refers to Feretrius.

18. *Inscr. It.* 13.3.86. See P. Zanker 1988: 202–3 and Putnam 1985: 238 and note 6.

19. See Barchiesi 2002 for a discussion of Ovid's representation of Augustus' Forum.

20. Other military honors and functions were transferred to the new temple of Mars Ultor; see Kockel in Steinby 1993–2000 s.v. Forum Augustum.

21. *M. Varro ait opima spolia esse, etiam si manipularis miles detraxerit, dummodo duci hostium* (M. Varro says that they are still *spolia opima*, even if a common soldier has taken them, provided he has taken them from the leader of the enemy).

22. As Rich 1999 demonstrates, Drusus may have aspired to dedicate *spolia opima* had he not died prematurely; in honor of Drusus' curtailed potential, Augustus dedicated the laurels from his fasces to Jupiter Feretrius rather than to Jupiter Optimus Maximus just after Drusus' death (Dio Cassius 55.5.1, and see Rich 1999: 354).

23. See Càssola 1970 *passim*, and especially pages 10 and 24–26.

24. Livy calls him Augustus in this chapter, which must therefore have been written after January 27 BCE.

25. No need to recreate the complete roster of cynics collected by Flower 2000: 53 and note 105 (and cf. 44 and note 55) , to which I would add now Forsythe 1999: 63–64 with note 22 who, though he believes the passage is not a later interpolation, nevertheless sees Livy's preference for his own annalistic evidence.

26. Miles 1995: 44–47.

27. *OLD* s.v. *auctor* 14a.

28. Harrison 1989: 411, and see also Hubbard 1975: 131.

29. To wet: *OLD* s.v. *imbuo* 1a (to wet), 1b (to stain), and 1c (to stain with blood).

30. Richardson 1977 *ad* 4.10.6.

31. See *OLD* s.v. *occupo* 11b for the violent connotations of this word. *Occupat* also appears at 4.4.84, in which either Tarpeia or Tatius silences the Capitol's watchdog—presumably by slitting its throat.

32. Richardson 1977 *ad* 4.10.15, responding to Camps 1965 *ad* 4.10.15; the latter believes that "nothing can be gained from analysis in such a case."

33. Camps 1965 *ad* 4.10.21 reads *neque* as common to *fulgebat* and *picta*, because the passage stresses the austerity of Romulus' equipment. Even a painted shield would be ostentatious.

34. At 4.1.61 this adjective describes Ennius' shaggy crown (as opposed to Bacchus' soft ivy garland), and at 4.4.28 bristly brambles damage Tarpeia in her

quest for love. At 4.9.49 Hercules contrasts the soft bra he wore in the service of Omphale with the shaggy breast it (surely unsuccessfully) tried to conceal.

35. Rothstein 1898 *ad* 4.10.13. *redis* at 4.1.6 supports Rothstein's sequence.

36. Similarly Romulus fights with a crude *parma*, while Aeneas bears the grand *clipeus*.

37. The presence of Roman horses—even the notion of cavalry (Acron's horse at 4.10.8 suggests the existence of mounted fighters)—need not indicate that Cossus was *magister equitum*, as Richardson 1977 suggests *ad* 4.10.38; nor need they be the horses of the triumphal chariot, a possibility that Camps 1965 *ad* 4.10.38 puts forward (albeit skeptically).

38. Fantham 1997: 132: " . . . the elegy depends for its effect as much on spatial as on temporal advance, from the first defence of the original city to the victory that ensured the safety of Italy itself from the barbarian."

39. As Richardson 1977 points out *ad* 4.10.25–26, Veii "was Rome's first serious invasion of Etruscan territory." Camps 1965 *ad* 4.10.25 also retains the original manuscript order, arguing that it heightens the pathos of Veii's fall.

40. Nethercut 1983: 1851. The phenomenon is also discussed by Janan 2001: 197–98 n. 13.

41. Coli 1996: 266, citing Plautus, Catullus, Ovid, and Tacitus among others.

42. Parker 1992 traces the image of agricultural fertility through human death back to Archilochus.

43. Umbria had long been part of Etruscan territory when Propertius was writing; see Richardson 1977 *ad* 1.21.9–10. See also Newman 1997: 54 n. 1 for a collection of sources about Propertius' Etrurian heritage, to whose bibliography should be added Guarducci 1986.

44. Nethercut 1983: 1839. On that same page Nethercut broadly connects elegies 4.10 with 1.21 and 1.22 through their "review of Rome's contacts with her neighbors in the peninsula." This connection and the book's ending on the death of a loved one and the solitude of the bereaved demonstrate the culmination in the fourth book of themes introduced earlier: "to set the rhythms of love—of desire, of possession, separation and death—within the context of life itself, the lives of other men and women, the life of Italy."

45. For example, in 1.7 Propertius refuses to campaign abroad with Tullus so that he can remain in Rome under Cynthia's thumb. Newman 1997: 68 n. 26 interprets the *sphragis* poems differently: Propertius is trying to curry favor with Etruscan Maecenas, and places responsibility for his kinsman's loss in the war on bandits, not Caesar. While Newman is here right that "at least two soldiers escaped with their lives, and perhaps more," words such as *dolor* and *miser* suggest a darker tone. In this interpretation he stands against Putnam 1976, Stahl 1985: 99–129, and others who see the *sphragis* poems as condemnatory.

46. Sullivan 1976: 137 n. 26.

47. The siege at Perusia is referred to in Appian *B Civ.* 5.5.49, Dio Cassius 48.14.3, Suetonius *Aug.* 15, Velleius 2.74.4, and Seneca *Clem.* 1.11.1.

48. See Gabba 1986 for land encroachment as the cause of the war.

49. See Syme 1960 (1939): 212 for the circulation of the legend of the *arae Perusinae*—an exaggeration of accounts of what Syme terms a few "judicial murders." Or, the legend may stem from a hostile (Italian or even Perusine) perspective on the incident.

50. The arch of the gate is Etruscan; the superstructure on the arch is Roman, of Augustan date. See Scullard 1967: 159–60 with plate 78.

51. See Janan 2001: 197–98 n. 13, following Weeber's 1977 dissertation. On Aeneas' shield (*Aen.* 8.659–62), the Gauls wear striped cloaks and golden necklaces (to match their gold hair and clothes). Oddly, they carry the *scutum*, which would not make such a striking contrast with their large bodies as does Propertius' *parma*.

52. Grimal 1953: 14.

53. Rich 1999 examines in great detail Drusus' intention to dedicate *spolia opima* from his German campaign, and the Princeps' corresponding attention to Jupiter Feretrius. See also Flower 2000.

54. *Causa* would soon be used by Ovid in marking out Callimachean territory as well (*Fast.* 1.1).

55. Pentad, if we include the allusion to Cicero, who had translated Aratus' text into Latin, and the Alexandrian, antiquarian Varro; as Newman points out (1997: 124–25), Cicero had eulogized Varro with the phrase *causas aperuisti* (*Acad.* 1.3). See J. F. Miller 1982: 385.

56. Camps 1965 and Richardson 1977, both *ad* 4.10.4, emphasize the difficulty.

57. For a sound overview, see J. F. Miller 1982. Redefinition of Callimacheanism in Book 4 is one of the theses of DeBrohun 2003 (see, e.g., 3).

58. See Coarelli in Steinby 1993–2000 s.v. Iuppiter Feretrius (*aedes*).

59. The elegist's approach toward and access to the temple of Jupiter Feretrius is all the more striking given that it was probably not open to the public; recall its caved-in roof before Augustus' restoration, and the fact that Livy did not see the spoils themselves but relied on Augustus' description of them. See Càssola 1977: 26–27, who speaks about the sanctity of armor dedicated to the gods, but cf. Rawson 1991 on the pervasive presence and importance of spoils in the city. Miles 1995: 45–47 offers a different, more cynical explanation for Livy's apparent lack of acquaintance with the spoils: whether he saw them or not, Livy deliberately effaces his own certainty about them in order to cast doubt on Augustus' certainty. Versnel 1970: 311–13, discussing the difference between the triumphal ceremony, Etruscan in origin, and the very Roman *spolia opima,* posits a different reason for the inaccessibility of the *spolia opima* once dedicated: they were trophies containing magical power; therefore, they were to be treated with caution as well as respect. It is also for this reason that they are so rare, to Versnel.

60. Galinsky 1969: 91. He catalogues the triumphal imagery in Arethusa's poem, in Cynthia's return from Lanuvium, and in Cornelia's praise for her husband. To these I would add the triumphal imagery in Tarpeia's poem, in which the troubled girl paces the triumphal route, and 4.2, in which Vertumnus watches from the sidelines.

61. Livy suggests *ferre* (1.10.5), Servius and Plutarch *ferire* (*ad Aen.* 8.641, Marcellus 8.4); Festus offers both (81L), and Dionysius of Halicarnassus posits the Greek ὑπερφερέτης (2.34.4), meaning "preeminent," from φέρω.

62. There is an embedded third option: Feretrius from *feretrum*, bier. Richardson 1977 *ad* 4.10.45–46 sees this etymology at work, as a result of which he does not capitalize *feretri* at 4.10.45. I subordinate this option because of its obvious connection to *ferre,* and because of the grammatical difficulties that must accompany a lowercase *feretri.*

63. Janan 2001: 197–98 n. 13 draws attention to the sure omen and to the poet's

silence about the gods' approval—or lack thereof—for the second etymology. For Janan, the rival etymologies resist masculine closure on the topic and betray instead the poet's persistent feminine—i.e., open—logic.

64. Richardson 1977 points to these and other playful clusters in his introductory note to poem 4.10.

65. See particularly Janan 2001: 197–98 n. 13 and Wyke 1987a: 171.

66. Other such titles were floating around as well; Ennius had called Romulus *custos patriae* (*Ann.* 108–9); Livy had called him *parens urbis Romae* (1.16). As Favro 1996: 225–26 points out, the abundance of images of the Princeps himself that adorned the city reminded those who moved through it that Augustus was the *pater urbis* as well as the *pater patriae*. Horace *C.* 3.24.27–29 connects the phrase with urban adornment and with a clear allusion to Augustus: *si quaeret pater urbium subscribi statuis, indomitam audeat refrenare licentiam* (if the patron of the cities seeks to be commemorated with statues, let him be bold enough to rein in unbridled excess).

67. Putnam 1985: 239 n.10 discusses Romulus' title as parent of the city in the context of Vergil *Aen.* 6.777–808, connecting Romulus to Augustus as renewer of the city and of virtue.

Epilogue

1. Tränkle 1983: 161 similarly contrasts the lively warmth of elegy 4.2 with the distant chill of elegy 4.10 to demonstrate that the poet's celebration of Roman rites, days, and places retains a certain aloofness vis-à-vis affairs of the state that his earlier poetry had expressed outright. Indeed, for Tränkle, elegy 4.2's appeal lies to a great extent in the fact that Vertumnus' monument lacks an ideological program.

2. Pound 1994 [1958]: 10.

3. See also Hardie 1992 on the poetic mutability of Rome in the Augustan age.

4. Janan 2001: 198 n. 13 takes the broadest view of the power of this pairing, as a comment on "the vicissitudes of fortune" in general. Rothwell 1996: 850 sees the pairing as proof of the inevitable triumph of nature over constructed culture. See also Newman 1997: 67–68, who draws no conclusions.

BIBLIOGRAPHY

Ahl, F. 1985. *Metaformations. Soundplay and Wordplay in Ovid and Other Classical Poets.* Ithaca: Cornell University Press.

Albertson, F. 1990. "The Basilica Aemilia Frieze: Religion and Politics in Late Republican Rome." *Latomus* 49: 801–15.

Alföldy, G. 1991. "Augustus und die Inschriften: Tradition und Innovation. Die Geburt der imperialen Epigrafik." *Gymnasium* 98: 289–324.

Alfonsi, L. 1979 (1945). *L'elegia di Properzio.* New York: Garland.

Anderson, M. L., A. Guiliano, and L. Nista. 1989. *Radiance in Stone: Sculptures in Colored Marble from the Museo Nazionale Romano.* Rome: De Luca Edizion d'Arte.

Anderson, W. S. 1964. "Hercules *Exclusus:* Propertius IV.9." *AJPh* 85: 1–12.

_____. 1992. "Limits of Genre: Response to Francis Cairns." In Karl Galinsky, ed. *The Interpretation of Roman Poetry: Empiricism or Hermeneutics?* 96–103. Frankfurt-am-Main: Peter Lang.

Arkins, B. 1989. "Language in Propertius 4.6." *Philologus* 133: 246–51.

Arya, D. A. 1996. "The Figural Frieze of the Basilica Aemilia: A New Perspective in Building Context and Pentelic Marble." Master's thesis, University of Texas at Austin.

Bal, M. 1985. *Narratology: Introduction to the Theory of Narrative.* C. van Boheemen, trans. Toronto: University of Toronto Press.

Barber, E. A. 1960. (1953). *Sexti Properti Carmina.* Oxford: Oxford University Press.

Barchiesi, A. 1997a. *The Poet and the Prince: Ovid and Augustan Discourse.* Berkeley: University of Califonia Press.

_____. 1997b. "Virgilian Narrative: Ecphrasis." In C. Martindale, ed. *Cambridge Companion to Vergil,* 271–81 Cambridge: Cambridge University Press.

_____. 2002. "Martial Arts. Mars Ultor in the Forum Augustum: A Verbal Monument with a Vengeance." In G. Herbert-Brown, ed. *Ovid's Fasti: Historical Readings at Its Bimillenium,*1–22. Oxford: Oxford University Press.

_____. 2003. "Learned Eyes: Poets, viewers, and image-makers." Online essay found at http://www.utexas.edu/depts/classics/events/barchiesi03.html.

Beard, M. 1980. "The Sexual Status of Vestal Virgins." *JRS* 70: 12–27.

_____. 1995. "Re-reading (Vestal) Virginity." In R. Hawley and B. Levick, eds., *Women in Antiquity: New Assessments,*166–77. London: Routledge.

_____, J. North, and S. Price. 1998. *Religions of Rome. Vols. I-II.* Cambridge: Cambridge University Press.

Becker, A. S. 1995. *The Shield of Achilles and the Poetics of Ekphrasis.* Lanham, MD: Rowman and Littlefield.

Beltrami, L. 1989. "Properzio 4.4: La colpa della Vestale." In G. Catanzaro and F. Santucci, eds., *Tredici Secoli di Elegia Latina,* 267–72. Assisi: Accademia Properziana del Subasio.

Benediktson, D. T. 1989. *Propertius: Modernist Poet of Antiquity.* Carbondale, IL: Southern Illinois University Press.

Bing, P. 1988. *The Well-Read Muse: Present and Past in Callimachus and the Hellenistic Poets.* Göttingen: Vanderboeck and Ruprecht.

Bo, Dominic. 1969. *A. Persi Flacci Saturarum Liber.* Turin: Paravia.

Bömer, F. 1957. *P. Ovidius Naso: Die Fasten I, II.* Heidelberg: Carl Winter Verlag.

Boucher, J.-P. 1965. *Études sur Properce: Problèmes d'inspiration et d'art.* Paris: de Boccard.

Boyd, B. W. 1984. "Tarpeia's Tomb: A Note on Propertius 4.4." *AJPh* 105: 85–86.

Boyle, A. J. 1986. *The Chaonian Dove: Studies in the Eclogues, Georgics, and Aeneid of Virgil.* Leiden: Brill.

_____. 2003. *Ovid and the Monuments: A Poet's Rome. Ramus* Monographs 4.

Bremmer, J. N., and N. M. Horsfall. 1987. *Roman Myth and Mythography. BICS* Supplement 52.

Brouwer, H. H. J. 1989. *Bona Dea: The Sources and a Description of the Cult.* Leiden: Brill.

Cairns, F. 1981. "L'elegia IV.6 di Properzio: Mannerismo ellenistico e classicismo Augusteo." *Colloquium Propertianum* 3: 97–115.

_____. 1984. "Propertius and the Battle of Actium (4.6)." In T. Woodman and D. West, eds. *Poetry and Politics in the Age of Augustus.* Cambridge: 129–68, 229–36.

_____. 1992. "Propertius 4.9: Hercules *Exclusus* and the Dimensions of Genre." In Karl Galinsky, ed., *The Interpretation of Roman Poetry: Empiricism or Hermeneutics?* 65–95. Frankfurt-am-Main: Peter Lang.

Calame, C. 1993. "Legendary Narration and Poetic Procedure in Callimachus' *Hymn to Apollo.*" In M. A. Harder, R. F. Regtuit, and G. C. Wakker, eds., *Callimachus,* 37–55. Groningen: Egbert Forster.

Cameron, A. 1995. *Callimachus and His Critics.* Princeton: Princeton University Press.

Camps, W. A. 1965. *Propertius Elegies Book IV.* Cambridge: Cambridge University Press.

_____. 1967. *Propertius Elegies Book II.* Cambridge: Cambridge University Press.

Carettoni, G. 1961. "Il fregio figurato della Basilica Emilia: rinvenimento, dati tecnici, collocazione." *RIA* 10: 5–78.

_____. 1988. "Die Bauten des Augustus auf dem Palatin." In M. Hofter, ed. *Kaiser Augustus und die verlorene Republik: Eine Ausstellung im Martin-Gropius-Bau, Berlin 7. Jun–14. August 1988,* 263–67. Berlin: Phillip von Zabern.

Càssola, F. 1970. "Livio, il tempio di Giove Feretrio, e la inaccessibilità dei santuari in Roma." *RSI* 82: 5–31.

Clausen, W. V. 1964. "Callimachus and Roman Poetry." *GRBS* 5: 181–96.

Coarelli, F. 1988. *Il Foro Boario: dalle origini alla fine della Repubblica.* Rome: Quasar.

_____. 1992 (1983). *Il Foro Romano: Periodo Arcaico.* Rome: Quasar.

Coli, E. 1978. "Properzio IV.9 e il culto della Bona Dea." *GIF* 9:298–305.

_____. 1996. "L'Umbria nell'elegia Latina." In G. Bonamente and F. Coarelli, eds.,

Assisi e gli Umbri nell'antichità, 265–75. Assisi: Minerva.

Colonna, G. 1981. "Quali Etruschi a Roma." In G. Colonna, ed. *Gli Etruschi e Roma*, 159–70. Rome: L'Erma de Bretschneider, 159–70.

_____, with responses from M. Cristofani, A. Prosdocimi, and M. Morandi. 1987. "Etruria e Lazio nell'età dei Tarquini." In M. Cristofani, ed. *Etruria e Lazio Arcaico*, 55–71. Rome: Istituto per l'Archeologia Etrusco-Italia.

Connor, P. J. 1978. "The Actian Miracle: Propertius 4.6." *Ramus* 7: 1–10.

Conte, G. B. 1986. *The Rhetoric of Imitation: Genre and Poetic Memory in Virgil and Other Latin Poets*. Ithaca: Cornell University Press.

Corbeill, A. C. 2005. "The Topography of *Fides* in Propertius 1.16." In G. Tissol and W. S. Batstone, eds., *Exploiting Genre and Gender in Latin Literature: Essays Presented to William S. Anderson on His Seventy-fifth Birthday*, 79–95. New York: Peter Lang.

Cornell, T. J. 1995. *The Beginnings of Rome: Italy and Rome from the Bronze Age to the Punic Wars (c. 1000–264 BC)*. London: Accordia Research Institute.

_____, and K. Lomas, eds. 1997. *Gender and Ethnicity in Ancient Italy*. London: Accordia Research Institute.

Crawford, J. 1994. *M. Tullius Cicero: The Fragmentary Speeches*. 2nd ed. Atlanta: Scholars Press.

Cristofani, M. 1985. *Dizionario della civiltà Etrusca*. Florence: Giunti Martello.

Cyrino, M. S. 1998. "Heroes in D(u)ress: Transvestism and Power in the Myths of Herakles and Achilles." *Arethusa* 31: 207–41.

D'Ambra, E. 1998. *Art and Identity in the Roman World*. London: Weidenfeld and Nicolson.

D'Anna, G. 1983. "Il rapporto di Properzio con Virgilio: Una sottile polemica col classicismo augusteo." *Colloquium Propertianum* 3: 45–57.

DeBrohun, J. B. 1994. "Redressing Elegy's *Puella*: Propertius IV and the Rhetoric of Fashion." *JRS* 84: 41–63.

_____. 2003. *Roman Propertius and the Reinvention of Elegy*. Ann Arbor: The University of Michigan Press.

Dee, J. 1974. "Propertius 4.2: Callimachus Romanus at Work." *AJPh* 95: 43–55.

Degrassi, A. 1963. *Fasti Anni Numani et Iuliani (Inscriptiones Italiae 13.2)*. Rome: Accademia Nazionale.

D'Elia, S. 1981. "I presupposti sociologici dell'esperienza elegiaca Properziana." *Colloquium Propertianum* 2: 59–80.

Della Corte, Francesco, ed. *Enciclopedia virgiliana*. Vol. I–V. 1984–1991. Rome: Istituto della Enciclopedia Vergiliana.

Depew, M. 1993. "Mimesis and Aetiology in Callimachus' *Hymns*." In M. A. Harder, R. F. Regtuit, and G. C. Wakker, eds., *Callimachus*, 57–78. Groningen:.Vandenboeck and Ruprecht.

Devoto, G. 1940. "Nomi di divinità Etrusche III: Vertumno." *Studi Etruschi* 14: 275–80.

Dufallo, B. 2003. "Propertian Elegy as 'Restored Behavior': Evoking Cynthia and Cornelia." *Helios* 30: 163–79.

Dumézil, G. 1947. *Tarpeia: Essais de philologie comparative indo-européenne*. Paris: Gallimard.

DuQuesney, I. M. leM. 1984. "Horace and Maecenas: The Propaganda Value of *Sermones* 1." In T. Woodman and D. West, eds., *Poetry and Politics in the Age of Augustus*, 19–58. Cambridge:.Cambridge University Press.

Dyson, S. L., and R. E. Prior. 1995. "Horace, Martial, and Rome: Two Poetic Outsiders Read the Ancient City." *Arethusa* 28: 245–63.

Edwards, C. 1993. *The Politics of Immorality in Ancient Rome.* Cambridge: Cambridge University Press.

————. 1996. *Writing Rome: Textual Approaches to the City.* Cambridge: Cambridge University Press.

Elsner, J. 1995. *Art and the Roman Viewer: The Transformation of Art from the Pagan World to Christianity.* Cambridge: Cambridge University Press.

————. 1996. "Inventing Imperium: Texts and the Propaganda of Monuments in Augustan Rome." In J. Elsner, ed., *Art and Text in Roman Culture,* 32–53, 284–87. Cambridge: Cambridge University Press.

Evans, J. D. 1992. *The Art of Persuasion. Political Propaganda from Aeneas to Brutus.* Ann Arbor: The University of Michigan Press.

Fantham, E. 1997. "Images of the City: Propertius' new-old Rome." In T. Habinek and A. Schiesaro, eds., 122–35. *The Roman Cultural Revolution.* Cambridge: Cambridge University Press.

————. 1996. *The Urban Image of Augustan Rome.* Cambridge: Cambridge University Press.

Fedeli, P., ed. 1984. *Sexti Properti Elegiarum Libri IV.* Stuttgart: Teubner.

————. 1988. " L'età augustea nel guidizio di Properzio." In E. Benedini, ed., *L' età augustea vista dai contemporanei e nel giudizio dei posteri,* 87–105. Mantua: Accademia Vergiliana.

Feeney, D. 1998. *Literature and Religion at Rome.* Cambridge: Cambridge University Press.

Flacelière, R., and P. Devambez. 1966. *Héraclès: Images & Récits.* Paris: de Boccard.

Flory, M. B. 1984. "*Sic exempla parantur:* Livia's Shrine to Concord and the Porticus Liviae." *Historia* 33: 309–30.

Flower, H. 2000. "The Tradition of the *Spolia Opima:* M. Claudius Marcellus and Augustus." *CA* 19: 36–64.

Forsythe, G. 1999. *Livy and Early Rome: A Study in Historical Method and Judgment.* Stuttgart: Franz Steiner.

Fowler, D. 1991. "Narrate and Describe: The Problem of Ekphrasis." *JRS* 81: 25–35.

————. 1996. "Even better than the real thing: a tale of two cities." In J. Elsner, ed., *Art and Text in Roman Culture,* 57–74, 287–93. Cambridge: Cambridge University Press.

Fox, M. 1998. "Transvestite Hercules at Rome." In R. Cleminson and M. Allison, eds., *In/visibility: Gender and Representation in a European Context,* 1–21. Bradford: University of Bradford.

————. 1999. "Propertius 4.9 and the Toils of Historicism." *MD* 43: 157–76.

Fredrick, D. 2002. "Mapping Penetrability in Late Republican and Early Imperial Rome." In D. Fredrick, ed., *The Roman Gaze: Vision, Power, and the Body,* 236–64. Baltimore: The Johns Hopkins University Press.

Gabba, E. 1986. "Trasformazioni politiche e socio-economiche dell'Umbria dopo il bellum Perusinum." In G. Catanzaro and F. Santucci, eds., *Bimillenario della morte di Properzio,* 95–104. Assisi: Accademia Properziana del Subasio.

Gagé, J. 1930. "Romulus-Augustus." *MEFRA* 47: 138–81.

Gale, M. R. 2000. *Virgil on the Nature of Things: The Georgics, Lucretius and the Didactic Tradition.* Cambridge: Cambridge University Press.

Galinsky, K. 1969. "The Triumph Theme in the Augustan Elegy." *WS* 82: 75–107.
_____. 1972. *The Herakles Theme. The Adaptations of the Hero in Literature from Homer to the Twentieth Century.* Oxford: Blackwell.
_____. 1996. *Augustan Culture: An Interpretive Introduction.* Princeton: Princeton University Press.
Gansiniec, Z. 1949. *Tarpeia: The Making of a Myth.* Wratislaviae: Kazimierz Majewski.
Genette, G. 1980. *Narrative Discourse: An Essay in Method.* J. E. Lewin, trans. Ithaca: Cornell University Press.
Gold, B. K. 1993. "But Ariadne Was Never There in the First Place: Finding the Female in Roman Poetry." In N. S. Rabinowitz and A. Richlin, eds., *Feminist Theory and the Classics,* 75–101. New York: Routledge.
Goldhill, S. 2001. *Being Greek under Rome: Cultural Identity, the Second Sophistic and the Development of Empire.* Cambridge: Cambridge University Press.
Goold, G. P. 1990. *Propertius Elegies.* Cambridge, MA: Harvard University Press.
Greene, E. 1995. "Elegiac Woman: Fantasy, *Materia,* and Male Desire in Propertius 1.3 and 1.11." *AJP* 116: 303–18.
_____. 1998. *The Erotics of Domination: Male Desire and the Mistress in Latin Love Poetry.* Baltimore: The Johns Hopkins University Press.
Griffin, J. 1977. "Propertius and Antony." *JRS* 67: 17–26.
Grimal, P. 1951. "Études sur Properce, II: César et la légende de Tarpéia." *REL* 29: 201–14.
_____. 1953. "Les intentions de Properce et la composition du livre IV des Elegies." *Collection Latomus* 12: 5–53.
_____. 1988. "Aeneas in Rom und der Triumph des Octavian." In G. Binder, ed. *Saeculum Augustum II: Religion und Literatur,* 240–54. Darmstadt: Wissenschaftliche Buchgesellschaft.
Gruen, E. S. 1992. *Culture and National Identity in Republican Rome.* Ithaca: Cornell University Press.
Guarducci, M. 1986. "La casa di Properzio ad Assisi." In G. Catanzaro and F. Santucci, eds., *Bimillenario della morte di Properzio,* 137–41. Assisi: Accademia Properziana del Subasio.
Gurval, R. A. 1995. *Actium and Augustus: The Politics and Emotions of Civil War.* Ann Arbor: The University of Michigan Press.
Hallett, J. P. 1973. "The Role of Women in Roman Elegy: Counter-Cultural Feminism." *Arethusa* 6: 103–24.
Hardie, P. 1986. *Virgil's Aeneid: Cosmos and Imperium.* Oxford: Oxford University Press.
_____. 1992. "Augustan Poets and the Mutability of Rome." In A. Powell, ed., *Roman Poetry and Propaganda in the Age of Augustus,* 59–82. London: Bristol Classical Press.
_____. 1993. "*Ut pictura poesis?* Horace and the Visual Arts." In N. Rudd, ed., *Horace 2000: A Celebration: Essays for the Bimillennium,* 120–39. Ann Arbor: The University of Michigan Press.
_____. 1998. *Virgil. Greece and Rome: New Surveys in the Classics No. 28.* Oxford: Oxford University Press.
Harris, W. V. 1971. *Rome in Etruria and Umbria.* Oxford: Oxford University Press.
Harrison, S. J. 1989. "Augustus, the Poets, and the *Spolia Opima.*" *CQ* 39: 408–14.
_____. 2001. "Picturing the Future: The Proleptic Ekphrasis from Homer to

Vergil." In S. J. Harrison, ed., *Texts, Ideas, and the Classics: Scholarship, Theory, and Classical Literature*, 70–92. Oxford: Oxford University Press.

Haslam, M. W. 1993. "Callimachus' *Hymns*." In M. A. Harder, R. F. Regtuit, and G. C. Wakker, eds., *Callimachus*, 111–25. Groningen: Vandenboeck und Ruprecht.

Haynes, S. 2000. *Etruscan Civilization: A Cultural History*. Los Angeles: The J. Paul Getty Trust.

Hexter, R. 1992. "Sidonian Dido." In R. Hexter and D. Selden, eds., *Innovations of Antiquity*, 332–84. London: Routledge.

Hinds, S. 1992a. "*Arma* in Ovid's *Fasti* Part 1: Genre and Mannerism." *Arethusa* 25: 81–112.

———. 1992b. "*Arma* in Ovid's *Fasti*, Part 2: Genre, Romulean Rome and Augustan Ideology." *Arethusa* 25: 113–53.

———. 2002. "Landscape with Figures: Aesthetics of Place in the *Metamorphoses* and Its Tradition." In P. Hardie, ed., *The Cambridge Companion to Ovid*, 122–49. Cambridge: Cambridge University Press.

Holleman, A. W. J. 1977. "Propertius IV.9: An Augustan View of Roman Religion." *RBPh* 55.1: 79–92.

Horsfall, N. 1989. *Cornelius Nepos: A Selection, Including the Lives of Cato and Atticus*. Oxford: Oxford University Press.

Hubbard, M. 1975. *Propertius*. London and New York: Duckworth.

Hutchinson, G. O. 1984. "Propertius and the Unity of the Book." *JRS* 74: 99–106.

Huttner, U. 1997. "Hercules und Augustus." *Chiron* 27: 369–91.

Jaeger, M. 1993. "*Custodia Fidelis Memoriae*: Livy's Story of M. Manlius Capitolinus." *Latomus* 52: 350–63.

———. 1995. "Reconstructing Rome: The Campus Martius and Horace, Ode 1.8." *Arethusa* 28: 177–91.

James, S. L. 2003. *Learned Girls and Male Persuasion: Gender and Reading in Roman Love Elegy*. Berkeley: University of California Press.

Janan, M. 1998. "Refashioning Hercules: Propertius 4.9." *Helios* 25: 65–77.

———. 2001. *The Politics of Desire: Propertius Book IV*. Berkeley: University of California Press.

Johnson, W. R. 1973. "The Emotions of Patriotism: Propertius 4.6." *CSCA* 6: 151–80.

———. 2001. "Imaginary Romans: Vergil and the Illusion of National Identity." In S. Spence, ed., *Poets and Critics Read Vergil*, 3–18. New Haven: Yale University Press.

Kampen, N. B. 1988. "The Muted Other." *Art J* 57:15–19.

———. 1991a. "Between Public and Private: Women as Historical Subjects in Roman Art." In S. B. Pomeroy, ed., *Women's History and Ancient History*, 218–44. Chapel Hill:.University of North Carolina Press.

———. 1991b. "Reliefs of the Basilica Aemilia: A Redating." *Klio* 73: 448–58.

———. 1996a. "Omphale and the Instability of Gender." In N. B. Kampen, ed., *Sexuality in Ancient Art: Near East, Egypt, Greece, and Italy*, 233–46. Cambridge: Cambridge University Press.

———. 1996b. "Gender Theory in Roman Art." In D. E. E. Kleiner and S. B. Matheson, eds., *I, Claudia: Women in Ancient Rome*, 14–25. New Haven: Yale University Press.

Kellum, B. 1993 (1986). "Sculptural Programs and Propaganda in Augustan Rome: The Temple of Apollo on the Palatine." In E. D'Ambra, ed., *Roman Art in Context:*

An Anthology, 75–84. Englewood Cliffs, NJ: Prentice Hall.

———. 1997. "Concealing/Revealing: Gender and the Play of Meaning in the Monuments of Augustan Rome." In T. Habinek and A. Schiesaro, eds., *The Roman Cultural Revolution*, 158–81. Cambridge: Cambridge University Press.

Kennedy, D. F. 1992. "'Augustan' and 'Anti-Augustan': Reflections on Terms of Reference." In A. Powell, ed., *Roman Poetry and Propaganda in the Age of Augustus*, 26–58. London: Bristol Classical Press.

———. 1993. *The Arts of Love: Five Studies in the Discourse of Roman Love Elegy.* Cambridge: Cambridge University Press.

King, R. 1990. "Creative Landscaping and Artifice in Propertius 4.4." *CJ* 85: 225–46.

Kleiner, D. E. E. 1978. "The Great Friezes of the Ara Pacis Augustae. Greek Sources, Roman Derivatives, and Augustan Social Policy." *MEFRA* 90: 753–85.

———. 1996. "Imperial Women as Patrons of the Arts in the Early Empire." In D. E. E. Kleiner and S. B. Matheson, eds., *I, Claudia: Women in Ancient Rome*, 28–41. Austin: University of Texas Press.

Konstan, D. 1986. "Narrative and Ideology in Livy: Book I." *ClAnt* 5: 198–215.

Krostenko, B. A. 2001. *Cicero, Catullus, and the Language of Social Performance.* Chicago: University of Chicago Press.

Laird, A. 1993. "Sounding Out Ecphrasis: Art and Text in Catullus 64." *JRS* 83: 18–30.

———. 1996. "*Ut figura poesis:* Writing Art and the Art of Writing in Augustan Poetry." In J. Elsner, ed., *Art and Text in Roman Culture*, 75–102, 293–300. Cambridge: Cambridge University Press.

Laurence, R., and J. Berry, eds. 1998. *Cultural Identity in the Roman Empire.* London: Routledge.

Leach, E. W. 1988. *The Rhetoric of Space: Literary and Artistic Representations of Landscape in Republican and Augustan Rome.* Princeton: Princeton University Press.

———. 2001. "Gendering Clodius." *CW* 94: 335–59.

LeFèvre, E. 1989. *Das Bild-Programm des Apollo-Tempels auf dem Palatin.* Konstanz: Universitätsverlage Konstanz.

Lentano, M. 2002. "La conferma di paternità. Properzio IV,6, 60 tra filologia e antropologia." *BStudLat* 32: 11–32.

Levick, B. 1975. "Primus, Murena, and *Fides:* Notes on Dio Cassius LIV.3." *G&R* 22: 156–63.

Lindheim, S. H. 1998. "Hercules Cross-Dressed, Hercules Undressed: Unmasking the Construction of the Propertian *Amator* in Elegy 4.9." *AJPh* 119: 43–66.

MacLeod, C. 1983. "Propertius 4.1." In *Collected Essays*, 141–53. Oxford: Clarendon Press.

Mader, G. 1990. "The Apollo Similes at Propertius 4.6.31–36." *Hermes* 118: 325–34.

Marquis, E. C. 1974. "Vertumnus in Propertius 4.2." *Hermes* 102: 491–501.

McDonough, C. M. 1999. "Forbidden to Enter the Ara Maxima: Dogs and Flies or Dogflies?" *Mnemosyne* 52: 464–77.

McParland, E. H. 1970. "Propertius 4.9." *TAPhA* 101: 349–55.

Miles, G. B. 1980. *Vergil's Georgics: A New Interpretation.* Berkeley: University of California Press.

———. 1995. *Livy: Reconstructing Early Rome.* Ithaca: Cornell University Press.

Miller, J. F. 1982. "Callimachus and the Augustan Aetiological Elegy." *ANRW* 2.30.1: 371–417.

_____. 2003. "Alternating Apollo's Bow and Lyre." Paper presented at the annual meeting of the Classical Association of the Middle West and South.

Miller, P. A., and C. Platter. 1999. "Crux as Symptom: Augustan Elegy and Beyond." *CW* 92: 445–54.

Miller, P. A. 2001. "Response." Paper presented at the annual meeting of the American Philological Association in response to the panel, "Gendered Dynamics in Latin Love Elegy," San Diego, January 2001.

_____. 2003. *Subjecting Verses: Latin Erotic Elegy and the Emergence of the Real.* Princeton: Princeton University Press.

Morel, J-P. 1962. "Thèmes sabins et thèmes numaïques dans le monnayage de la république romaine." *MEFRA* 74: 7–59.

Mueller, H.-F. 2002. "The Extinction of the Potitii and the Sacred History of Augustan Rome." In D. S. Levine and D. P. Nelis, eds., *Clio and the Poets: Augustan Poetry and the Traditions of Ancient Historiography*, 313–29. Leiden: Brill.

Murgia, C. E. 1989. "Propertius 4.1.87–88 and the Division of 4.1." *HSPh* 92: 257–72.

Nethercut, W. R. 1983. "Recent Scholarship on Propertius." *ANRW* 2.30.3: 1813–57.

Newlands, C. E. 1995. *Playing with Time: Ovid and the Fasti.* Ithaca: Cornell University Press.

Newman, J. K. 1997. *Augustan Propertius: The Recapitulation of a Genre.* Hildesheim: Olms.

O'Hara, J. J. 1996. "Sostratus *Suppl. Hell.* 733: A Lost, Possibly Catullan-Era Elegy on the Six Sex Changes of Tiresias." *TAPA* 126: 173–219.

O'Neill, K. 1995. "Propertius 4.4 and the Burden of Aetiology." *Hermathena* 158: 53–60.

_____. 2000. "Propertius 4.2: Slumming With Vertumnus." *AJPh* 121: 259–77.

Orlin, E. M. 1997. *Temples, Religion and Politics in the Roman Republic.* Leiden: Brill.

_____. 2002. "Foreign Cults in Republican Rome: Rethinking the Pomerial Rule." *MAAR* 47: 1–18.

Papanghelis, T. 1987. *Propertius. A Hellenistic Poet on Love and Death.* Cambridge: Cambridge University Press.

Parker, H. N. 1992. "The Fertile Fields of Umbria: Propertius 1.22.10." *Mnemosyne* 45: 88–92.

Perkell, C. G. 1989. *The Poet's Truth: A Study of the Poet in Virgil's Georgics.* Berkeley: University of California Press.

Perrone, G. 1991. "Un problema testuale nel monologo di Tarpeia (Prop. IV 4, 34)." *Civiltà Classica e Cristiana* 12: 83–86.

Pillinger, H. E. 1969. "Some Callimachean Influences on Propertius, Book 4." *HSCP* 73: 171–99.

Pinotti, P. 1977. "Properzio IV.9: Alessandrinismo e arte allusiva." *GIF* 8: 50–71.

_____. 1983. "Properzio e Vertumno: antioconformismo e restaurazione augustea." *Colloquium Propertianum* 3: 75–96.

Platner, S. B., and T. Ashby. 1929. *A Topographical Dictionary of Ancient Rome.* Oxford: Clarendon Press.

Pound, E. 1994 (1958). *Diptych Rome-London.* New York: New Directions.

Purcell, N. 1986. "Livia and the Womanhood of Rome." *PCPhS* 32: 78–105.

Putnam, M. C. J. 1967. "The Shrine of Vortumnus." *AJA* 71: 177–79.

_____. 1976. "Propertius 1.22: A Poet's Self-Definition." *QUCC* 23: 93–123.

_____. 1985. "Romulus *Tropaeophoros* (*Aeneid* 6.779–80)." *CQ* 35: 237–40.

Raditsa, L. F. 1980. "Augustus' Legislation Concerning Marriage, Procreation, and Adultery." *ANRW* 2.13: 278–339.

Radke, G. 1979 (1965). *Die Götter Altitaliens*. Munster: Die Universität Munster.

Rawson, E. 1985. *Intellectual Life in the Late Roman Republic*. Baltimore: Johns Hopkins University Press.

_____. 1991. "The Antiquarian Tradition: Spoils and the Representation of Foreign Armour." In *Roman Culture and Society. Collected Essays*. Oxford: 582–98.

Rich, J. W. 1996. "Augustus and the *Spolia Opima*." *Chiron* 26: 85–127.

_____. 1999. "Drusus and the *Spolia Opima*." *CQ* 49: 544–55.

Richardson, L. 1977. *Propertius Elegies I-IV*. Norman: University of Oklahoma Press.

_____. 1992. *A New Topographical Dictionary of Ancient Rome*. Baltimore: Johns Hopkins University Press.

Ross, D. O. 1987. *Virgil's Elements: Physics and Poetry in the Georgics*. Princeton: Princeton University Press.

Rothstein, M. 1898. *Die Elegien des Sextus Propertius*. Berlin: Weidmann.

Rothwell. K. S. 1996. "Propertius on the Site of Rome." *Latomus* 55: 829–54.

Schmeling, G. 2000. "*Urbs Aeterna*: Rome, Monument of the Mind." In S. K. Dickison and J. P. Hallett, eds., *Rome and Her Monuments: Essays on the City and Literature of Rome in Honor of Katherine Geffcken*, 89–98. Wauconda, IL: Bolchazy-Carducci.

Schultz, C. E. 2000. "Modern Prejudice and Ancient Praxis: Female Worship of Hercules at Rome." *ZPE* 133: 291–97.

Scivoletto, N. 1979. "La città di Roma nella poesia di Properzio." *Colloquium Propertianum* 2: 27–38.

Scott, R. T. 1997. "The Shield of Aeneas and the Problem of Ecphrasis." In B. Magnusson, S. Renzetti, P. Vian, and S. J. Voicu, eds., *Vltra terminum vagari: Scritti in onore di Carl Nylander*, 301–8. Rome: Quasar.

Scullard, H. H. 1967. *The Etruscan Cities and Rome*. London: Thames and Hudson.

Severy, B. 2003. *Augustus and the Family at the Birth of the Roman Empire*. New York: Routledge.

Sharrock, A. R. 1991. "Womanufacture." *JRS* 81: 36–49.

_____. 2000. "Constructing Characters in Propertius." *Arethusa* 33: 263–84.

Shea, C. 1988. "The Vertumnus Elegy and Propertius IV." *ICS* 13: 63–71.

Simpson, C. J. 1977. "The Date of Dedication of the Temple of Mars Ultor." *JRS* 67: 91–94.

Spence, S. 1991. "Clinching the Text: the Danaids and the End of the *Aeneid*." *Vergilius* 37: 11–19.

Spencer, D. 2001. "Propertius, Hercules, and the Dynamics of Roman Mythic Space in *Elegy* 4.9." *Arethusa* 34: 259–84.

Stahl, H.-P. 1985. *Propertius "Love" and "War": Individual and State under Augustus*. Berkeley: University of California Press.

Stambaugh, J. E. 1988. *The Ancient Roman City*. Baltimore: Johns Hopkins University Press.

Staples, A. 1998. *From Good Goddess to Vestal Virgins. Sex and Category in Roman Religion*. London: Routledge.

Stehle, E. 1989. "Venus, Cybele, and the Sabine Women: The Roman Construction of Female Sexuality." *Helios* 16: 143–64.

Steinby, E. M. 1993–2000. *Lexicon Topographicum Urbis Romae Vol. I–VI.* Rome: Quasar.

Strazulla, M. J. 1990. *Il Principato di Apollo: Mito e propaganda nelle lastre "Campana" dal tempio di Apollo Palatino.* Rome: L'Erma edi Bretschneider.

Suits, T. A. 1969. "The Vertumnus Elegy of Propertius." *TAPhA* 100: 475–86.

Sullivan, J. P. 1976. *Propertius: A Critical Introduction.* Cambridge: Cambridge University Press.

Sweet, F. 1972. "Propertius and Political Panegyric." *Arethusa* 5: 169–75.

Syme, R. 1960 (1939). *The Roman Revolution.* Oxford: Oxford University Press.

———. 1959. "Livy and Augustus." *HSPh* 64: 43–47.

Tatum, W. J. 1999. *The Patrician Tribune: Publius Clodius Pulcher.* Chapel Hill: University of North Carolina Press.

Thomas, R. F. 1982. *Lands and Peoples in Roman Poetry: The Ethnographical Tradition.* Cambridge: Cambridge University Press.

———. 1988. *Vergil: Georgics. Vols. I–II.* Cambridge: Cambridge University Press.

Tissol, G. 1997. *The Face of Nature: Wit, Narrative, and Cosmic Origins in Ovid's Metamorphoses.* Princeton: Princeton University Press.

Torelli, M. 1995. *Studies in the Romanization of Italy* (trans. H. Fracchia). Alberta: University of Alberta Press.

Tränkle, H. 1983. "Properzio poeta dell'opposizione politica?" *Colloquium Propertianum* 3: 149–62.

Treggiari, S. 1991. *Roman Marriage: Lusti coniuges from the Time of Cicero to the Time of Ulpian.* Oxford: Oxford University Press.

Valladares, H. 2001. "Breaking Gender Boundaries: Elegiac Pleasure and the Ambiguous Power of the Gaze in Propertius 1.3." Paper presented at the annual meeting of the American Philological Association, San Diego, January 2001.

Vasaly, A. 1993. *Representations: Images of the World in Ciceronian Oratory.* Berkeley: University of California Press.

Vermeule, C. C. 1977. *Greek Sculpture and Roman Taste: The Purpose and Setting of Graeco-Roman Art in Italy and the Greek Imperial East.* Ann Arbor: The University of Michigan Press.

Versnel, H. S. 1970. *Triumphus: An Inquiry into the Origin, Development and Meaning of the Roman Triumph.* Leiden: Brill.

Veyne, P. 1988. *Roman Erotic Elegy: Love, Poetry, and the West.* D. Pellauer, trans. Chicago: University of Chicago Press.

Walker, S. 2000. "The Moral Museum: Augustus and the City of Rome." In J. Coulston and H. Dodge, eds. *Ancient Rome: The Archaeology of the Eternal City,* 61–77. Oxford: Oxford University Press.

Wallace-Hadrill, A. 1986. "Image and Authority in the Coinage of Augustus." *JRS* 76: 66–87.

———. 1997. "*Mutatio morum:* The Idea of a Cultural Revolution." In T. Habinek and A. Schiesaro, eds., *The Roman Cultural Revolution,* 3–22. Cambridge: Cambridge University Press.

Warden, J. 1978. "Another Would-be Amazon: Propertius 4.4.71–72." *Hermes* 106: 177–87.

———. 1980. *Fallax Opus: Poet and Reader in the Elegies of Propertius.* Toronto: University of Toronto Press.

_____. 1982. "Epic into Elegy: Propertius 4.9.70f." *Hermes* 110: 228–42.

Weeber, K. W. 1977. *Das 4. Properz-Buch: Interpretationen zu seiner Eigenart und seiner Stellung im Gesamtwerk.* Doctoral dissertation, Ruhr-Universität Bochum.

_____. 1978. "Properz IV 1,1–70 und das 8. Buch der *Aeneis.*" *Latomus* 37: 489–506.

Whitaker, R. 1983. *Myth and Personal Experience in Roman Love-Elegy: A Study in Poetic Technique.* Göttingen: Vandenboeck and Ruprecht.

White, P. 1993. *Promised Verse: Poets in the Society of Augustan Rome.* Cambridge, MA: Harvard University Press.

Wiedemann, T. 1986. "The Fetiales: A Reconsideration." *CQ* 36: 482–83.

Williams, G. 1968. *Tradition and Originality in Roman Poetry.* Oxford: Oxford University Press.

Winter, J. G. 1910. "The Myth of Hercules at Rome." In H. A. Sanders, ed., *Roman History and Mythology. University of Michigan Studies. Humanistic Series* 4: 171–273.

Wiseman, T. P. 1995. *Remus: A Roman Myth.* Cambridge: Cambridge University Press.

Wyke, M. 1987a. "The Elegiac Woman at Rome." *PCPhS* 33: 153–78.

_____. 1987b. "Written Women: Propertius' *Scripta Puella.*" *JRS* 77: 47–61.

_____. 1989. "Mistress and Metaphor in Augustan Elegy." *Helios* 16: 25–47.

Zanker, G. 1987. *Realism in Alexandrian Poetry: A Literature and Its Audience.* London: Croom Helm.

Zanker, P. 1968. *Forum Augustum.* Tübingen: Verlag Ernst Wasmuth.

_____. 1983. "Der Apollontempel auf dem Palatin: Ausstattung und politische Sinnbezüge nach der Schlacht von Actium." In *Città e Architettura nella Roma Imperiale. ARID* Supplement 10: 21–40.

_____. 1988. *The Power of Images in the Age of Augustus.* A. Shapiro, trans. Ann Arbor: The University of Michigan Press.

Ziolkowski, A. 1992. *The Temples of Mid-Republican Rome and Their Historical and Topographical Context.* Rome: L'Erma di Bretschneider.

INDEX LOCORUM

Only primary authors and works are included. Endnotes are indexed only if a passage is discussed in some detail.

GENERAL INDEX

Acanthis, 43, 110

Acron, 133–34, 144–46, 148–50, 159

Actium, battle of, 2, 103, 106, 114, 126, 137–38, 188 n.52; and elegy 4.6, 14, 79–81, 96–98; and the temple of Palatine Apollo, 83, 85–89; 110

Aeneas, 30; and Augustus, 7, 102–3, 116, 139–40; evoked in elegy 4.10, 147–50, 199 n.36

aetiology, 22–23, 127, 174 n.10

Alexandrianism, 63, 81, 83, 105, 107–8. *See also* Callimacheanism

alumnus, 25, 50–52, 176 n.16

Amazon, 61–62, 185 n.67, 187 n.22

amor (vs. *Roma*), 57, 63–64, 67, 76, 182–83 n.29, 183 n.32

antiquarianism, 136–37, 144, 193 n.40, 196 n.4, 200 n.55

Anton, 115, 125

Antonius, M., 81, 98, 109, 131; and Atticus, 135–36, 196–97 n.4; evoked in the temple of Palatine Apollo, 86–87; and Hercules, 87, 114–16, 125–26, 149–50, 191 n.8, 194 n.48; and Remus, 101–2

Apollo, 14, 42, 80–81, 84 fig. 7, 86 fig. 8, 88 with fig. 9, 91–93, 105–6, 109, 160; aspects of, 98–100, 102, 104, 189 n.57 and n. 73; and Augustus, 87–88, 92, 115, 186 n.13; and Callimachus, 106–8; cult image in

the temple of Palatine Apollo, 84–85, 87, 91–93, 94; 186 n.13; and Horos, 32, 176 n.34; as poetic inspiration, 28, 89, 106, 108, 110, 178 n.33, 188 n.47

Ara Maxima, 14–15, 112–17, 113 fig. 10, 120–22, 124, 126–27, 129, 131–32, 167, 191 n.11

Ara Pacis, 60, 182 n.20, 193 n.37

Aratus, 161

Archytas, 33, 176 n.34

Arethusa, 11, 17, 42–43, 54–55, 175–76 n.31

Ariadne, 64, 75, 195 n.65

arma, 22

Arria, 30, 33

assimilation, 39–41

astrology, 13, 20

Asylum, 71

Atticus, 136–37

Augustus, 2, 14, 26, 48, 59, 62, 67–68, 74, 79, 89, 92–93, 96–97, 100, 109, 113–114, 126, 134–35, 160, 164–65, 167–68, 182 n.25; and Aeneas, 103; and Apollo, 87, 92, 102–3, 109–10, 186 n.13; and gender, 119–20, 126–27, 131–32; and Hercules, 87, 113–16, 196 n.65; house of, 82–83, 82 fig. 6, 87, 92, 165; mausoleum of, 167; and monuments, 2, 15, 54, 59–60, 72, 80–83, 85, 116, 135–44,